D1880346

Production and Operation Management

Production and Operation Management

Dr. Virender S. Poonia

genNEXT Publication

Production and Operation Management

© Dr. Virender S. Poonia

ISBN : 978-93-80222-31-8

All rights reserved. No Part of this book may be reproduced in any manner without written permission.

Published in 2010 in India by
Gennext Publication
23 Main Ansari Road, Darya Ganj,
E-Mail : GenNextpublication@hotmail.com
Phone : 23282060

Laser Type Setting : Shubh Deep Laser Printers

Printed at : Chawla Offset Printers, Delhi

Contents

Preface *ix*

1. **Production and Operation Management** 1

Application, Customization, Product, Plant, Processes, Programmes, People, Physiocracy of Factors, Entrepreneurship, Human capital, Intellectual capital, Social capital, History of Modes of Production, LTV and Labor Process, Risk assessment, Risk Analysis, Approaches to Scheduling, Loading, Approaches to Loading, Sequencing, Priority Rules, Gantt Charts, Production and Operations Management: a Case Study, Benchmarking in an Organization, Aspects of Product Management, Product Planning, Product Marketing, Case Study

2. **Operations as a Working Tool** 31

Generating Recurring Income, Increase the Value of Business's Assets, Securing the income and value of the business, Manager of a Printing Services Firm, Conceptualization of business models, Formats of Business Plan, Problems in Operational Planning, Principles of ORM, Benefits of ORM, Process of ORM, Facilitated Risk Analysis Process, Risk reduction, Risk retention, Creation of RMP, Implementation of RMP, Limitations of RMP, Risk-management activities as applied to project management, Risk Management and Business continuity, Benefits and Barriers of Risk Communication, Rules of Risk Communication, How to Use the Tool, Example to represent the Decision Tree, Evaluating the Decision Tree, Calculating Tree Values, Calculating the Value of Decision Nodes, Conclusion of

Decision Tree, General Description of Decision Tree, Case Study

3. **Operation Strategies** **61**

Shorter Product Cycle, Low Cost Process, Convenience and Location, Production Flexibility, Quality, Product Variety and Facility Size, Designing the Production System, Technology Selection and Process Development, Allocation of Resources to Strategic Alternatives, Facility Planning, Accounting vs opportunity costs, Quality, Dimension of Quality, In Manufacturing, Case Study

4. **Decision Making Process and Decision Theory** **77**

How to Use the Tool, Example of Measured Criteria, Force Field Analysis, Principles of Costs Benefits Analysis, Decision Criteria for Projects, Evaluating Quantitatively whether to follow a Course of Action, How to Use the Tool?, Brainstorming, Brainstorming and Lateral Thinking, Individual Brainstorming, Group Brainstorming, How to Use the Tool?, How to Use the Tool?, Advantages and Disadvantages, Steps to Conduct this Analysis, Example of Paired Comparison Analysis, How to Use the Tool?, Setting Priorities for Action, How to Use the Tool?, Example of Grid Analysis, Reactive Decision, How to List Your Risks, Determination of Utility, Decision Theory under Various Conditions, Degrees of Uncertainty, Set of States, Paradoxes of Uncertainty, Measures of Incompletely Known Probability, Decision-making under Ignorance, Decision Rules for Classical Ignorance, Various Decision Rules, For example, Case Study

5. **Process Analysis** **129**

Business Process Modeling Tools, Life-cycle of BPM, Advantages of Business Rules, Implementation of ERP, Format of BOM, Advancements in Cross-Platform, How Cloud Computing will Change Capacity Management, Case Study

6. **Project Management** **145**

Extreme Project Management, Event Chain Methodology, I stage: Initiation, IInd stage: Planning and Design, IIIrd stage: Executing, IVth stage: Monitoring and Controlling, Vth stage: Closing, Formal System Development, Historical Development, Execution, Monitoring, Methods of Determining Risk, Case Study

7. **Process Performance and Quality Management** 165

How to Measure Customer Satisfaction, Statistical Process Control, Usage of Chart, Performance of Control Charts, Measure the Process, Capability Study, DMAIC, DMADV, Implementation Roles, Quality Assurance versus Quality Control, Case Study

8. **Supply Chain Strategy** 185

Organization Challenges, How to Develop Supply Chain Strategy, Step I: Understand the Business Strategy, Step II: Assess the Extended Supply Chain, Goals of Supply Chain Strategy, Strategic Levels, Tactical Levels, Operational Levels, 1. Location Decisions, 2. Production Decisions, 3. Inventory Decisions, 4. Transportation Decisions, Aspects of CRM, Network Design Model, Rough Cut Methods, Product Development, Customers, Manufacturing, Suppliers, Logistics, Manufacturing, Suppliers, Logistics, Features of Consignment, Structural Elements, Control Elements, Case Study

9. **Inventory Management** 213

1. Raw Materials, 2. Work-in-Process, 3. Finished Goods, 4. MRO goods Inventory, Various Assumptions of this Model includes, Used Variables, Total Cost Function, Extensions in EOQ, Future of Inventory Control System, Warehouse Layout and Operation, Finished Goods Inventory, Inventory Analysis, Inventory Turnover, Cost of Ordering, Costs of Carrying, Case Study

10. **Product Process Strategy** 235

Equivalent or Interchangeable Product, Lots or Batches, Categories, Sizes and Colors, Product line, Production Function as an Equation, Shifting a Production Function, Classes of Production Function, Diminishing Returns of Product, Methods of Economies of Scale, Product Planning, Product Marketing, Product Life Cycle Curve, Introduction Stage, Growth Stage of PLC, Maturity Stage of PLC, Decline Stage of Product Life Cycle, Request for Deviation, Market Identification, Theories of Diffusion,

Rate of Diffusion, Models of Diffusion, Process, Capabilities of PDM, Effective Production Management, Manufacturing Process Management, Types of Scheduling, Important functions of a Service Product Manager, Case Study

11. Maintenance Management **267**

Implementation of TPM, Step A - Preparatory Stage, Step B - Introduction Stage, Step C – Implementation Stage, Step D - Institutionalizing Stage, Case Study

12. Constraint Management **277**

Five Focusing Steps, Thinking Processes of TOC, Diseconomies of Scale

Bibliography **289**

Index **295**

Preface

As we all know that Production and Operation Management is one of the most important topics in today's world. Many books have been written in this topic. This modest effort is another pearl in the sequence. This book has been designed in mind the mentality of the general reader's language which is easy to understandable. The aim of this book is to provide students and lectures with a clear concise and comprehensive introduction to the theory and practice of production and operation management.

The book explains, in a simple but thorough manner, the fundamental concepts and techniques involved in both production and operations management. Sufficient examples are included throughout the text to illustrate these concepts and techniques. This comprehensive text retains the core concepts, models and managerial orientation of previous editions and reflects current production and operations management practices and research results. It emphasizes practice through new chapter highlights. The text continues to offer problems which can be solved by the computer.

This textbook on Production and Operations Management addresses the impact of operations decisions on the firm and emphasizes cross-functional decision making. The text provides materials of interest to general business students and operations management majors. By stressing cross-functional decision making, the text provides a unique and current business perspective for all students.

A significant characteristic of the recent times has been that the different economies of the world are getting increasingly integrated with each other. For the emerging economies of the world—that have been of late showing rapid rates of economic growth – such as India, Production and Operations is a vital management discipline.

We hope that the discussion made in this book will help the readers to understand and learnt about the different concept of "Production and Operations Management" in a most comprehensive way to face the present and future challenges which are occurred in this field.

1

Production and Operation Management

This chapter includes the key concepts which are shown below:

- Introduction
- Scope of Production and Operation Management
- Main features of POM
- Production's Overview
- Production Line
- Efficiency and Cross-efficiency in Production
- Factors of Production
- Four Factors of Production
- Mode of Production
- Labor Theories of Value
- Relation between Values and Prices
- Production Process
- Operational Management
- Operational Planning
- Operational Risk
- Risk Management
- Operations Scheduling
- Scheduling Service Operations
- Production Management System

INTRODUCTION

Production and Operations Management ("POM") is about the transformation of production and operational inputs into "outputs" that, when distributed, meet the needs of customers. There are some relation between production and operation which are held on that production. These productions are processed by operations with the help of input and outputs.

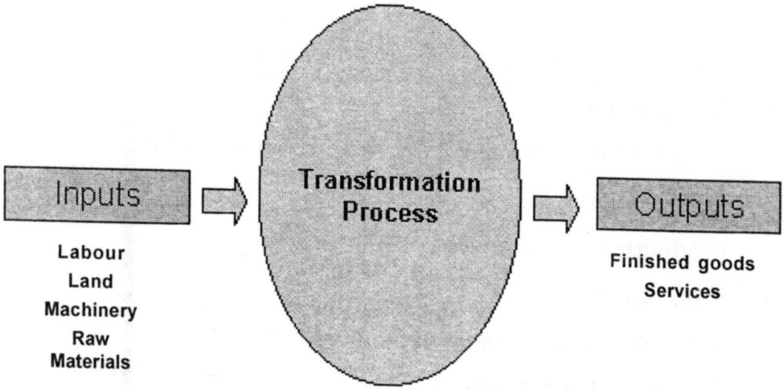

This figure shows the processing of input and output.

The process in the above diagram is often referred to as the "Conversion Process". There are several different methods of handling the conversion or production process - Job, Batch, Flow and Group.

In order to fulfill three basic tasks, which need to be accomplished for an enterprise to achieve success, it is necessary to appropriately manage production processes. These tasks include:

- ensuring quality in production processes - ensures that Customer will receive a product of desired, guaranteed quality
- effective management of production orders - ensures that a product will be manufactured and delivered on time
- control of production costs - enables cost control and optimization.

Effective fulfillment of these tasks is impossible without precise tracing and controlling of the stages of production processes. This requires information about production process which is detailed enough for the system of controlling production stages. Such information says:

- who (worker/shift/team) manufactured
- where (plant/post/section)
- when (date, time)
- by means of what (machines, tools)
- from what (raw materials, semi-finished products)

Here input refers to the labor, land, machinery and row materials as well and when these inputs are processed then, they convert into outputs which refers to finished goods and services.

A lot of such data is frequently gathered in the form of paper (operation card, shop guides, etc.). Entering it into the system carries the risk of errors which are occurring during this process, and consumes workers' time. In certain branches of production, the amount of data that should be registered is so huge that it is virtually impossible to register it manually. The question arises whether it is possible to quickly and reliably register a huge amount of data, to combine it into a coherent whole, and to enable further processing of this data in order to manage the production, control quality, or conduct analyses. Is it possible to use this data in logistic areas to ensure the proper cooperation of raw material warehouses (ensuring continuity of supplies to production line), or finished product warehouses (production planning, optimization of logistic costs) with production?

SCOPE OF PRODUCTION AND OPERATION MANAGEMENT

The scope of production and operations management is indeed vast .Commencing with the selection of location production management covers such activities as acquisition of land, constructing building, procuring and installing machinery, purchasing and storing raw material and converting them into saleable products.

Production and operation management has very vast scope. It has various applications and customization which are described below:-

Application

There are several application of production and operations management, i.e.

1 Production monitoring
2 Production supply
3 Processing ware house documents
4 Track and trace

- *Production monitoring includes the various features, i.e.*

  - automatic, semi-automatic or manual registration of events at the production
  - registration and visualization of production order status
  - registration of production stages
  - gathering data from the course of production process
  - reporting basic indicators (worktime, downtime, progress of order fulfillment) and efficiency

- *Production supply includes the several features like*

  - ensuring continuity of supplies of materials to production line
  - visualization of an order directly in a warehouse
  - generating documents concerning issuance of goods and linking them with orders
  - monitoring the progress of order fulfillment

- *Processing warehouse documents refers to linking warehouse operations with production orders*

- *Track&Trace includes these characteristics like*

  - forming logistic units (defining pallet composition)
  - manual and automatic printing of logistic labels
  - reporting the origin of logistic unit

Customization

These solutions are designed for any production company, regardless of branch in which it operates. They can be quickly adapted to the needs of Customer and implemented in various stages in terms to minimize the effect on current processes which are carried out in an enterprise or organization.

The system for production monitoring are responsible for completeness of the data gathered, that can enforce the entering of certain information at a given stage of production process, and make the actual functioning of production system conditional on dynamic data gathered in real time. It can be deeply integrated with industrial equipment systems, with two-way information communication. On the other hand, the system for production tracing is integrated with systems of ERP class (Enterprise Resource Planning), MRP/MRP II (Material requirements / Manufacturing Resource Planning), or WMS (Warehouse Management System). Its functionality allows to use modern technologies (e.g. automatic identification) to register and supervise processes in an enterprise, and consequently to extend the functionality of management systems.

MAIN FEATURES OF POM

Here POM tends to production and operations management which have some features that are independent. Its features are categorized into five categories namely product, plant, process, programmes, people.

Product

Marketers in a business must ensure that a business sells the products that fulfill the customer needs and wants. The role of Production and Operations is to ensure that the business actually makes the required products in accordance with the plan. Therefore, the role of PRODUCT in POM therefore concerns areas such as:

- Performance
- Aesthetics
- Quality
- Reliability
- Quantity
- Production costs
- Delivery dates

This is major features of POM because it is the major aim of an enterprise to begin the production whenever product arise, then production begins according to it.

Plant

To make PRODUCT, PLANT of some kind is needed. This will

comprise the bulk of the fixed assets of the business. In determining which PLANT to use, management must consider areas such as:

- Future demand (volume, timing)
- Design and layout of factory, equipment, offices
- Productivity and reliability of equipment
- Need for (and costs of) maintenance
- Heath and safety (particularly the operation of equipment)
- Environmental issues (e.g. creation of waste products)

Plant is another features which includes the all the needed fixed assets of the business which are generally required to make a product.

Processes

There are many different ways of producing a product. Management must choose the best process, or series of processes. They will consider:

- Available capacity
- Available skills
- Type of production
- Layout of plant and equipment
- Safety
- Production costs
- Maintenance requirements

Process are important to make the better production. There are various methods are used to produce a product.

Programmes

There are main concern of a programme in production because without making a programme to develop the product, it is all tends to be bad management.

The production PROGRAMME concerns the dates and times of the products that are to be produced and supplied to customers. The decisions made about programme will be influenced by following factors are:

- Purchasing patterns (e.g. lead time)
- Cash flow

- Need for / availability of storage
- Transportation

People

Production depends on PEOPLE, whose skills, experience and motivation vary. Key people-related decisions will consider the following areas:

- Wages and salaries
- Safety and training
- Work conditions
- Leadership and motivation
- Unionisation
- Communication

People has also a major part of production. It needs those people who have skills and experiences.

PRODUCTION'S OVERVIEW

Production refers to the economic process of converting of inputs into outputs and is a field of study in microeconomics. Production uses the resources to create a goods or service that is suitable for exchange. This can include manufacturing, storing, shipping, and packaging. Some economists define the production broadly as all economic activity other than consumption. They see every commercial activity other than the final purchase as some form of production.

Production is a process, and as such it occurs through time and space. Because it is a flow concept, production is measured as a "rate of output per period of time". There are three aspects to production processes:

1. the quantity of the good or service produced,
2. the form of the good or service created,
3. the temporal and spatial distribution of the good or service produced.

A production process can be defined as any activity that increases the similarity between the pattern of demand for goods and services, and the quantity, form, and distribution of these goods and services available to the market place.

Mainly production refers to the process or way which is used to make a product. It is the process which occurs through time and space. These three aspects of production processes includes all the ways or methods which are made to be success to develop a product.

PRODUCTION LINE

A Production line is a set of sequential operations which are established in a factory whereby materials are put through a refining process to produce an end-product that is suitable for onward consumption; or components which are assembled to make a finished article.

Typically, raw materials such as metal ores or agricultural products such as foodstuffs or textile source plants (cotton, flax) require a sequence of treatments to render them useful. For metal, the processes include the crushing, smelting and further refining. For plants, the useful material has to be separated from husks or contaminants and then treated for onward sale.

EFFICIENCY AND CROSS-EFFICIENCY IN PRODUCTION

Production is more efficient when the same output concludes from less input. Some economists (specifically Leibenstein) use the term X-efficiency to indicate that production processes tend to be inherently inefficient due to satisficing behaviour. The "rate of efficiency" is simply the amount of (or value of) outputs divided by the amount of (or value of) inputs. If a production process uses 50 units of input (or $5000 worth of inputs) to produce one unit of output it is more efficient than a process that uses 55 units of input (or $5500 worth of inputs) to produce the same level of output. It is said to be 10% more efficient ({55-50}/50=1/10=10%).

FACTORS OF PRODUCTION

Factors of Production are the resources employed to produce goods and services. They facilitate production but do not become part of the product (as with raw materials) or significantly transformed by the production process (as with fuel used to power machinery). To 19th century economists, the factors of production were land (natural resources, gifts from nature), labor (the ability to work), and capital goods (human-made tools and equipment).

Recent textbooks have added entrepreneurship and "human capital" (labor's education and skills). "Land" can include ecosystems while sometimes the overall state of technology is seen as a factor of production. In any event, it is the scarcity of the factors of production which poses humanity's economic problem, often forcing us to choose between competing goals. The number and definition of factors varies, depending on theoretical purpose, empirical emphasis, or school of economics.

Factors of production refers to the productive inputs that tends to be the resources. These inputs or resources are broadly categorized into sex groups. Theses categorize are:-

1. Row materials
2. Machinery
3. Labor services
4. Land
5. Capital goods
6. Entrepreneur

The inputs or resources we generally used in the production process are called factors of production that are proposed by economists. The myriad of possible inputs are usually grouped into six categories. These factors are:

1. *Raw materials* : A raw material is something that is acted upon or used by or by human labor or industry which is for use as a building material to obtain some product or structure. Frequently the term is used to denote those material that came from nature and is in an unprocessed or minimally processed state. Iron ore, logs, and crude oil, would be examples. A non-human related raw material would include twigs and found objects as used by birds to make nests.

2. Machinery : A machine is any device that uses the energy to perform some activity. In common usage, the meaning is that of a device having parts that perform or assist in performing any type of work. A simple machine is a device that transforms the direction or magnitude of a force without consuming any energy.

3. Labor services : labor is a measure of the work done by human beings. It is conventionally contrasted with such other factors of production as land and capital. There are theories which

have created a concept called human capital that are referring to the skills that workers possess, not necessarily their actual work, although there are also counter posing macro-economic system theories that think human capital is a contradiction in terms.

4. Land : Location values must not be confused with values imparted by fixed capital improvements. In classical economics, land is considered one of the three factors of production (along with capital, and labor). Income derived from ownership or control of natural resources is referred to as rent.

5. Capital goods : Capital goods usually referred to the means of production. Individuals, organizations and governments use capital goods in the production of other goods or commodities. Capital goods include factories, machinery, tools, equipment, and various buildings which are used to produce other products for consumption. Then Capital goods are products which are not produced for immediate consumption; rather, they are objects that are used to produce other goods and services. These types of goods are important economic factors because they are the key to developing a positive return from manufacturing other products and commodities.

6. Entrepreneur : An entrepreneur is a person who has the possession of an enterprise, or venture, and assumes the significant accountability for the inherent risks and the outcome. It is an ambitious leader who combines land, labor, and capital to create obtain and market new goods or services.

In the "long run", all of these factors of production can be adjusted by management. The "short run", however, is defined as a period in which at least one of the factors of production is fixed.

There are two type of factors of production, i.e., fixed factors of production and variable factors of production. Here fixed refers to the constant and variable refers to the changeable.

A fixed factor of production is one whose quantity cannot readily be changed. Examples include major pieces of equipment, suitable factory space, and key managerial personnel.

A variable factor of production is one whose usage rate can be changed easily. Examples include electrical power consumption, transportation services, and most raw material inputs. In the short run, a firm's "scale of operations" determines the maximum number of outputs that can be produced. In the long run, there are no scale limitations.

Physiocracy of Factors

Physiocracy of factors includes three classes means to capital, labor, land. These classes are further distinct in two types of economics, i.e., classical and neoclassical microeconomics.

Further distinctions from classical and neoclassical microeconomics include the following:

- Capital - This has many meanings, including the financial capital that are raised to operate and expand a business. However, in much economics "capital" without any qualification means the goods that can help produce other goods in the future, the conclusion of investment. It refers to the machines, roads, factories, schools, infrastructure, and office buildings which humans have produced in order to produce goods and services.
- Labor - human effort used in production which also includes technical and marketing expertise. The payment for someone else's labor and all income received from ones own labor is wages. Labor can also be classified as the physical and mental contribution of an employee to the production of the good(s).
- Land or natural resource - naturally-occurring goods such as water, air, soil, minerals, flora and fauna that are used in the creation of products. The payment for land use and the received income of a land owner is rent.

FOUR FACTORS OF PRODUCTION

There are four factors of production. These factors are contributing to production of goods and services. These factors including entrepreneurship, human capital, intellectual capital, social capital.

Entrepreneurship

Consider entrepreneurship as a factor of production, leaving debate aside. In markets, entrepreneurs combine the other factors of production, land, labor, and capital in order to make a profit. Often these entrepreneurs are seen as innovators, developing new ways to produce and new products. In a planned economy, central planners decide how land, labor, and capital should be used to provide for maximum benefit for all citizens. Of course, just as with market entrepreneurs, the benefits may mostly accrue to the entrepreneurs themselves.

The word has been used in other ways. The sociologist C. Wright Mills refers to "new entrepreneurs" who work within and between corporate and government bureaucracies in new and different ways. Others (such as those practicing public choice theory) refer to "political entrepreneurs," i.e., politicians and other actors.

Human capital

Contemporary analysis distinguishes the tangible, physical, or nonhuman capital goods from other forms of capital such as human capital. Human capital is embodied in a human being and is acquired through education and training, whether formal or on the job. Human capital is important in modern economic theory. Education is a key element in explaining economic growth over the time.

Intellectual capital

Intellectual capital is especially used as to information technology, recorded music, written material. This property is protected by copyrights, patterns and trademarks.

Social capital

Social capital is frequently defined as the stock of trust, mutual understanding, shared values, and socially held knowledge that facilitates the social coordination of economic activity.

Knowledge, ideas, and values, and human relationships are transmitted as part of the culture. This type of capital cannot be owned by individuals and is instead part of the common stock owned by humanity. But they often crucial to maintaining a peaceful society in which normal economic transactions and production can occur.

MODE OF PRODUCTION

Mode of production is a specific combination of production forces and social and technical relations of production.

1. Productive forces includes human labor power and the means of production, i.e., tools, equipment, buildings and technologies, materials, and improved land.

2. Social and technical relations of production include the property, power and control relations which governing are society's productive assets, frequently codified in law, cooperative work relations and forms of association, relations between people and the objects of their work, and the relations between social classes.

Marx regarded the productive ability and participation in social relations as two essential characteristics of human beings and that the particular modality of these relations in capitalist production are inherently in conflict with the increasing development of human productive capacities.

According to Marx, the combination of forces and relations of production means that the way of people that relate to the physical world and the way in which people relate to each other socially are bound up together in specific and necessary ways. People must consume to survive, but to consume they must produce, and in producing they necessarily enter into relations which exist independently of their will.

However, When new productive forces or new social relations develop then they conflict with the existing mode of production, this mode of production will either evolve without losing its basic structure, or else begin to break down. This then gives rise to a transitional era of social instability and social conflict, until a new social order is finally consolidated, with a new mode of production.

History of Modes of Production

• *"Primitive communism"*. Primitive communism is the stage of mode of production. It is Ist stage. Human society is seen as organized in traditional tribe structures, typified by shared production and consumption of the entire social product. As no permanent surplus product is produced, there is also no possibility of a ruling class coming into existence. As this mode of production lacks differentiation into classes, it is said to be classless. Palaeolithic and Neolithic tools, pre- and early-agricultural production, and rigorous ritualized social control have often been said to be the typifying productive forces of this mode of production. However, the foraging mode of production still exists, and often typified in contemporary hunter-gatherer societies. Past theories of the foraging mode of production have focused on lack of control over food production (Meillassoux, 1973). More recent scholarship has argued that hunter-gatherers use the foraging mode of production to maintain a specific set of social relations that, perhaps controversially, are said to emphasize egalitarianism and the collective appropriation of resources (Tim Ingold, 1987, 1988; Robert Kelly, 1995).

• *The Antique mode of production.* Antique mode of production is historic stage of production. It is some as the Asiatic mmode which is described below but variate in the form of property. It is similar to the Asiatic mode, but differentiated in that the form of property is the direct possession of individual human beings. Additionally, the ruling class usually avoids the more outlandish claims of being the direct incarnation of a god, and prefers to be the descendants of gods, or seeks other justifications for its rule. Ancient Greek and Roman societies are the most typical examples of this mode. The forces of production associated with this mode include advanced (two field) agriculture, the extensive use of animals in agriculture, and advanced trade networks.

• *The Asiatic mode of production.* This is a controversial contribution to Marxist theory, initially used to explain pre-slave and pre-feudal large earthwork constructions in China, India, the Euphrates and Nile river valleys and named on this basis of the primary evidence coming from greater "Asia". The Asiatic mode of production is said to be the initial form of class society, where a small group extracts social surplus through violence which are aimed at settled or unsettled band communities within a domain. Exploited labor is extracted as forced corvee labor during a slack period of the year that allowing for monumental construction such as the pyramids, ziggurats, ancient Indian communal baths or the Chinese Great Wall. Exploited labor is also extracted in the form of goods which are directly seized from the exploited communities. The primary property form of this mode is the direct religious possession of communities villages, bands, hamlets and all those within them. The ruling class of this society is generally a semi-theocratic aristocracy which claims to be the incarnation of gods on earth. The forces of production are associated with this society include basic agricultural techniques, massive construction and storage of goods for social benefit (granaries).

• *The feudal mode of production.* It is the last mode of production which is commonly feudalism in Western Europe. These non-animal power devices are clockwork, wind-mills and the intensification of specialization in the crafts and craftsman exclusively producing are specialized class of product. It is usually typified by high feudalism in Western Europe. The primary form of property is the possession of land in reciprocal contract relations: the possession of human beings as peasants or serfs is dependent upon their being entailed upon the land. Exploitation occurs through reciprocated contract (though ultimately resting on the threat of forced extractions). The ruling class is usually a nobility or aristocracy. The primary forces of production include highly complex agriculture (two, three field, lucerne fallowing and manuring) with the addition of non-human and non-animal power devices.

• *The capitalist mode of production.* It is usually associated with modern industrial societies. The initial form of property is the possession of objects and services through state guaranteed contract. The initial form of exploitation is wage labor. The ruling class is the bourgeoisie, which exploits the proletariat. Capitalism may produce one class (bourgeoisie) who possess the means of production for the whole of society and another class who possess only their own labor power, which they must sell in order to survive. The key forces of production include the overall system of modern production with its supporting structures of bureaucracy, and the modern state, and above all finance capital. Capitalist mode of production is commonly associated with industrial societies.

LABOUR THEORIES OF VALUE

Labor theories Labour Theories of Value(LTV) of value are economic theories of value according to which the values of commodities are related to the labor which of commodities are related to the labor which are needed to produce them.

There are many different accounts of labor value, with the common element that the "value" of an exchangeable good or service is, or tends to be, or can be considered as, or "is to be measured as" equal or proportional to the amount of labor which are needed to produce it that including the labor required to produce the raw materials and machinery which are used in production). Different labor theories of value prevailed amongst classical economists through to the mid-19th century.

Value "in use" is the usefulness of this commodity, its utility. There is a classical paradox which is often expressed when considering this type of value. Here, according to the Adam Smith:

The word VALUE, it is to be observed that has two different meanings, and sometimes expresses the utility of some particular object, and sometimes the power of purchasing other goods which the possession of that object conveys. The one may be called 'value in use ;' the other, 'value in exchange.' The things which have the greatest value in use have frequently little or no value in exchange; and on the contrary, those which have the greatest value in exchange have frequently little or no value in use. Nothing is more useful than water: but it will purchase scarce any thing; scarce any thing can be had in exchange for it. A diamond, on the contrary, has scarce any value in use; but a very great quantity of other goods may frequently be had in exchange for it.

There are some relationship between "value in exchange" and " value in use", i.e., when the value in exchange is greater as much, then, the there is nothing the value in use.

Value "in exchange" is the relative proportion with which this commodity exchanges for another commodity (in other words, its price in the case of money). It is relative to labor as explained by Adam Smith:

The value of any commodity, ... to the person who possesses it, and who means not to use or consume it himself, but to exchange it for other commodities which is equal to the quantity of labor which it enables him to purchase or command. Therefore, labor is the real measure of the exchangeable value of all commodities. Without qualification, value as intrinsic worth which stands without the process of exchange.

LTV and Labor Process

Since the term value is understood in the LTV as denoting something created by labor, and its "magnitude" as something proportional to the quantity of labor performed, it is important to explain how the labor process both preserves value and adds new value in the commodities it creates.

The value of a commodity increase in proportion to the duration and intensity of labor performed on average for its production.

Part of what the LTV means by "socially necessary" is that the value only increases in proportion to this labor as it's performed with average skill and average productivity. So though workers may labor with greater skill or more productivity than others, these more skillful and more productive workers will thus produce more value through the production of greater quantities of the finished commodity: each unit still bearing the same value as all the others of the same class of commodity. By working sloppily, the unskilled workers may drag down the average skill of labor, thus increasing the average labor time required for the production of each unit commodity. But these unskillful workers cannot hope to sell the conclusion of their labor process at a higher price (as opposed to value) simply because they have spent more time than other workers producing the same kind of commodities.

However, production not only involves labor, but also few means of labor: includes tools, materials, power plants and so on. These means of labor are also known as means of production which are frequently the product of another labor processes as well. Therefore, the labor process inevitably involves these means of production that already enter the process with a certain amount of value. Labor also requires other means of production that are not created with labor and therefore bear no value: such as sunlight, air, uncultivated land, unextracted minerals, etc. While useful, even crucial to the production process, these bring no value to that process. In terms of means of production resulting from another labor process, LTV treats the magnitude of value of these produced means of production as constant throughout the labor process. Due to the constancy of their value, these means of production are referred to, in this light, as constant capital.

Labor process are the major part of labor theories of values. These processes are help to obtained the values.

RELATION BETWEEN VALUES AND PRICES

One major issue facing the LTV is the relationship between value quantities on one hand and prices on the other. If a commodity's value is not the same as its price, and therefore the magnitudes of each likely differ, then what is the relation between the two, if any? Various LTV schools of thought provide the different answers to this question. For example, some argue that value in the sense of the amount of labor embodied in a good which acts as a center of gravity for price. As counter-intuitive as this may seem to those accustomed to neoclassical price theory, some empirical evidence suggests the labor values are better predictor of empirically recorded prices than prediction by any other means.

However, most economists would say that cases where pricing is even approximately equal to the value of the labor embodied are only special cases, and not the general case. In the standard formulation, prices also normally include a level of income for "capital" and "land". These incomes are known as "profit" and "rent" respectively. (It should be kept in mind that like the terms "labor" and "value", the terms "price", "capital", "land", "profit" and "rent" here are being used in a theoretical way which will not always correspond to everyday use, even by accountants.)

PRODUCTION PROCESS

It is the process that business create the products and services are known as production.

The way that businesses create products and services is known as the production process.

A firm must purchase all the necessary **inputs** and then **transform** them into the product **(outputs)** that it wishes to sell. For example a football shirt manufacturer must buy the fabric, pay someone for a design, invest in machinery, rent a factory and employ workers in order for the football shirts to be made and then sold.

How well-organised a firm is at undertaking this transformation process that will determine its success. This is known as the **productive efficiency** of a firm and it will want to be as efficient as possible in transforming its inputs into outputs, i.e., using the minimum number of inputs as possible to achieve a set amount of output. This will decrease the cost per unit of production and allow the firm to sell at a lower price.

Ultimately, the **objective of the production process is to obtain the goods and services that fulfill the needs and wants of customers.** The needs and wants of customers will be met, if a business can produce the correct number of products, in the shortest possible time, to the best quality and all at a competitive price.

This process is already discussed in first topic of this chapter. Production process transforms the inputs into outputs.

OPERATIONS MANAGEMENT

Operations management is defined as the performance of the managerial activities which are entailed in selection, design, operating, controlling, and updating production systems. The process of selection involves the strategic decision of choosing the process by which some good or service is to be made or performed. For example, in a steel mill that produces railway wheels, the choice may be between forging or casting the wheels. "Design" encompasses the tactical decisions which are involved in the creation of methods to carry out a production operation. "Operating" consists of the decisions of planning of long-term output levels in light of the forecast demand and the short-term decisions of scheduling jobs and allocating workers. In the railway plant, this activity would range from forecasting to the growth in rail car sales for the next five years, to determining which order process first out of the array of orders on hand. "Controlling" entails the procedures involved in taking corrective measures as the product or service is created. Here, operation means to the process or performance of each activity which entailed by the management.

Here, operations traditionally refers to the production of goods and services separately, although the variation between these two main types of operations is increasingly typical to make as manufacturers tends to merge the product and service which are offerings. More generally, Operations Management aims to increase the content of value-added activities in any given process. Fundamentally, these value-adding creative activities should be aligned with market opportunity for optimal enterprise performance.

Operations Management is an area of business which are concerned with the production of goods and services, and involves the responsibility of ensuring that business operations are efficient in terms of using as little resource as needed, and effective in terms of meeting customer requirements. It is concerned with managing the process that converts inputs (in the forms of materials, labor and energy) into outputs (in the form of goods and services).

Operations management is in regard to all operations within the organization. Related activities includes the managing purchases, inventory control, quality control, storage, logistics and evaluations.

A great deal of focus is on the efficiency and effectiveness of processes. Therefore, operations management frequently includes substantial measurement and analysis of internal processes. Ultimately, the nature of how operations management is carried out in an organization which highly depends on the nature of products or services in the organization, for example, retail, manufacturing, wholesale, etc.

OPERATIONAL PLANNING

An operational planning is a subset of strategic work plan. It explain the short-term methods of achieving the milestones and explains how, or which part of, a strategic plan will be put into operation during a given operational period, in the case of commercial application, a fiscal year or another given budgetary term. An operational plan is the basis for, and justification of an annual operating budget request.

OPERATIONAL RISK

When we plan for an operation then we have to take some risk to complete that tasks or operation. An operational risk is a risk which are arising from execution of business functions of a company. As such, it is a very broad concept including e.g. fraud risks, legal risks, physical or environmental risks, etc. The term operational risk is generally found in risk management programs of financial institutions that must organize their risk management program. Operational planning explain the methods of achieving the milestones and describes which part of planning will be put into that operation.

RISK MANAGEMENT

When operational risk arises then that time we have to manage that risk through the help of management concerning risks.

Risk Management is the identification, assessment, and prioritization of risks which are followed by coordinated and economical application of resources which is to minimize, monitor, and control the probability and/or impact of unfortunate events. Risks can come from uncertainty in financial markets, project failures, legal liabilities, credit risk, accidents, natural causes and disasters as well as deliberate attacks from an adversary.

Risk assessment

Risk assessment is a step in a risk management process. Risk assessment is the determination of quantitative or qualitative value of risk related to a concrete situation and a recognized threat is also called hazard. Quantitative risk assessment needs the calculations of two components of risk: R, the magnitude of the potential loss L, and the probability p that the loss will occur Risk assessment is the step of risk management process which determines the quantitative as well as qualitative values of risks.

Risk Analysis

It is also the major step of risk management process. It is the method to analyze the factors of achieving the goals of an organization. Risk analysis is a way to identify and assess the factors that may jeopardize the success of a project or achieving a goal of a company. This technique also helps to define preventive measures to decrease the probability of these factors from occurring and identify the countermeasures to successfully deal with these constraints when they develop to avert the possible negative effects on the competitiveness of the company.

OPERATIONS SCHEDULING

Here, scheduling means the use of resources with in the time. Scheduling pertains to establishing both the timing and use of resources within an organization. Under the operations function including both manufacturing and services, scheduling relates to use of equipment and facilities, the scheduling of human activities, and receipt of materials.

While issues relating to facility location and plant and equipment acquisition are considered the long term and aggregate planning which is considered the intermediate term, operations scheduling is considered to be a short-term issue.

It has the purpose of balancing the timing and the use of resources with in an organization. As such in the decision-making hierarchy, scheduling is commonly the final step in the transformation process before the original or expected output including goods and services which is to produced.

Consequently, scheduling decisions are made within the constraints which are established by these longer-term decisions. Generally, scheduling objectives deals with trade-offs among the conflicting goals for efficient utilization of labor and equipment, lead time, inventory levels, and processing times.

Approaches to Scheduling

There are two common approaches to scheduling naming forward scheduling and backward scheduling.

There are two general approaches to scheduling includes forward scheduling and backward scheduling. As long as the concepts are applied properly, the choice of methods is not significant. In fact, if process lead the times to move, queue and setup times then add to the job lead time and process time is to be assumed to occur at the end of process time, then forward scheduling and backward scheduling yield the same result. With forward scheduling, the scheduler selects a planned order release date and schedules all activities from this point forward in time.

With backward scheduling, the scheduler begins with a planned receipt date or due date and moves backward in time, according to the required processing times, until he or she reaches the point where the order will be released.

Of course there are other variables to consider other than due dates or shipping dates. Other factors which directly impact the scheduling process include: the types of jobs to be processed and the different resources that can process each, process routings, processing times, setup times, changeover times, resource availability, number of shifts, downtime, and planned maintenance.

Forward and backward scheduling yields the secure or common result, when the process lead time is add to the job lead time and process time is assumed to occur at the end of process time. The underline text in important or main concepts of this above paragraph.

Loading

Loading involves the process of the assigning jobs to work centers and to various machines in the work centers. If a job can be processed on only one machine then there is no difficulty is presented. However, if a job can be loaded on multiple work centers or machines, and there are multiple jobs to process, the assignment process becomes more complicated. The scheduler needs some methods to assign jobs to the centers in such a way that processing and setups are minimized along with idle time and throughput time.

Loading is another and alternative concept of scheduling. Loading refers to the way of assigning the job can be processed on only single machine, then at that time there is no difficulty is arise, whenever if the job can be processed on the assignment becomes more complicated.

Approaches to Loading

There are also two approaches are used for loading the machine work namely infinite loading and finite loading. Two approaches are used for loading work centers including infinite loading and finite loading. With infinite loading jobs are assigned to work centers without regard for capacity of the work center. Priority rules are appropriate for use under the infinite loading approach. Jobs are loaded at work centers according to the chosen priority rule. This is known as vertical loading. Infinite loading are much variate from finite loading. Infinite loading follows the priority rules.

Finite loading projects the actual start and stop times of each job at each work center. Finite loading considers the capacity of each work center and compares the processing time so that process time does not exceed the capacity. With finite loading the scheduler loads the job that has the highest priority on all work centers it will require. Then the job with the next highest priority is loaded on all needed work centers, and so on. This process is known to as horizontal loading. The scheduler using finite loading can then project the number of hours the each work center will operate. A drawback of horizontal loading is that jobs may be kept waiting at a work center, even though the work center is idle. This happens when a higher priority job is expected to arrive shortly. The work center is kept idle so that it will be ready to process the higher priority job as soon as it arrives. With vertical loading the work center would be fully loaded. Of course, this would mean that a higher priority job would then have to wait to be processed since the work center was already busy. The scheduler will have to weigh the relative costs of keeping higher priority jobs waiting, the cost of idle work centers, the number of jobs and work centers, and the potential for disruptions, new jobs and cancellations.

If the firm has limited capacity (e.g., already running three shifts), finite loading would be appropriate since it reflects an upper limit on capacity. If infinite loading is used, capacity may have to be increased through overtime, subcontracting, or expansion, or work may have to be shifted to other periods or machines.

There are difference between infinite loading and finite loading are infinite loading prefers to the priority rules because of the infinite numbers of jobs whereas finite loading prefers the capacity of each work centers and compare this capacity with the processing time. Infinite loading are known as vertical loading whereas finite loading are known as horizontal loading.

Sequencing

Sequencing is also not the part of scheduling, as well as loading.

Sequencing is concerned with determining the order in which jobs are processed. Not only must the order be determined for processing jobs at work centers but also for work processed at individual work stations. When work centers are heavily loaded and lengthy jobs are involved, the situation can become complicated. The order of processing can be crucial when it comes to the cost of waiting to be processed and the cost of idle time at work centers.

Sequencing is mainly consider in terms of determine that which jobs are processed. It takes the all the responsibility either it is to determine the processing jobs at work centers or is to determine the processing of jobs at a specific or individual work stations. These are some priority rule which are followed by infinite job processings.

Priority Rules

There are various priority rules which are followed by infinite loading and these rules are proposed by Vollmann, Berry, Whybark and Jacobs in 2005. these rules are following below:-

- *Random (R)*. Pick any job in the queue with equal probability. This rule is frequently used as a benchmark for other rules.
- *First come/first served (FC/FS)*. This rule is sometimes deemed to be fair whenever jobs are processed in the order in which they arrive.
- *Shortest processing time (SPT)*. The job with the shortest processing time requirement goes first. This rule tends to reduce work-in-process inventory, average throughput time, and average job lateness.
- *Earliest due date (EDD)*. The job with the earliest due date goes first. This seems to work well if the firm performance is judged by job lateness.
- *Critical ratio (CR)*. To use this rule one must calculate a priority index using the formula (due date-now)/(lead time remaining). This rule is widely used in practice.
- *Least work remaining (LWR)*. An extension of SPT, this rule dictates that work be scheduled according to the processing time remaining before the job is considered to be complete. The less work remaining in a job, the earlier it is in the production schedule.
- *Fewest operations remaining (FOR)*. This rule is another variant of SPT; it sequences jobs based on the number of

successive operations remaining until the job is considered complete. The fewer operations that remain, the earlier the job is scheduled.

- *Slack time (ST)*. This rule is a variant of EDD; it utilizes a variable known as slack. Slack is computed by subtracting the sum of setup and processing times from the time remaining until the job's due date. Jobs are run in order of the smallest amount of slack.
- *Slack time per operation (ST/O)*. This is a variant of ST. The slack time is divided by the number of operations remaining until the job is complete with the smallest values being scheduled first.
- *Next queue (NQ)*. NQ is based on machine utilization. The idea is to consider queues (waiting lines) at each of the succeeding work centers at which the jobs will go. One then selects the job for processing that is going to the smallest queue, measured either in hours or jobs.
- *Least setup (LSU)*. This rule maximizes utilization. The process calls for scheduling first the job that minimizes changeover time on a given machine.

These rules are assume that setup time and setup cost are independent of the processing sequence. However, this is not always the case. Jobs that require the similar setups can reduce setup times if sequenced back to back. In addition to this assumption, the priority rules also assume that setup time and processing times are deterministic and not variable, there will be no interruptions in processing, the set of jobs is known, no new jobs arrive after processing begins, and no jobs are cancelled. While little of this is true in practice, it does make the scheduling problem manageable.

Gantt Charts

Gantt chart is the type of visual aid. This chart was proposed by Henry Gantt in early 1990s. Gantt charts are named for Henry Gantt, a management pioneer of the early 1900s. He proposed the use of a visual aid for loading and scheduling. Appropriately, this visual aid is known as a Gantt chart. This Gantt chart is used to organize and clarify the actual or intended use of resources within a time framework. Usually, time is represented horizontally with scheduled resources which are listed vertically. Managers are able to use the Gantt chart to make trial-and-error schedules to get some sense of the impact of different arrangements.

There are a number of different types of Gantt charts, but the most common ones, and the ones most appropriate to our discussion, are the load chart and schedule chart. A load chart displays the loading and idle times for machines or departments; this shows when certain jobs are scheduled to start and finish and where idle time can be expected. This can help the scheduler redo loading assignments for better utilization of the work centers. A schedule chart is used to cheek job progress. On this type of Gantt chart, the vertical axis shows the orders or jobs in progress while the horizontal axis represents the time. A quick glance at the chart reveals which jobs are on schedule and which jobs are on time.

Gantt charts are the job broadly used scheduling the tools. However, they do have some limitations. The chart must be repeatedly updated to keep it current. Also, the chart does not directly reveal the costs of alternate loadings nor does it consider that processing times may vary among work centers.

SCHEDULING SERVICE OPERATIONS

The scheduling of services frequently encounters problems not seen in manufacturing. Much of this is due to the nature of service, i.e., the intangibility of services and the inability to inventory or store services and the fact that demand for services is generally random. Random demand makes the scheduling of labor extremely typical as seen in restaurants, movie theaters, and amusement parks. Since customers don't like to wait, labor must be scheduled, so that customer wait is minimized. This sometimes requires the use of queuing the theory or waiting line theory. Queuing theory uses the estimate arrival rates and service rates to evaluate an optimum staffing plan. In addition, flexibility can often be built into the service operation through the use of casual labor, on-call employees, and cross-training.

These scheduling can also be complies when it is required to coordinate or schedule more than one resource.

Scheduling of services can also be complicated when it is necessary to coordinate and schedule more than one resource. For example, when hospitals schedule the surgery, not only is the scheduling of surgeons involved but also the scheduling of operating room facilities, support staff, and special equipment. Along with the scheduling of classes, universities must also schedule faculty, classrooms, labs, audiovisual and computer equipment, and students. To further complicate the matters, cancellations are also a general concept and can add further disruption and confusion to the scheduling process.

Instead of scheduling labor, service firms frequently try to facilitate their service operations by scheduling the demand of the consumer. This is done through the use of appointment systems and reservations.

PRODUCTION MANAGEMENT SYSTEM

This system is an order-based production type system for manufacturers' use. Based on order information arriving in the form of fax or electronic data, the system creates the production plans for parts of production development, set-aside inventory, etc. in consideration of delivery schedules and processing loads.

A production management system has a plurality of pieces of production apparatus, a production controller connected online to the production apparatus, and a simulator. The simulator performs a simulation of physical distribution for a specified period of time through use of a simulation parameter, apparatus information, and process information, which are acquired from the production controller. A re-simulation of physical distribution is performed while taking, as parameters for optimizing physical distribution, time-series data pertaining to the availability factor of each apparatus and the load factor of each apparatus obtained as a result of the simulation, as well as the start and termination times of an event which is to arise in the period of a simulation. A dispatch rule set for each apparatus or a group of pieces of apparatus having a single function is dynamically changed, thus feeding back the change to control of real physical distribution.

Under the system, clearly specified processing instructions are delivered to each production site, and in the case of process outsourcing, etc. outsourcing arrangement orders are also issued.

Workers read into the system initiation completion, inventory receipt and other information using a barcode reader. In this way, factory information is reflected on the office side in realtime, allowing unit production costs to be calculated based on the products' progress situation and processing time. Each time a product lot is completed and delivered a delivery slip is issued, and on the day of closure a bill is issued.

With regard to sales and purchasing, the system performs a series of management tasks up to deposit/disbursement management.

The information is stored in the archive in a form in which the relations between different pieces of information are preserved. This feature is very helpful when repeat orders are received.

This system is a low-cost, easy-to-use integrated system that was designed after first considering the opinions of customers, based on our unique know-how as a long experienced manufacturer.

Production and Operations Management: A Case Study

PRODUCTION AND OPERATIONS MANAGEMENT: A CASE STUDY DESCRIBING, ANALYZING, AND DEVELOPING THE RECOMMENDATIONS IN RELATION TO OPERATIONS MANAGEMENT AT WKK TECHNOLOGY LTD.

This is the case study of WKK technology ltd. In order to describe, analyze and development of production and operation management.

In recent months, WKK Technology has experienced increasingly serious problems associated with production operations. The most salient issues are (a) falling manufacturing productivity and (b) increasing overtime costs for both line workers and engineering staff. These operations management problems are related to one another (e.g., overtime costs affect productivity measures). The probability, however, is that an underlying problem is the root cause of both manifestations of the production problem at WKK Technology. Further, it is possible that actions at WKK (Holding) Ltd. in Hong Kong have an impact on production efficiency at WKK technology (all marketing operations, including customer specified product requirements are handled at corporate headquarters).

An investigation identified the specific nature of the operations management problems confronting the company. Specific recommendations were made for implementation by the company to correct the production and operations management problems identified.

These recommendations are following below:-

- Introduction to the Company and Problem
- External Factors Affecting the Problem
- Description and Analysis of the Problem
- Assessment of the Problem

Benchmarking in an Organization

Benchmarking is a process, not an outcome.

- This process is closely associated with and derived from the quality movement.
- Both total quality management (TQM) and ISO 9000 seek to improve quality, and in turn, organizational productivity through the formalization of best practices.
- Strategic benchmarking links the benchmarking concept to organizational strategy (Brockett, Golden, Sarin, and Gerberman, 2001). Applying strategic benchmarking to the application of technology in operations management allows the operational manager to apply specific technology to a process only at those points in the process and at the appropriate times to assure that organizational benchmarks are met. This approach, as is the case in the application of capacity planning to the application of technology in organizational management, can lead to improved operations at lower costs. Knowledge management is an increasingly important element of organizational strategy.

Aspects of Product Management

Depending on the company size and history, product management has a variety of functions and roles. Sometimes there is a product manager, and sometimes the role of product manager is held by others. Frequently there is Profit and Loss (P&L) responsibility as a key metric for evaluating product manager performance. In some companies, the product management function is the hub of many other activities around the product. In others, it is one of many things that need to happen to bring a product to market.

Product management often serves an inter-disciplinary role, bridging gaps within the company between teams of different expertise, most notably between engineering-oriented teams and business-oriented teams. For example product managers often translate business objectives set for a product by Marketing or Sales into engineering requirements. Conversely they may work to explain the capabilities and limitations of the finished product back to Marketing and Sales.

Product Planning

- Building product roadmaps, particularly Technology roadmaps
- Determine business-case and feasibility
- Detailed Product planning
- Evangelizing new products within the company
- Gathering market requirements
- Identifying new product candidates
- Product Life Cycle considerations
- Product differentiation
- Scoping and defining new products at high level

Product Marketing

- Bringing new products to market
- Monitoring the competition
- Product positioning and outbound messaging
- Promoting the product externally with press, customers, and partners

Case Study

Note : knowing more about "Production and Operation Management" reader can study documentation process of Microsoft company by visiting their site : www.members.microsoft.com

http://www.lotsofessays.com/viewpaper/1708824.html

http://www.allbusiness.com/production-management/3236575-1.html

http://www.managementportal.net/Knowledgebase/Operations/Operations.htm

http://www.icmrindia.org/casestudies/catalogue/Operations/OPER043.htm

http://www.icmrindia.org/casestudies/catalogue/Operations/OPER040.htm

2

Operations as a Working Tool

This chapter includes the key concepts which are described below:-

- Defining Operation
- Processing Work
- Nature and Scope of Operations Management
- Business Operation
- Decision Process
- Business Model
- Business Plan
- Operational Planning
- Operational Risk Management
- Approaches in Operations Management
- Risk Analysis
- Risk Management Plan
- Risk Communication
- Decision Tree

DEFINING OPERATION

In general, an operation is a term which represents a function (or instruction), rather than a term or name. But here, we represents the term operation in order to the business point of view, i.e., business operations.

Business operations are those ongoing recurring activities that are involved in the running of a business for the purpose of producing value for the stakeholders. They are contrasted with project management, and consist of business processes. The condusion of business operations is the harvesting of value from assets which are owned by a business. Assets can be either physical or intangible. An example of value derived from a physical asset like a building is rent. An example of value derived from an intangible asset like an idea is a royalty. The effort involved in "harvesting" this value is what constitutes the business operations.

Business operations encompasses three fundamental management imperatives that collectively aims to maximize the value which are harvested from business assets, this has frequently been referred to as "sweating the assets":

1. Generate recurring income.
2. Increase the value of the business assets.
3. Secure the income and value of the business.

These three imperatives are mutually dependent each other. There are following tenets which illustrate this interdependency:

- The more recurring income an asset generates, the more valuable it becomes. For example, the products that sell at the highest volumes and prices are commonly considered to be the most valuable products in of a business product portfolio.
- The more valuable a product becomes the more recurring income it generates. For example, a luxury car can be leased out at a higher rate than a normal car.
- The intrinsic value and income-generating potential of an asset cannot be realized without a way to secure it. For example, petroleum deposits are worthless unless processes and equipment are developed and employed to extract, refine, and distribute it profitably.

These three management imperatives are achieved by described the means of a business. These business operations is the execution of business model.

Generating Recurring Income

This is first imperative of business operations. It very straight forward and well-understood management imperative.

This is the most straightforward and well-understood management imperative of business operations. The major aim of this imperative is to implement or a sustained delivery of goods and services to the customers business at a cost that is less than the funds which establish are acquired in exchange for said goods and services — in short, making a profit.

These funds are directly acquired by the business in exchange for the goods and services it delivers the revenue of business. The cost of producing, developing and delivering these goods and services is the expenses of business.

Business's Profit = Revenues> Expenses

Above statement is true, which means a business whose revenues are greater than its expenses makes a profit. These business tends to do profitable.

Increase the Value of Business's Assets

This is second imperative of business operations. It is well known and utilized form of management imperative. Harvesting of value from assets are deride from the outcomes of business operations. These assets are categorized into two forms, i.e., physical or intangible.

Securing the income and value of the business

A business that can harvest a significant amount of value from its assets but cannot demonstrate an ability to sustain this effort that cannot be taken as a viable business. This is third and last management imperative which is the major issue in each and every business operations. This imperative has some many features that includes:-

- Desirability or demand for its goods and services
- Ability of its customers to pay for its goods and services
- Uniqueness and competitiveness of its business model
- Control exerted over the quality and efficiency of production activities
- Public regard for the business as a member of the community

PROCESSING WORK

Here processing work is concerned with how best to manage

the set of business process that are directly responsible for converting a variety of resources such as materials, money and the effort of people into outputs (such as manufactured goods or delivered goods). This processing deals with the strategic aspects of these operations management issues, covering:-

- Why the operations function is so critically important to the organization;
- What the organization should be seeking to achieve from effective management of its business processes ; and
- The crucial role which are played by the design of the operations system.

Here, an example which proves the meaning of operations in terms of their managers:-

Manager of a Printing Services Firm

We provide the full range of service— everything from copying a dog-eared black and white photo of someone's granny through to 4-color printing of a thousand copies of a glossy brochure. We're in the town center, so we have quite a bit of what you might call passing trade— we're useful when the office photocopier breaks down, for example!

Most of our business comes from regular clients. We have a few quite large contracts with companies who use us for almost all their printing except low-volume photocopying. For example, for one customer, we are currently working on their training manuals— 200 loose-leaf pages in a customized ring binder. They provide us with the content electronically and we do the rest. We're also working on a marketing leaflet for them—that's the design of the leaflet as well as the production.

At the moment we've more work than we can handle comfortable on the design side, as we've only one person who can really use the software properly. But at the same time we could do with more high-quality printing jobs— we spent a lot of money on printing equipment last year and it needs to earn its keep. You always want more business, but it doesn't take much to tip the balance— the phone could ring now and if one of our regulars wanted a large job doing quickly we'd be pushed—but we'd manage it somehow because they need to know they can rely on us.

According to the Johnston et al in 2003, p.15, operations management is usually with the design, planning, control and improvement of resources of an organization to produce goods or services for customers.

Whereas according to waters, 2002, p.4, operations have been defined that:-

At the heart of every organization are the activities that make their products. These activities are the operations. To put it simply, the operations describe what the organization does...operations are the activities that are primarily concerned with making an organization's products. Operations transform inputs to outputs. Effective operations system do not just happen. Whether or not stakeholders achieve the value that they seek from an operation which depends in the design of the operations systems and the methods in which those systems are operated or performed. Operations management is about both "doing the right thing" and doing things right.

Te method in which customers gets benefits from operations is through the products. Goods and services needs be designed to provide the features that customers want. These are frequently at least partly, and sometimes entirely, a function of the processes that are involved in making and delivering the product. For example, clearly, the quality of the printed items produced by the print service firm is directly affected by the printing process which are employed. Internet-based services such as travel booking or music download consists almost entirely of the processes which are involved the exchanges of information in the form of digital data. Consequently, product and process are closely intertwined concepts, and operations processes are difficulty in ensuring that the product that achieve the customer satisfaction.

Technology plays an important as well as inevitable role in operations system and strongly associated with both product and process. Latest changes and recent ways of applying the technology to meet the demands of the market place that give rise to entirely new products as well as new ways of producing and providing traditional goods and services.

Advanced manufacturing processes, the internet, and other aspects of information and communications technologies do not just enhance the existing processes, that they offer radically in different manners or doing business and innovative methods of creating value for all stakeholders. For example, computerized manufacturing processes have provide the means of 'mass customization' whereby an individual item can be tailor-made for a particular customer, but without the prohibitively high process costs that the traditional techniques would have required. An understanding of how technology can best be deployed—designed or selected, implemented and managed—to serve that operations is therefore crucial to effective design and management of operations systems.

Operations management is fundamentally about the management of processes that is their design, planning, operation and control and for this reasons it is sometimes referred as business process management.

NATURE AND SCOPE OF OPERATIONS MANAGEMENT

Generally operations refers to the production of goods and services separately, although the difference between these two main types of operations is increasingly typical to make as manufacturers that tends to merge the product and service offerings. More generally, Operations Management aims to increase the content of value-added activities in any given process. Fundamentally, these value-adding creative activities should be aligned with market opportunity for optimal enterprise performance.

Operations management is an area of business are concerned with the production of goods and services and involves the responsibility of ensuring that business operations are efficient in terms of using resources.

It is concerned with managing the process that converts inputs (in the forms of materials, labour and energy) into outputs (in the form of goods and services). Inputs refers to the data in the form of materials, labor and energy whereas the outputs refers to the data in the form of goods and services. Operations management is frequently used along with production management, therefore, it is useful to understand the nature of operations management.

Operations management mainly focuses on carefully managing the processes which are used to produce and distribute the products and services. Usually, small businesses don't talk about "operations management", but they carry out the activities that management schools typically associate with the phrase "operations management." Major, overall activities frequently include product creation, development, production and distribution. These activities are also associated with Product and Service Management. However product management is usually in regard to one or more closely related product — that is, a product line. Operations management is in regard to all operations within the organization. Related activities include managing purchases, inventory control, quality control, storage, logistics and evaluations. A great deal of focus is on efficiency and effectiveness of processes. Therefore, operations management frequently includes substantial measurement and analysis of internal processes. Ultimately, the nature of how operations management is carried out in an organization that depends very much on the nature of products or services in the organization, for example, retail, manufacturing, wholesale, etc.

There is hardly any difference between production management and operation management. First difference is occurred, in the terms of production management is more used for a system where tangible goods are produced. Whereas operations management is more frequently used where different inputs are transformed into tangible services.

Viewed from this perspective, operations management will cover such services organization as banks ,airlines ,utilities ,pollution control agencies super bazaars, educational institutions ,libraries ,consultancy firm and police departments, in addition ,of course ,to manufacturing enterprises. The second distinction relates to the evolution of the subject. Operation management is the term that is used now a days .Production management precedes the operations management in the historical growth of the subject.

BUSINESS OPERATIONS

Business operation are defined as the recurring activities which are involved in running of a business for the purpose of producing value for the stakeholders. This topic is earlier discussed as well as described in this chapter, business operations encompasses three fundamental management imperatives that aims to maximize the value which are harvested from business assets. These imperatives are shown below:-

1. Generate recurring income.
2. Increase the value of the business assets.
3. Secure the income and value of the business.

All these management imperatives are also discussed early in this chapter.

BUSINESS MODEL

A business model is a framework for creating economic, social, and/or other forms of value. The term business model is used for a broad range of informal and formal descriptions to represent the core aspects of a business which includes the purpose, offerings, strategies, infrastructure, organizational structures, trading practices, and operational processes and policies.

Business model consists of all economic social and other forms of value. Models are used to maintain the business policies and strategies.

Conceptualization of business models

Conceptualization of business models try to formalize the informal descriptions into building blocks and their relationships. While many different conceptualizations exist, Osterwalder proposed a synthesis of different conceptualizations into a single reference model which are based on the similarities of a large range of models, and constitutes a business model design template which allows enterprises to describe their business model:

Infrastructure :

- Value configuration: The rationale which makes a business mutually beneficial for a business and its customers.
- Partner network: The business alliances which complement other aspects of the business model.
- Core capabilities: The capabilities and competencies necessary to execute the business model of a company.

Customers :

- Target customer: The target audience for a business' products and services.
- Distribution channel: The means by which a company delivers the products and services to the customers. This includes marketing and distribution strategy of the company.
- Customer relationship: The links a company establishes between itself and its different customer segments. The process

of managing customer relationships is referred to as customer relationship management.

These three above customers are the concept of business model.

Finances :

- Cost structure: The monetary consequences of the means which are employed in the business model. A company's DOC is the example of lost structure.
- Revenue: The way a company makes money through a variety of revenue flows. A company's income is the example of revenue.

The process of business model design is part of business strategy. The implementation of a company's business model into organizational structures (e.g. organigrams, workflows, human resources) and systems (e.g. information technology architecture, production lines) is part of business operations of a company. It is inevitable to understand that business modeling which generally refers to the business process design at the operational level, whereas business models and business model design refer to the defining of business logic of a company at the strategic level.

Business strategy includes the designing of business model. Business modeling tends to the design of business process at operational level while business model and design tends to define the business logic of a company.

BUSINESS PLAN

Planning is major issue in starting any business process. Business plan acts statement of achieving the business goals.

A business plan is a formal statement of setting of business goals, the reasons why they are believed attainable, and the plan for reaching those goals. It may also contain the background information about the organization or team which are attempting to reach that goals.

There are two types of organization like profit or non-profit organization. These organization has typically focus on financial goals. Non-profit organization mainly focus on organizational mission.

The business goals may be defined for the for-profit or for non-profit organizations. For-profit business plans generally focus on financial goals, such as profit or creation of wealth. Non-profit and government agency business plans tends to focus on organizational mission which is the basis for their governmental status or their non-profit, tax-exempt status, respectively — although non-profits may also focus on optimizing the revenue. In non-profit organizations, creative tensions may develop in the effort to balance the mission with "margin" or revenue. Business plans may also keeps the target changes in perception and branding by the customer, client, tax-payer, or larger community. A business plan having the changes in perception and branding as its primary goals which is called a marketing plan.

Business plans are of two types of focus, i.e., internally and externally. External focus refers to the external stakeholders specifically financial stakeholders. Internal focus targets the immediate goals which are necessary any to achieve the external goals.

Business plans may be internally or externally focused. Externally focused plans target the goals that are important to external stakeholders, particularly financial stakeholders. They typically have detailed information about the organization or team that are attempting to reach the goals. With for-profit entities, external stakeholders include the investors and customers. External stake-holders of non-profits include the donors and the clients of the non-profit's services. For government agencies, external stakeholders include tax-payers, higher-level government agencies, and international lending bodies such as the IMF, the World Bank, various economic agencies of the UN, and development banks.

Internally focused business plans target the intermediate goals which are required to reach the external goals. They may includes the development of a new product, a new service, a new IT system, a restructuring of finance, the refurbishing of a factory or a restructuring of the organization. An internal business plan is frequently developed in conjunction with a balanced scorecard or a list of critical success factors. This allows the success of the plan is to be measured using non-financial measures. Business plans that identify and target the internal goals, but provide only general guidance on how they will be met are called strategic plans.

Operational plans describes the goals of an internal organization, working group or department. Project plans are known as project frameworks which describes the goals of a particular project. They may also address the project's place within the organization's larger strategic goals.

Formats of Business Plan

Format of structure of business plan always depends on its presentation context. It is not usual for business. These formats are generally categorized into four formats.

The format of a business plan depends on its presentation context. It is not uncommon for businesses, especially start-ups to have three or four formats for the same business plan:

- An "elevator pitch" - a three minute summary of the business plan's executive summary. This is frequently used as a teaser to awaken the interest of potential funders, customers, or strategic partners.
- An oral presentation - a hopefully entertaining slide show and oral narrative that is meant to trigger the discussion and interest potential investors in reading the written presentation. The content of the presentation is commonly limited to the executive summary and a few key graphs showing the financial trends and key decision making benchmarks. If a new product is being proposed and time permits, a demonstration of the product may also be included.
- A written presentation for external stakeholders - a detailed, well written, and pleasingly formatted plan that are targeted at external stakeholders.
- An internal operational plan - a detailed plan describing the planning details that are needed by management but may not be of interest to external stakeholders. Such plans have a somewhat higher degree of candor and informality than the version targeted at external stakeholders.

Typical structure of business plan includes:-

cover page and table of contents

- executive summary
- business description
- business environment analysis
- industry background

- competitive analysis
- market analysis
- marketing plan
- operations plan
- management summary
- financial plan
- attachments and milestone

These are brief details of maintaining a business plan.

OPERATIONAL PLANNING

As we discuss earlier that planning must be important to create a new business project. These planning are used to achieve the business goals and objectives. Operational plan should establish the activities and budgets for each portion of the organization.

An operational planning is a subset of strategic work plan. It describes the short-term methods of achieving the milestones and explains how, or what portion of, a strategic plan will be put into operation during a given operational period, in the case of commercial application, a fiscal year or another given budgetary term. An operational plan is the basis for, and justification of an annual operating budget request. Therefore, a five-year strategic plan would need five operational plans funded by five operating budgets.

Operational plans are always funded by operational budget, i.e., five year strategic plan would need the five operational plans which are funded by five operating budgets.

Operational plans should establish the activities and budgets for each part of the organisation for the next 1 - 3 years. They link the strategic plan with the activities the organization will deliver and the resources which are required to deliver these activities.

An operational plan draws directly from agency and program strategic plans which are used to describe agency and program missions and goals, program objectives, and program activities. Like a strategic plan, an operational plan addresses four questions:

- Where are we now?
- Where do we want to be?

- How do we get there?
- How do we measure our progress?

Sometimes operational planning is abbreviated as OP. for preparing the operating budget request, OP is the initial and ending step.

The OP is both the first and the last step in preparing an operating budget request. As the first step, the OP provides a plan for resource allocation; as the last step, the OP may be modified to reflect the policy decisions or financial changes made during the budget development process.

Operational plans should be prepared by the people who will be involved in implementation. There is frequently a need for significant cross-departmental dialogue as plans are created by one part of the organisation inevitably have implications for other parts.

Operational plans should contain:

- quality standards
- desired outcomes
- clear objectives
- activities to be delivered
- a process for monitoring progress.
- staffing and resource requirements
- implementation timetables

When there is a planning, then it also has some risk, i.e., operational risk.

An operational risk is a risk which are arising from the execution of business functions of a company. As such, it is a very broad concept including e.g. fraud risks, legal risks, physical or environmental risks, etc. The term operational risk is most commonly found in risk management programs of financial institutions that must organize their risk management program according to Basel II. In Basel II, risk management is divided into credit, market and operational risk management. In many cases, credit and market risks are handled through financial department of a company, whereas operational risk management is perhaps coordinated centrally but most commonly implemented in different operational units (e.g. the IT department takes care of information risks, the HR department takes care of personnel risks, etc)

More specifically, Basel II defines the operational risk as the risk of loss resulting from inadequate or failed internal processes, people and systems, or from external events. Although the risks apply to any organisation in business, this particular way of framing risk management is of particular relevance to the banking regime where regulators are responsible for establishing safeguards to protect against systemic failure of the banking system and the economy.

Problems in Operational Planning

It is relatively straightforward for an organisation to set and observe the specific, measurable levels of market risk and credit risk. By contrast, it is relatively difficult to identify or assess the levels of operational risk and its many sources. Historically, organisations have accepted the operational risk as an unavoidable cost of doing business.

OPERATIONAL RISK MANAGEMENT

Operational risk includes the risk of loss resulting which are occurred from inadequate or failed internal systems or processes and these risks are managed by operational risk management. It is also abbreviated as ORM.

The term Operational Risk Management (ORM) is the oversight of operational risk including the risk of loss resulting from inadequate or failed internal processes and systems, human factors, or from external events. ORM is defined as a continual cyclic process resulting in acceptance, mitigation, or avoidance of risk.

Principles of ORM

The U.S. Department of Defense summarizes the principles of ORM as follows:

1. Anticipate and manage risk by planning.
2. Accept no unnecessary risk.
3. Make risk decisions at the right level.
4. Accept risk when benefits outweigh the cost.

Benefits of ORM

1. Early detection of unlawful activities.

2. Lower compliance/auditing costs.
3. Reduced exposure to future risks.
4. Reduction of operational loss.

Process of ORM

Risk management process defined by the International Organization for Standardization in four-step model:

1. Establish context
2. Risk assessment
    - Risk identification
    - Risk analysis
    - Risk evaluation
3. Risk treatment
4. Monitor and review

This process is cyclic as any changes to the situation (such as operating environment or needs of the unit) requires re-evaluation per step one.

The U.S. Department of Defense summarizes the ORM process in a five-step model:

1. Identify hazards
2. Assess hazards
3. Make risk decisions
4. Implement controls
5. Supervise (and watch for changes)

APPROACHES IN OPERATIONAL RISK MANAGEMENT

There are three approaches in ORM which are proposed by Basel II. These includes basic indicator approach, standardized approach and advanced measurement approaches.

Basel II and various Supervisory bodies of the countries have prescribed various soundness standards for Operational Risk Management for Banks and similar Financial Institutions. To complement these standards, Basel II has given guidance to 3 broad methods of Capital calculation for Operational Risk

- Basic Indicator Approach are based on annual revenue of the Financial Institution
- Standardised Approach are based on annual revenue of each of the broad business lines of the Financial Institution
- Advanced Measurement Approaches are based on the internally developed risk measurement framework of the bank adhering to the standards prescribed (methods include IMA, LDA, Scenario-based, Scorecard etc.)

The Operational Risk Management framework should include the identification, measurement, monitoring, reporting, control and mitigation frameworks for Operational Risk.

Basic Indicator Approach :

It is first approach of ORM which are proposed by Basel II capital adequacy rules. The basic approach or basic indicator approach is a set of operational risk measurement techniques which are proposed under Basel II capital adequacy rules for banking institutions.

Basel II needs all banking institutions to set aside the capital for operational risk. Basic indicator approach is much simpler compared to the alternative approaches (i.e. standardized approach (operational risk) and advanced measurement approach) and this has been recommended for banks without significant international operations.

It is the simplest approach as compared to other, i.e., standardized and advanced measurement approach.

Based on the original Basel Accord, banks using the basic indicator approach that must hold the capital for operational risk which are equal to the average over the previous three years of a fixed percentage of positive annual gross income. Figures for any year in which annual gross income is negative or zero should be excluded from both the numerator and denominator when calculating the average. The fixed percentage 'alpha' is typically 15 percent of annual gross income.

Standardized Approach :

It is second approach of ORM which are also predicted by Base II under adequacy rules for banking institutions.

The standardized approach or standardised approach is a set of operational risk measurement techniques that are proposed under Basel II capital adequacy rules for banking institutions.

Basel II needs all banking institutions to set aside capital for operational risk. Standardized approach falls between basic indicator approach and advanced measurement approach in terms of degree of complexity.

Degree of complexity lies between the basic indicator approach and advanced measurement approach.

Based on the original Basel Accord, under the Standardised Approach, activities of bank are divided into eight business lines: corporate finance, trading & sales, retail banking, commercial banking, payment & settlement, agency services, asset management, and retail brokerage. Within each business line, gross income is a broad indicator that serves as a proxy for the scale of business operations and thus the likely scale of operational risk exposure within each of these business lines. The capital charge for each business line is formulated by multiplying gross income by a factor (denoted beta) that are assigned to that business line. Beta serves as a proxy for the industry-wide relationship between the operational risk loss experience for a given business line and the aggregate level of gross income for that business line.

The total capital charge is formulated as 3-year average of summation, i.e., total of the regulatory capital charges across each of the business lines in each year.

The negative capital charges which are resulting from negative gross income in any business line may offset the positive capital charges in other business lines without limit.

In order to qualify for use of the standardised approach, a bank must satisfy its regulator that, at a minimum:

- Its board of directors and senior management, as appropriate, are actively involved in the oversight of the operational risk management framework;
- It has an operational risk management system that is conceptually sound and is implemented with integrity; and
- It has sufficient resources in the use of the approach in the major business lines as well as the control and audit areas.

Advanced Measurement Approach

It is third as well as last approach of ORM which are also proposed by Basel II capital adequacy rules like two approaches which are above described.

The advanced measurement approach (AMA) is a set of operational risk measurement techniques which are proposed under Basel II capital adequacy rules for banking institutions.

Under this approach, the banks are allowed to create their own empirical model to quantify the needed capital for operational risk. Banks can use this approach only subject to approval from their local regulators.

Also, according to section 664 of original Basel Accord, In order to qualify for use of the AMA a bank must satisfy its supervisor that, at a minimum:

- Its board of directors and senior management, as appropriate, are actively involved in the oversight of the operational risk management framework;
- It has an operational risk management system that is conceptually sound and is implemented with integrity; and
- It has sufficient resources in the use of the approach in the major business lines as well as the control and audit areas.

Advanced measurement approach may be abbreviated as AMA. This approach can be used by banks which allow to develop the empirical model to quantity the AMA.

RISKS ANALYSIS

Risk analysis is method to identify the risk or factors that affects the business policies and strategies.

Risk analysis is a technique to identify and assess those factors that may jeopardize the success of a project or achieving a goal of a business or organization. This technique also helps to define the preventive measures to reduce or decrease the probability of these factors from occurring and identify countermeasures to successfully deal with these constraints when they develop to avert the possible negative effects on the competitiveness of the company.

There is a process which helps to analyze the risk and it is possible by using the facilitated risk analysis process.

Facilitated Risk Analysis Process

It is abbreviated as FRAP and use to analyze the risk which occurs in business strategy.

FRAP analyzes one system, application or segment of business processes at time.

FRAP assumes that additional efforts to develop the precisely quantified risks which are not cost effective because:

- such estimates are time consuming
- risk documentation becomes too voluminous for practical use
- specific loss estimates are generally not needed to determine if controls are needed.

After identifying and categorizing risks, a team identifies the controls that could mitigate the risk. The decision for what controls are needed lies with the business manager. The conclusions of a team as to what risks exists and what controls needed are documented along with a related action plan for control implementation.

Three of the most important risks a software company faces are unexpected changes in revenue and costs from those budgeted and amount of specialization of the software planned. Risks that affect the revenues can be unanticipated competition, privacy, intellectual property right problems, and unit sales that are less than forecast; unexpected development costs also create the risk that can be in the form of more rework than anticipated, security holes, and privacy invasions.

Narrow specialization of software with a large amount of research and development expenditures can lead both business and technological risks since specialization does not lead to lower the unit costs of software. Combined with the decrease in the potential customer base, specialization risk can be significant for a software firm. After probabilities of scenarios have been calculated with risk analysis, the process of risk management can be applied to help manage the risk.

Risk reduction

When risk analysis tends to be completed, then the first thing is to reduce the risk. Risk reduction involves the methods that reduce the severity of the loss or the likelihood of the loss from occurring. For example, sprinklers are designed to put out a fire to reduce the risk of loss by fire. This method may cause a greater loss by water damage and therefore may not be suitable. Halon fire suppression systems may mitigate that risk, but the cost may be prohibitive as a strategy. Risk management may also take the form of a set policy, such as only allow the use of secured IM platforms (like Brosix) and not allowing personal IM platforms (like AIM) to be used in order to reduce the risk of data leaks.

Modern software development methodologies reduce the risk by developing and delivering the software incrementally. Early methodologies suffered from the fact that they only delivered the software in the last phase of development; any problems encountered in earlier phases meant the costly rework and often jeopardized the whole project. By developing in iterations, software projects can limit the effort which are wasted to a single iteration.

Outsourcing could be an example of risk reduction if the outsourcer can demonstrate the higher capability at managing or reducing the risks. In this case companies outsource only some of their departmental needs. For example, a company may outsource only its software development, the manufacturing of hard goods, or customer support which needs to another company, while handling the business management itself. This way, the company can concentrate more on business development without having to worry much more about the manufacturing process, managing the development team, or finding a physical location for a call center.

Risk retention

Here retention involves the acceptance of that loss which occurs during the processing. This Involves accepting the loss when it occurs. True self insurance falls in this category. Risk retention is a viable strategy for small risks where the cost of insuring against the risk that would be greater over time than the total losses sustained. All risks that are not avoided or transferred are retained by default. This includes risks that are so large or catastrophic that they either cannot be insured against or the premiums which would be infeasible. War is an example since most property and risks that are not insured against war, so the loss attributed by war is retained by the insured. Also any amounts of potential loss or risk over the amount which are insured is retained risk. This may also be acceptable if the chance of a very large loss is small or if the cost to insure for greater coverage amounts that is so great it would hinder the goals of the organization too much.

Some ways of managing risk fall into multiple categories. Risk retention pools are technically retaining the risk for the group, but spreading it over the whole group that involves the transfer among individual members of the group. This is different from traditional insurance, in that case where no premium is exchanged between members of the group up front, but instead those that losses are assessed to all members of the group.

In the terminology of practitioners and scholars alike, the purchase of an insurance contract is often described as a "transfer of risk." However, technically speaking, the buyer of the contract generally retains legal responsibility for the losses "transferred", meaning that insurance may be described more accurately as a post-event compensatory mechanism. For example, a personal injuries insurance policy does not transfer the risk of a car accident to the insurance company. The risk still lies with the policy holder namely the person who has been in the accident. The insurance policy simply provides that if an accident (the event) occurs involving the policy holder then some compensation may be payable to the policy holder that is commensurate to the suffering/damage.

RISK MANAGEMENT PLAN

A Risk Management Plan is a document which are prepared by a project manager to foresee the risks, to calculate the effectiveness, and to create response plans to mitigate them. It also consists of the risk assessment matrix.

A risk is defined as "an uncertain event or condition that, has a positive or negative effect on a project's objectives if it occurs." Risk is inherent with any project, and project managers that should assess the risks continually and develop plans to address them. The risk management plan contains an analysis of likely risks with both high and low impact, as well as mitigation strategies to help the project that avoid being derailed should common problems arise.

Risk is a condition which some positive as well as some negative impact on a project of a business. Risk management plan is a statement that are developed by project manager which is used to evaluated the effectiveness of risk on the project.

Risk management plans should be periodically reviewed by the project team in terms to avoid having the analysis become stale and not reflective of actual potential project risks.

Most critically, risk management plans include a risk strategy. Broadly, there are four potential strategies, with numerous variations. Projects may choose to:

- Accept risk; simply take the chance that the negative impact will be incurred
- Avoid risk; changing plans in order to prevent the problem from arising
- Mitigate risk; lessening its impact through intermediate steps
- Transfer risk; outsource risk to a capable third party that can manage the outcome

Creation of RMP

Select appropriate controls or countermeasures to measure the each risk. Risk mitigation needs to be approved by the appropriate level of management. For example, a risk concerning the image of the organization should have top management decision behind it whereas IT management would have the authority to decide on computer virus risks.

The risk management plan should propose applicable and effective security controls for managing the risks. For example, an observed high risk of computer viruses could be mitigated by acquiring and implementing antivirus software. A good risk management plan should contain a schedule for control implementation and responsible persons for those actions.

Risk management plan is used to proposed the applicable and effective security controls for managing the risks. These plans are implemented and created by the project manager.

According to ISO/IEC 27001, the stage immediately after completion of the Risk Assessment phase consists of preparing a Risk Treatment Plan, which should document the decisions about how each of the identified risks should be handled. Mitigation of risks frequently means the selection of security controls, which should be documented in a Statement of Applicability, which identifies the particular control objectives and controls from the standard that have been selected, and why.

Implementation of RMP

Follow all of the planned methods for mitigating the effect of the risks. Purchase insurance policies for the risks that have been decided to be transferred to an insurer and avoid all risks that can be avoided without sacrificing goals of the entity, reduce others, and retain the rest.

Review and evaluation of the plan :

Initial step of risk management plans will never be perfect. Practice, experience, and actual loss results that will necessitate the changes in the plan and contribute information to allow the possible various decisions which are to be made in dealing with the risks being faced.

Risk analysis results and management plans should be updated periodically. There are two primary reasons for this:

1. to evaluate whether the previously selected security controls are still applicable and effective, and
2. to evaluate the possible risk level changes in the business environment. For example, information risks are a good example of rapidly changing business environment.

Limitations of RMP

There are some limitations of risk management plan. If risks are improperly assessed and prioritized, time can be wasted in dealing with risk of losses that are not likely to occur. Spending too much time assessing and managing unlikely risks that can divert those resources that could be used more profitably. Unlikely events do occur but if the risk is unlikely enough to occur it may be better to simply retain the risk and deal with the result if the loss does in fact occur. Qualitative risk assessment is subjective and lack consistency. The primary justification for a formal risk assessment process is legal and bureaucratic.

Prioritizing too highly the risk management processes could keep an organization from ever completing a project or even getting started. This is especially true if other work is suspended until the risk management process is considered complete.

It is also important to keep in mind the distinction between risk and uncertainty. Risk can be measured by impacts x probability.

Risk-management activities as applied to project management

In project management risk management includes various activities like planning, assigning a risk officer, maintaining live project risk database, creating anonymous risk reporting channel, preparing mitigation plan, summarizing planned. Project management is also a separate chapter which are described in detailed.

In project management, risk management includes the following activities:

- Planning how risk will be managed in the particular project. Plan should include risk management tasks, responsibilities, activities and budget.
- Assigning a risk officer - a team member other than a project manager who is responsible for foreseeing potential project problems. Typical characteristic of risk officer is a healthy skepticism.
- Maintaining live project risk database. Each risk should have the following attributes: opening date, title, short description, probability and importance. Optionally a risk may have an assigned person responsible for its resolution and a date by which the risk must be resolved.
- Creating anonymous risk reporting channel. Each team member should have possibility to report risk that he foresees in the project.
- Preparing mitigation plans for risks that are chosen to be mitigated. The purpose of the mitigation plan is to describe how this particular risk will be handled - what, when, by who and how will it be done to avoid it or minimize consequences if it becomes a liability.
- Summarizing planned and faced risks, effectiveness of mitigation activities, and effort spent for the risk management.

Risk Management and Business continuity

Risk management is simply a practice of systematically selecting cost effective approaches for minimising the effect of threat realization to the organization. All risks can never be fully avoided or mitigated simply because of financial and practical limitations. Therefore all organizations have to accept some level of residual risks.

Whereas risk management tends to be preemptive, business continuity planning (BCP) was invented to deal with the consequences of realised residual risks. The necessity to have BCP in place arises because even very unlikely events will occur if given enough time. Risk management and BCP are often mistakenly seen as rivals or overlapping practices. In fact these processes are so tightly tied together that such separation seems artificial. For example, the risk management process creates important inputs for the BCP (assets, impact assessments, cost estimates etc). Risk management also proposes applicable controls for the observed risks.

RISK COMMUNICATION

This term refers to the concept in which people are uncomfortable to talk about risk. Risk communication refers to the idea that people are uncomfortable to make talking about risk. People tends to put off admitting that risk is involved, as well as communicating about risks and crises. Risk Communication can also be linked to Crisis communication.

Benefits and Barriers of Risk Communication

"Some of the Benefits of risk communication include, improved collective and individual decision making. Both the purpose of the exchange, and the nature of the information have an impact on the benefits. Depending on the situation, personal and community anxieties about environmental health risks can be reduced or increased. For example, a goal might be raising concern about radon and prompting action."

Rules of Risk Communication

There are seven rules for practice of risk communication which are following below:-

1. Accept and involve the public as a legitimate partner.
2. Plan carefully and evaluate your efforts.
3. Listen to the public's specific concerns.
4. Be honest, frank, and open.
5. Coordinate and collaborate with other credible sources.
6. Meet the needs of the media.
7. Speak clearly and with compassion.

DECISION TREE

Decision tree is a way for visualizing a complex chain of decision.

A decision leads to a new choice and therefore to a new decision that in term focus with a new choice and so on. Decision trees are the useful tools for helping you to choose between several courses of action.

These trees shows the parent-child relationship if can be represented by circles, sequences, etc. To prepare the decision tree, it is important to understand how to use this tool.

How to Use the Tool

You start a Decision Tree with a decision that you need to make. Draw a small square to represent this on the left hand side of a large piece of paper, half way down the page.

From this box draw out lines towards the right for each possible solution, and write a short description of the solution along the line. Keep the lines apart as far as possible so that you can expand your thoughts.

At the end of each line, consider the results. If the result of taking that decision is uncertain, draw a small circle. If the result is another decision that you need to make, draw another square. Squares represent decisions, and circles represent uncertain outcomes. Write the decision or factor above the square or circle. If you have completed the solution at the end of the line, just leave it blank.

Starting from the new decision squares on your diagram, draw out lines representing the options that you could select. From the circles draw lines representing possible outcomes. Again make a brief note on the line saying what it means. Keep on doing this until you have drawn out as many of the possible outcomes and decisions as you can see leading on from the original decisions.

Once you have done this, review your tree diagram. Challenge each square and circle to see if there are any solutions or outcomes you have not considered. If there are, draw them in. If necessary, redraft your tree if parts of it are too congested or untidy. You should now have a good understanding of the range of possible outcomes of your decisions.

Example to represent the Decision Tree

Let's go on with the example and look at the next drawing which illustrates decision tree.

DRAWING 6

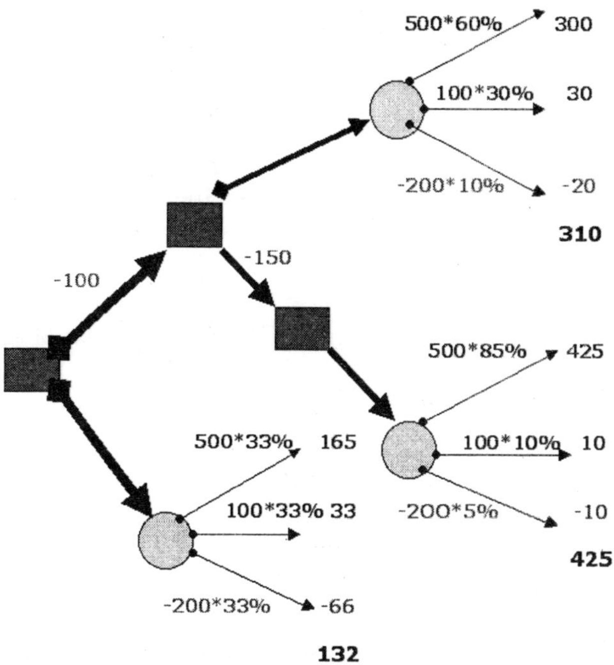

Let's suppose that you decide to start a biz. This decision is not submitted to uncertainty and is represented conventionally by a square. Then you have to choose if you will follow up a training or not.

If you decide to do not, you go to a circle that represents an uncertainty because it leads to three probabilities which are represented by three arrows. Conserving the same % of probability and the same expected incomes than in our first example, we know that the sum is **132.**

Now if you decide to take a training, you have to pay its cost that is to say **-100**. There is not uncertainty about the cost, so you go to a new Square. Here, according to our previous example, you meet three probabilities: 60% for the best, 30% for the medium and 10% for the worst. The result of the calculation is 310 but you have to substrate the cost of the learning **(-100)**. The net result is therefore **210.**

Now, let's suppose that a consulting group proposes you to realize a complex market study costing 150. Thanks to this study, you can highly improve your probabilities: 85% for the best, 10% for the medium and only 5% for the worst: It's quite a deterministic probability!

Now look at the results. Of course, you get 425 but going back on the tree, you have to deduce the cost of the market study **(-150)** and the cost of the training **(-100)**. It means that the net result amounts only **175**. Despite the increase of the success probabilities, you have better in this case to not order the market study.

Be aware that when there is a long chain of decisions and events you should need a computer program and a bit of time.

Evaluating the Decision Tree

Now you are ready to evaluate the decision tree. This is where you can work out which option has the greatest worth to you. Start by assigning a cash value or score to each possible outcome. Make your best assessment of how much you think it would be worth to you if that outcome came about.

Next look at each circle (representing an uncertainty point) and estimate the probability of each outcome. If you use percentages, the total must come to 100% at each circle. If you use fractions, these must add up to 1. If you have data on past events you may be able to make rigorous estimates of the probabilities. Otherwise write down your best guess.

Calculating Tree Values

Once you have worked out the value of the outcomes, and have assessed the probability of the outcomes of uncertainty, it is time to start calculating the values that will help you make your decision.

Start on the right hand side of the decision tree, and work back towards the left. As you complete a set of calculations on a node (decision square or uncertainty circle), all you need to do is to record the result. You can ignore all the calculations that lead to that result from then on.

Calculating the Value of Decision Nodes

When you are evaluating a decision node, write down the cost of each option along each decision line. Then subtract the cost from the outcome value that you have already calculated. This will give you a value that represents the benefit of that decision.

Note that the amounts that already spent do not count for this analysis – these are 'sunk costs' and (despite the emotional cost) should not be factored into the decision.

When you have calculated these decision benefits, choose the option that has the largest benefit, and take that as the decision made. This is the value of that decision node.

Conclusion of Decision Tree

By applying this technique, we can see that the most and very important option is to develop a new product. It is worth much more to us to take out time and get the product right, than to rush the product to market. And its better just to improve our existing products than to botch a new products even through it costs useless.

Decision trees provide an effective way of decision making because they:

- Clearly lay out the problem so that all options can be challenged.
- Allow us to analyze the possible consequences of a decision fully.
- Provide a framework to quantify the values of outcomes and the probabilities of achieving them.
- Help us to make the best decisions on the basis of existing information and best guesses.

As with all decision making methods, decision tree analysis should be used in conjunction with common sense - decision trees are just one important part of your decision making tool kit.

General Description of Decision Tree

A **decision tree** (or **tree diagram**) is a decision support tool that uses a tree-like graph or model of decisions and their possible consequences, including chance event outcomes, resource costs, and utility. Decision trees are commonly used in operations research, specifically in decision analysis, to help identify a strategy most likely to reach a goal. Another use of decision trees is as a descriptive means for calculating conditional probabilities.

Decision tree is a part of decision analysis, it includes the closely related influence diagram which is used as a visual and analytical decision support tool, where the expected values or expected utilities of competing the alternatives which are calculated.

A decision Tree consists of 3 types of nodes:-

1. Decision nodes - commonly represented by squares
2. Chance nodes - represented by circles
3. End nodes - represented by triangles

These are drawn from left to right, a decision tree has only burst nodes (splitting paths) but no sink nodes (converging paths). Therefore, they are used manually, and can grow very big and are then frequently hard to draw fully by hand.

Case Study

Note : knowing more about "Operations as a Working Tool" reader can study documentation process of Microsoft company by visiting their site : www.members.microsoft.com

http://www.osha.gov/dcsp/success_stories/compliance_assistance/tocas_case_study.html

http://www.moldmakingtechnology.com/articles/0607case1.html

3

Operation Strategies

This chapter includes the key concepts which are shown below:

- Introduction
- Need for Operation Strategies
- Operation Strategy as a Competitive Weapon
- Elements of Operation Strategy
- Developing an Operation Strategy
- Corporate Strategy
- Global Strategies
- Cost and Quality
- Market Analysis

INTRODUCTION

We are discussed in previous chapter that how the operation are useful tool to make a product to apply these operations, a company have to follow some operation strategies.

This chapter explores the advantages of implementing operations strategies to improve the efficiency and effectiveness of company. Operations strategies include the actions which are taken by various companies and industries to maintain the capacity and future of their company which provide the information about the specific project to the employees and workers of that company which perform these operation.

NEED FOR OPERATION STRATEGY

An organization that wants to succeed in a competitive business environment needs a sound strategy. A strategy is a broad, long-term plan which are conceived in terms to achieve business objectives. Strategies are developed at three levels: the corporate level, the business level and the functional level. In this chapter, we look at functional strategies, and specifically, strategies decision concerning the operation function. Many operation decision are developed in compliance with business objectives, and with the functional objectives of the marketing finance and human resources departments. Operations strategies such as the choice of operating structure are

Influenced by the nature of goods or services which are to be produced and the markets to be served.

In the early 1990s, following the liberalization of the Indian economy, many companies from Japan, Europe, North America and Korea started operations in India. Most Indian companies were not in a position to compete against them as their products were either costlier or of lower quality. At this point, many Indian companies realized that they had to improve their operations strategies in order to improve the productivity of their company. Today, operation strategies from an integral part of the strategic planning process of most companies. They deal with the development of operational plans for the manufacturing facilities of an organization.

Operation strategies are major required of any organization. These are influenced by the nature of goods or services that are produced and the markets which are to be served . These strategies are developed at three levels; the corporate level, the business level and third is functional level.

OPERATIONS STRATEGIES AS A COMPETITIVE WEAPON

There are some objectives of an organization in these objectives, one objective is to reach a position where it is able to attract more customers than its competitors their business rivals.

One of the key objectives of any business organizations to reach the position where it is able to attract more and more customers than its competitors. In terms to gain such a competitive advantage, organization try to identify their distinct competencies. The characteristics of company's operation function are important in determining its choice of product and markets, and the elements of its competitive strength. The following example show how operational strength can be used effectively as competitive weapons:

Product/Process Expertise: An organization can employ its strengths in some areas of product functionalities and process capabilities to achieve a competitive advantage over its competitors. For instance, Intel corporation, USA, has superior computer chip design due to its technological expertise in producing microchips.

Quick Delivery: An organization with flexible capacity and an adaptive production process can produce a product and satisfy the customer needs quickly. One-hour eye glass shoe repair services are some examples of quick delivery.

There are some competitive weapon of operations strategy which includes short product cycle, low-cost process, convenience and location, production flexibility, quality as well as product variety and facility size.

Shorter Product Cycle

The first that enters a market generally gains a significant market share over the subsequently entrants. The speed of product introduction is dependent on the flexibility and adaptability of the production system. A company, which is more adaptable than its competitors, can untapped market demand and as a conclusion that will able to corner a significant market share.

When a company firstly enters into a market then first of all, if gains the significant market share. Production introduction because of their flexibility and adaptability.

Low Cost Process

An organization with an efficient production system or access to low-cost resources can make the standard product at costs which are lower than its competitors. For example, steel companies, such as Nucor in the United States, have competed successfully with larger integrated steel producers like Nippon and US steel by using mini-mill (a smaller version of a steel reining mill that can process scrap). The mini-mill production process allowed Nucor to gain a substantial price advantage over the competitors by reprocessing scrap steel rather then producing primary steel from iron ore.

Convenience and Location

Facility location can provide substantial competitive advantage. For example, local courier and parcel company, Desk TO Desk Couriers (DTDC), is a strong competitor to foreign multinationals like DHL and FedEx in India, as it has deep penetration and covers a larger number of Indian towns and cities.

Production Flexibility

Some organizations specialize in having a highly flexible and responsive operations environment which is not fixed or constant to the floor. This enable production lines to be reconfigured within hours or days to make new and different products. This flexibility has allowed Celestica to expand from manufacturing a few product for single customer (IBM) to making hundreds of products for over 40 different companies.

Quality

An organization that produces a product of higher quality than its competitors can increase its sale volume even while commanding a higher price. Such an example is found in Sundaram Fasteners of the Sundaram Clayton Group. Their radiator caps are standard equipment in major automobile companies like Daimler Chrysler and General Motors

Quality is tasks for manufacturing a product. When an organization process high quality product to the market against their business rival then they can increase the sales volume.

Product Variety and Facility Size

In certain industries, the variety of product offered and the size of operations can provide competitive advantage. Grocery stores and supermarket retailers compete by having larger stores that allow them to show a vast variety of product and to benefit from economies of scale.

ELEMENTS OF OPERATION STRATEGY

An operations strategy is a high-level integrated plan for business effectiveness competitiveness. Key elements of operations strategy are described below:

- Designing the production system
- Product/service design and development
- Technology selection and process development
- Allocation of resources to strategic alternatives
- Facility planning.

There are the elements of operations strategy which helps for business effectiveness and competitiveness.

Designing the Production System

Designing the production system is one of the key responsibilities of any operations manager. It involve selecting the product design, the production system, and the inventory policy for finished goods each product line.

(a) Product design : Product design are categorized into two types naming customized product design and standard product design.

Operations managers customized the product design when the level of customization is high and the quality to be product is low. Product are designed to satisfy the needs or requirements of customer. The emphasis in this type of product design in on the quality and on-time delivery, rather than on cost. Industrial products like boilers and turbines are example of customized products.

Standardized product design is employed when an organization is involved in the production of limited variety of product, which are produced in large batch sizes. In such system, importance is given to cost-control and quality rather than on the flexibility of the system. Consumer durable like coolers, fans, and television are example of standardized products.

(b) Production System : Production system can also categorized into two type naming product focused system and process-focused systems.

Product-focused systems are usually employed in mass production organizations where there groups of machines tools and workers are arranged according to their respective process in terms to put together a product. These system are appropriate for producing standardized products like cars, television, computer system, etc.

Process-focused system are designed to support the production departments that perform a single performances like painting or packing. These system are highly flexible and can easily be modified to support other product design. Hence, they are used in the production of customized products.

(c) Finished Goods Inventory Policy : These policy are of two types including produce-to-stock policy and produce-to-order policy.

In a produce-to-stock policy, products are produced well in advance and are stored in warehouses, from where they are dispatched as per customer orders. This policy is suitable demand (like refrigerators and air-coolers) or those, which have general applications (like bolts and nuts).

A produce-to-order policy allows the production to start only after when the company receives customer orders and halts the production until another order is received. This policy is appropriate for organizations that produce the product, parts or components of high value (like spares of an aircraft engine) or those that are meant exclusively for particular purposes (like dyes, casting, etc.).

(d) Product/service Design and Development : Every product has a life cycle. The life cycle of a typical product is shown in Figure 2.1. the first stage in the life cycle of a product, after it is designed and developed, is the *introduction stage*. In this stage, sales are dependent on promotion and other marketing efforts. Profits are either negative or quite insignificant. The products that successfully survive on this stage enter the growth stage. In the growth stage, sales volume increases exponentially. During the growth stage, organizations take decisions regarding production capacity expansion. These decision are dependent on the response to the product in the market. In the maturity stage, sales growth becomes stagnant. During the maturity stage, organizations focus on improving the efficiency of the processes, minimizing costs, etc. finally, the product enters the decline stage. In this stage, sales show a downward trend, because of obsolescence of technology which are used in the product, changing customer requirements, and the availability of substitute or complementary products.

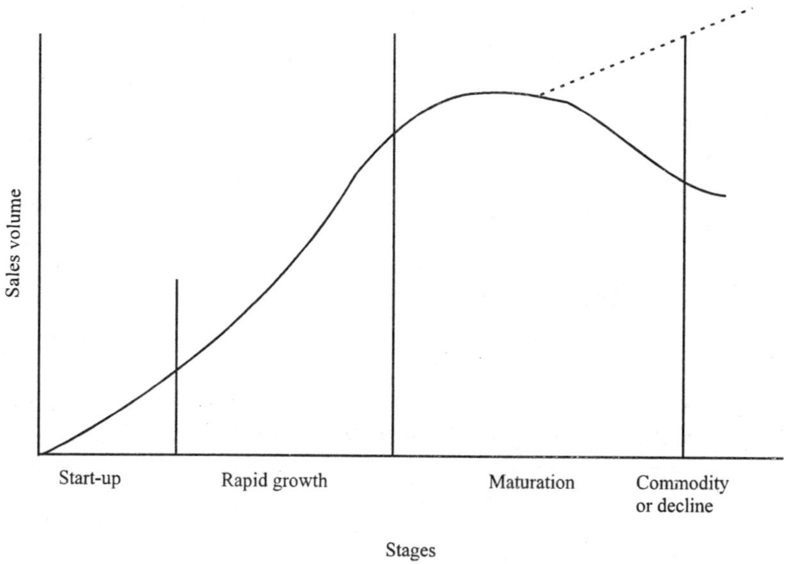

Figure 2.1 : Characteristics of the Product Life Cycle

The operation department plays an inevitable role in initial stage of the product life cycle. Its role diminishes as the product moves up in the life cycle.

The organization focus shifts towards maintaining or increasing the market share and improving the quality of the product and the production process.

The following are the important steps in the development of new products:

- Idea Generation
- Feasibility Studies
- Prototype Design
- Initial Design of Production Model
- Economic Evaluation
- Market Testing
- Final Design of Production Model

New product development always starts with idea generation. Ideas can come from several sources such as employees, customers, intermediaries, vendors, market research and so on. After a new idea is selected, it is screened to ascertain its feasibility in implementation.

Feasibility studies consider whether the idea which are generated is feasible both technically and economically. Such studies test whether the production of the products is technically feasible and profitable to produce and market. If the idea is found to be both technically and economically feasible, then a prototype of the product is developed. The prototype may not have all the features of the final product, but it has all the basic characteristics of the products. The prototype is tested under standard condition and defects are noted. On the basic of the conclusion of testing, the required changes are made in the prototype. Then the prototype is tested again. This process is carried out until the performance of the prototype reaches a satisfactory level. Once the final structure of the prototype is in place, the prototype design is evaluated for profitability. If the production of the model is profitable, then the prototype enters the production design stage. The initial production design is transformed into final production design after the performance testing, production trials and testing, economic studies and test marketing. These steps ensure that the final product performs satisfactorily and can be produced efficiently in the desired quantities. The product development process continues even after the launch of the product. The product is modified or upgraded to adapt to changing market conditions and/or adopt new technology.

Technology Selection and Process Development

Once the design of the product is finalized, managers concentrate on determining how the product will be produced. This involves through analysis and planning of the production processes and facilities. Every step in the process of production is planned in detail. The technology to be used in the production process is selected from a variety of options.

Allocation of Resources to Strategic Alternatives

Production companies have to continuously deal with the problem of scarce resources like capital, machine and materials and so on. As involves resources inputs are essential production activities, their shortages can influence production performance significantly. Hence operation managers have to plan the optimal use of resources, both in terms of minimizing wastage, and in terms of their allocation to the best strategic use.

Facility Planning

The location of the production facilities is one of the key decision an operation manager has to make since it is critical to the competitiveness of the organization.

Setting up production facilities with adequate capacity includes initial investment. So that, strategically right option should be carefully weighed against all available alternatives. These decision also influence the future decisions on probable capacity expansions plans. Managers have to take into account factors like the availability of raw materials and access to the market when making their decision. Operations managers also make layout decisions, i.e., decisions on the internal arrangement of workers and departments within the facility. All these decision are crucial for the success of the organization.

DEVELOPING AN OPERATION STRATEGY

We have already discussed about the operation strategy, what are its needs and how these are important and what are the elements of it but the main task into how to develop it.

These operations strategy should be in line with the organization strategy, and the organization strategy should be in line with the corporate vision and mission. If the organization strategy is not consistent with the corporate vision and mission, the organization cannot survive in the competitive marketplace. For example, let us assume that the operation strategy of an organization focuses on cost reduction by specializing production and process and utilizing long production runs, while the marketing strategy focuses on product customization and quick response. These strategies are in conflict with each other. In such a case, it will be difficult for the organization to achieve its corporate vision and mission. Figure below, shows the process of developing an operations strategy in atypical production organization. Long-term operations strategy decision are concerned with developing new products, determining the appropriate production capacity, establishing new production facilities, adopting new technology, location plants and warehouses and so on. The objective of an operation strategy is to achieve the long-term goals established by the business strategy.

Operation strategy— organization strategy—corporate vision and mission. There are some process for developing operation strategies.

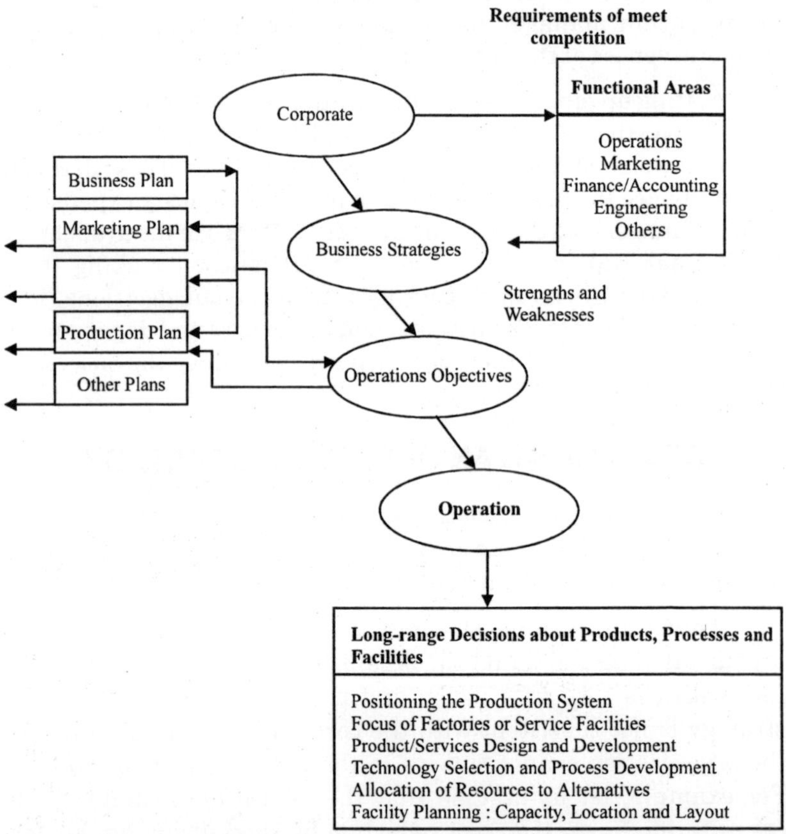

There is a distinction between strategic planning and operational planning in the scope of its application. Strategic planning is concerned with long-term planning and involves the selection of target markets and distribution channels, whereas operational planning is concerned with short term, day-to-day planning.

Selections of markets is the key concept for any strategy. After markets are analyzed for their attractiveness, operations managers develop suitable processes and design to achieve objectives of the organization as mentioned earlier, the operations strategy is developed in the line with organization strategy, which, in turn is derived from corporate objectives.

Organization strategies focus on achieving the corporate objectives by utilizing current strengths of a company and identifying, capability to improve the competitive position of the company.

The operations strategy should be flexible enough to support a product or service of a organization through its entire life cycle and be able to accommodate the future changes in market demand or business objectives. In addition, operation strategies should be consistent with strategies in other functional areas such as marketing, finance and human resources. Operational superiority is critical for maintaining the competitive position of manufacturing and service organizations

CORPORATE STRATEGY

We believe this is the most realistic strategic objectives for us partly because of the strength and depth of our product portfolio, and also because we currently compete against the vendors that have substantial business scale in areas where we have not traditionally been active like system integration services.

It should be noted that product sales is the primary driver for our other revenue streams: professional services and recurring income.We intend to continue working towards this objective through a number of well-established strategic approaches:

- Continuing the growth of market share in the core product lines through our traditionally strong sales and marketing focus;
- Cross-selling of additional products to existing exceeding 400 customers, the majority of whom have only one or two products;
- Expansion within these core product lines by developing and commercializing the additional solution which offers that all expanded potential customer base;
- Diversification into non-telecom markets where our product strengths have proven the application, like financial services; and
- Addition of new product capabilities, by acquisition or internal development, that we can sell to new and existing customers.

In addition to this product-oriented strategy, we are also now focusing more resources on building our Managed Services business, as we believe there is continuing stable demand for this offering, and by its regular nature it offers some insulation against the typically lumpy revenue characteristic of a large-scale software licence business.

GLOBAL STRATEGY

Global strategies require firms to tightly coordinate their produce and pricing strategies across international markets and locations and therefore, firms that pursue a global strategy are typically highly centralized.

A global strategy may be appropriate in industries where firms are faced with strong pressures for cost reduction but with weak pressures for local responsiveness. So that, it allows these firms to sell a standardized product worldwide. However, fixed costs (capital equipment) are substantial. Nevertheless, these firms are able to take advantage of scale economies and experience curve effects, because it is able to mass-produce a standard product which can be exported the providing that demand is greater than the costs involved.

Global strategy as defined in business terms is strategic guide of an organization to globalization. A sound global strategy should address these questions: what must be (versus what is) the extent of market presence in the world's major markets? How to build the necessary global presence? What must be (versus what is) the optimal locations around the world for the various value chain activities? How to run global presence into global competitive advantage?

Academic research on global strategy came of age during the 1980s, including work by Michael Porter and Christopher Bartlett & Sumantra Ghoshal. Among the forces perceived to bring about the globalization of competition were convergence in economic systems and technological change, especially in information technology, that facilitated and required the coordination of a multinational firm's strategy on a worldwide scale.

COST AND QUALITY

Cost is the value of money that has been used up to produce something. Generally, cost refers to the money.

In business, retail, and accounting, a **cost** is the value of money that has been used up to produce something, and hence is not available for use anymore. In economics, a cost is an alternative that is given up as a result of a decision. In business, the cost may be one of acquisition, in which case the amount of money expended to acquire it is counted as cost. In this case, money is the input that is gone in terms to acquire the thing. This acquisition cost may be the sum of the cost of production as incurred by the original producer, and further costs of transaction as incurred by the acquirer over and above the price paid to the producer. Usually, the price also includes a mark-up for profit over the cost of production. Costs are often further described based on their timing or their applicability.

Accounting vs opportunity costs

In accounting, costs are the monetary value of expenditures for supplies, services, labour, products, equipment and other items are purchased for use by a business or other accounting entity. It is the amount denoted on invoices as the price and recorded in bookkeeping records as an expense or asset cost basis.

Opportunity cost are also known as *economic cost* is the value of the best alternative that was not chosen in terms to pursue the current endeavour—i.e, what could have been accomplished with the resources expended in the undertaking. It represents the opportunities forgone.

In theoretical economics, **cost** used without qualification frequently means opportunity cost.

There are four costs naming private costs, external costs, social costs and psychic costs. When a transaction takes place, it typically involves both private costs and external costs.

Private costs are the costs that the buyer of a good or service pays the seller. This can also be described as the costs internal to the firm's production function.

External costs are also called externalities, in contrast, are the costs that people other than the buyer are forced to pay as a conclusion of the transaction. The bearers of such costs can be either specific individuals or society at large. Note that external costs are frequently both non-monetary and problematic to quantify for comparison with monetary values. They include things like pollution, things that society will likely have to pay for in some way or at some time in the future, but that are not included in transaction prices.

A psychic cost is a subset of social costs that specifically represent the costs of added stress or losses to quality of life.

Quality

The common element of the business definitions is that the quality of a product or service refers to the perception of the degree to which the product or service meets the expectations of customers. Quality has no meaning unless related to a particular function and object. Quality is perceptual, conditional and somewhat subjective attribute.

Quality in business, engineering and manufacturing has a pragmatic interpretation as the *non-inferiority* or *superiority* of something. Quality is a perceptual, conditional and somewhat subjective attribute and may be understood differently by different people. Consumers may focus on the **specification quality** of a product/service, or how it compares to competitors in the marketplace. Producers might measure the **conformance quality**, or degree to which the product/service was produced correctly.

Dimension of Quality

The dimensions of quality refer to the attributes that quality achieves in Operations Management

- Quality supports dependability
- Dependability supports Speed
- Speed supports Flexibility
- Flexibility supports Cost

Quality ↔ Dependability ↔ Speed ↔ Flexibility ↔ Cost

In Manufacturing

In the manufacturing industry, it is generally stated that "Quality drives the productivity." Improved productivity is a source of greater revenues, employment opportunities and technological advances. However, this has not been the case historically, and in the early 19th century it was recognised that some markets,such as those in Asia, preferred cheaper products to those of quality. Most discussions of quality refers to a finished part, wherever it is in the process. Inspection, which is what quality insurance usually means, is historical, since the work is done. The best way to think about quality is in process control. If the process is under control, inspection is not necessary.

MARKET ANALYSIS

A large number of market analysis methods are related to sales forecasting, others are more general techniques for analyzing markets. The literature defines various areas in which market analysis is important. These include: sales forecasting, market research, and marketing strategy. Sales forecasting and market analysis are complementary skills that any marketing manager should possess.

A **Market analysis** is a documented investigation of a Market which are used to inform a planning activities of a firm specifically around decision of: inventory, purchase, work force expansion/ contraction, facility expansion, purchases of capital equipment, promotional activities, and many other aspects of a company.

Not all managers are asked to conduct a market analysis, but all managers must make decisions using market analysis data and understand how the data was derived. So all managers need a reasonable understanding of the tools which are most used for making sales forecasts and analyzing markets.

The most progressive view of quality is that it is defined eternally by the customers or and user and is based upon that evaluation of the person entire customer experience. The customer experience is the aggregate of all the touch point's that customers that have with products and services of the company.

Case Study

Note : knowing more about "*Operation Strategies* " reader can study documentation process of Microsoft company by visiting their site : www.members.microsoft.com

http://www.globalfuture.com/scenario2.htm

http://www.robustdecisions.com/decision-making/case-studies.php

http://www.infozee.com/channels/mba/casestudy/decision.htm

http://www.icmrindia.org/casestudies/catalogue/Human%20Resource%20and%20Organization%20Behavior/HROB053.htm

http://www.flipkart.com/clinical-decision-making-case-studies/143543983x-tox3fqovid

http://www.chemcases.com/

4

Decision Making Process and Decision Theory

This chapter includes the key concepts which are shown below:-

- Introduction to Decision Making Process
- Planning for Decision Making
- Decision Levels
- Techniques for Decision Making
- Cost Benefit Analysis
- Paired Comparison Analysis
- Pareto Analysis
- Grid Analysis
- Decision Theory
- Problems in Decision Theory
- Types of Decision
- Normative and Descriptive Decision Theory
- Decision under Certainty
- Decision under Uncertainty
- Probability
- Decision under Unknown Non-zero Possibilities

INTRODUCTION TO DECISION MAKING PROCESS

A business man have to make decisions under the pressure of

time and circumstances. The decision making process is a key to leadership.

The techniques in this chapter ranges from the very simple to the rather sophisticated. Which technique you choose for a given decision will be influenced by the importance and complexity of the decision. As a preview to a discussion of techniques, then, let's consider a few preliminary ideas that will help identify some decision making levels.

PLANNING FOR DECISION MAKING

While decision making without planning is fairly common, it is often not pretty. The terms used to describe it—crisis management, putting out fires, seat-of-the-pants governing—all reveal the inelegance and awkwardness of this way of life. Planning allows decisions to be made in a much more comfortable and intelligent way. Planning even makes decisions easier by providing guidelines and goals for the decision. We might even say that planning is a type of decision simplification technique.

Without the use of planning, decision making is not fairly comfortable and easiest. With the help of planning, i.e., to make a plan, then this plan makes decisions easier by providing the guidelines and goals for the decision.

There are four types of benefits to planning that will find by the decision makers, these are following below:-

1. Planning allows the establishment of independent goals. The vision which will shape the decisions is set apart from surrounding events. Decisions are not made only as reactions to external stimuli. "Management by firefighting" which is replaced by a conscious and directed series of choices. Managers now steer the organization, individuals now steer their lives, rather than being steered by external forces. Sometimes the difference between planning and not planning is described as "proactive" means of taking the control of the situation versus "reactive" means of responding to stimuli.

2. Planning provides a standard of measurement. A plan provides something to measure against, so that you can discover whether or not you are achieving or heading toward the goals. As the proverb says, *If you don't know where you're going, it doesn't matter which way you go.*

3. Planning converts values to action. When you are faced with a decision, you can consult your plan and determine that which decision will help to advance your plan best. Decisions made under the guidance of planning can work together in a coherent manner to advance the company or individual goals.

Planning is too useful in emergency situations. When a crisis arises, a little thought about the overall plan will help to determine which decision is to make that will not only help to resolve the crisis but will also help to advance the overall plan. Without a plan, crises are dealt with haphazardly and decisions are made which may ultimately be in conflict with each other.

4. Planning allows limited resources to be committed in an orderly way. Budgets, time, effort, manpower—all are limited. Their best use can be made when a plan governs their use.

A simple example would be planning to buy a house or a car. Rather than having to decide between buying the item right now with all cash or never having it, you can plan to buy it over several years by making payments. Or, you might combine this plan with the plan to buy a smaller house and add rooms later as they could be afforded. By planning, you can thus accomplish things that might otherwise look impossible.

DECISION LEVELS

Each things has their to do anything. These levels are helpful to achieve the goals. Decision have their own levels. Decision levels are also categorized into three levels such as strategic, tactical and operational.

We all recognize that some decisions are more important than others, whether in their immediate impact or long term significance. As a means of understanding the significance of a decision so that we can know how much time and resources are to spend on it, three levels of decision have been identified:

1. Strategic. Strategic decisions are the highest level. Here a decision concerns in general direction, long term goals, philosophies and values. These decisions are the least structured and most imaginative; they are the most risky and of the most uncertain outcome, partly because they reach so far into the future and partly because they are of such importance.

For example: Decisions about what to do with your life, what to learn, or what methods to use to gain knowledge (travel, work, school) that would be strategic. Whether to produce a low priced product and gain market share or produce a high priced product for a niche market would be a strategic decision.

Strategic decision is the first level of decisions in which decision makers gets the ability to take decision but in general directions.

2. Tactical. Tactical decisions support strategic decisions. They tend to be medium range, medium significance, with moderate consequences.

For example: If your strategic decision were to become a forest ranger, a tactical decision would include where to go to school and what books to read. Or if your company decided to produce a low priced product, a tactical decision might be to build a new factory to produce them at a low manufacturing cost.

These types of decision support the strategic decisions. It is medium of strategic and operational level that's why they supports the medium direction, medium significance.

3. Operational. These are every day decisions which are used to support the tactical decisions. They are frequently made with little thought and are structured. Their impact is immediate, short term, short range, and usually low cost. The consequences of a bad operational decision will be minimal, although a *series* of bad or sloppy operational decisions can cause harm. Operational decisions can be preprogrammed, pre-made, or set out clearly in policy manuals.

For example: If your tactical decision is to read some books on forestry, your operational decision would involve where to shop for the books. You might have a personal policy of shopping for books at a certain store or two. Thus, the operational decision is highly structured: "Whenever books are needed, look at Joe's Books."

Operational decision are used to support the tactical decision. It is that level of decision which supports the short range and short term direction of firections and apply in everyday life.

TECHNIQUES FOR DECISION MAKING

There are some techniques which are used for decision making. These techniques can be applied to simple or complex decision.

This is a list of easy, practical techniques or methods that can be applied to simple or complex decisions. They share the assumption that circumspect analysis is the key to making good decisions. Many decisions are made with too little information and too little thought, in a non-deliberate manner.

Note, how these techniques provide a visible, structured, orderly set of factors which are involved in a decision, so that the decision maker can consider them in a thoughtful and coherent way.

There are five techniques for decision making including T-chart, PMI, Buriden's Ass, Measured criteria and Decision Matrix or Weighted decision table.

T-chart, PMI and Buriden's Ass are first three techniques which are especially for those types of decision, which involves yes/no. either/or, or two-possibility decision.

1. T-Chart. A T-Chart is an orderly, graphic representation of alternative features or points involved in a decision. In one form, it can be a list of positive and negative attributes surrounding a particular choice. Drawing up such a chart insures that both the positive and negative aspects of each direction or decision will be taken into account.

T-chart are used to make decision that what are its five as well as aspects of this decision.

For example, what are the pros and cons of deciding to buy a sport utility vehicle?

MERITS	DEMERITS
better visibility	higher insurance
safer structure	poorer gas mileage
can take off road	moreexpensive maintenance

In another form, two possible choices are listed, with the good points or arguments or effects are listed for each. Suppose a company is trying to decide whether to create its own advertising agency or hire an agency.

Use Outside Agency	Write Ads In-House
professional work	faster product
expertise of ideas	better knowledge of product
media connections	use same ad in flyers

To fill out this latter form, more than two choices can be included, and a list of negatives for each choice can be added as well.

2. PMI. Edward de Bono refines the T-Chart idea into a three part structure, which he calls PMI for plus, minus, and interesting. Here you first list all the plus or good points of the idea, then all the minus or bad points, and finally all the interesting points—consequences, areas of curiosity or uncertainty, or attributes that you simply don't care to view as either good or bad at this point (consequences that some people might view as good and others might view as bad, for example). The "interesting" category also allows exploration of the idea or choice outside the context of judgment—you don't have to evaluate the attribute into a positive or negative category.

PMI is the second techniques for decision making and described as plus, minus and interesting. It was proposed by Edward de Bowo. Here, plus refers to the merits, advantages or good points and minus refers to the bad points, demerits or disadvantages and finally interesting refers to those points which provides the curiosity uncertainty and also creates consequences.

PMI stands for 'Plus/Minus/Interesting'. It is a valuable improvement was to the 'weighing of pros and cons' technique used for centuries.

PMI is an important Decision Making tool: the mind tools used so far in this section have focused on selecting a course of action from a range of options. It is important to check that it is going to improve the situation (it may actually be best to do nothing!) PMI is a useful tool for doing this.

How to Use the Tool

In the column underneath 'Plus', write down all the positive results and conclusion of taking the action. Underneath 'Minus' write down all the negative effects. In the 'Interesting' column write down the implications and possible outcomes or results of taking the action, whether positive, negative, or uncertain.

By this stage it may already be obvious whether or not you should implement the decision. If it is not, consider each of the points you have written down and assign a positive or negative score to it appropriately. The scores you assign may be quite subjective.

Once you have done this, add up the score, a strongly positive score shows that an action should be taken, a strongly negative score that it should be avoided.

PMI is a good way of weighing the pros, cons and implications of a decision. When you have selected a course of action, PMI is a good technique to use to check that it is worth taking.

To use the technique, draw up a table with three columns headed Plus, Minus and Interesting. Within the table write down all the positive points of following the course of action, all the negatives, and all the interesting implications and possible outcomes.

If the decision is still not obvious, you can then score the table to show the importance of individual items. The total score should show whether it is worth implementing the decision.

Example :

A young professional is deciding where to live. Her question is 'Should she move to the big city?'

She draws up the PMI table below:

Plus	**Minus**	**Interesting**
More going on (+5)	Have to sell house (-6)	Easier to find n job? (+1)
Easier to see friends (+5)	More pollution (-3)	Meet more peo] (+2)
Easier to get places (+3)	Less space (-3)	More difficult t own work done (-4)
	No countryside (-2)	
	More difficult to get to work? (-4)	
+13	**-18**	**-1**

She scores the table as 13 (Plus) - 18 (Minus) - 1 (Interesting) = - 6

For her, the comforts of a settled rural existence outweigh the call of the 'bright lights' - it would be much better for her to live outside the city, but close enough to travel in if necessary.

3. Buriden's Ass. This method of decision making is used when two or more equally attractive alternatives are faced. The method is simply to list all the negative points or drawbacks about each decision. That is, when two or more alternatives seem very desirable, we become blinded to any drawbacks. The Buriden's Ass method simply focuses on the drawbacks.

This is the third technique for decision making which mainly focus on drawbacks or negative points.

For example, suppose a young lady about to become engaged. Mr. Right asks her that, " would you rather have a $4,000 diamond engagement ring or $4,000 worth of furniture for our new Swiss chalet?" she find these to be both very attractive alternatives, so she decide to use the Buriden's Ass method to decide between them. What are the drawbacks of the ring? It might get stolen or lost; it isn't useful like furniture; people might think her married Mr. Right for his money (or that he had to buy your consent with a big rock); it might make her friends feel bad because they have little rings; you might worry about damaging it. And so on.

Now, what are the drawbacks of the furniture? It will wear out eventually and be gone, while the ring should last a lifetime; you might worry about staining or damaging the furniture; furniture isn't "romantic" like diamonds; and so on.

4. Measured Criteria. With this technique, you list the criteria that you want your decision to meet and assign points to each criterion which are based on its relative importance in the decision. Then, each alternative is given a certain number of points according to how it fully meets the criterion. For points you can use a scale of 1 to 10, 1 to 100, or any other range that makes sense to you.

Measured criteria is the fourth techniques of decision making which is used when we want to their decision to meet and design points to each criteria of our decision.

Example of Measured Criteria

In the example below, traveling by train is rated at 25 out of 30 points for the "comfort" criterion, while the plane is ranked a little less comfortable, at 21 out of 30. Once all the alternatives have been assigned their due points for each criterion, all the points for each alternative are added up and the alternative with the highest total points is the one chosen. In the example below, that would be the plane.

Example:

	Possible Points	Train	Plane	Car
Comfort	30	25	21	18
Speed	15	7	15	3
Safety	20	13	17	9
Food	10	6	2	10
Total	75	51	55	40

5. Decision Matrix or Weighted Decision Table. This is a slightly more sophisticated version of the measured criteria technique. Here a table is set up with each criterion given a weight depending on its importance in the decision and with each alternative given a ranking for that criterion.

This is fifth techniques of decision-making which is more sophisticated. It is described in the format of table.

Force Field Analysis

A good tool to value these strengths and weaknesses is the force field analysis. Force Field Analysis is a useful technique for looking at all the forces for and against a decision. In effect, it is a specialized method of weighing pros and cons.

By carrying out the analysis you can plan to strengthen the forces supporting a decision, and reduce the impact of opposition to it.

As people are often opposed to change, be sure that you will never make any decision if you just follow the conclusions of a force field analysis.

To carry out a force field analysis, first download our free worksheet and then use it to follow these steps:

- Describe your plan or proposal for change in the middle.
- List all forces for change in one column, and all forces against change in another column.
- Assign a score to each force, from 1 (weak) to 5 (strong).

Once you have carried out an analysis, you can decide whether your project is viable. Where you have already decided to carry out a project, Force Field Analysis can help you to work out how to improve its probability of success. Here you have two choices:

- To reduce the strength of the forces opposing a project, or
- To increase the forces pushing a project

Often the most elegant solution is the first: just trying to force change through may cause its own problems. People can be uncooperative if change is forced on them.

Force Field Analysis is a useful method or technique which are used for looking at all the forces for and against a plan. It helps you to weigh the importance of these factors and decide whether a plan is worth implementing. Where you have decided to carry out a plan, Force Field Analysis helps you to identify the changes that you could make to improve it.

COST BENEFIT ANALYSIS

As the name suggests, it easier to understand that first of all this analysis supports the positive factors, good points as well as advantages, then it finds and reduce the all negative factors as well as costs.

A cost benefit analysis finds, quantifies, and adds all the positive factors. These are the benefits. Then it identifies, quantifies, and subtracts all the negatives, the costs. The difference between the two indicates whether the planned action is advisable. The real trick to doing a cost benefit analysis well is making sure you include all the costs and all the benefits and properly quantify them.

Should we hire an additional sales person or assign overtime? Is it a good idea to purchase the new stamping machine? Will we be better off putting our free cash flow into securities rather than investing in additional capital equipment? Each of these questions can be answered by doing a proper cost benefit analysis.

Cost benefits analysis is a powerful, widely used and relatively easy tool for deciding whether to make a change. To use the tool, firstly work out how much the change will cost to make. Then calculate the benefit you will from it. Where costs or benefits are paid or received over time, work out the time it will take for the benefits to repay the costs.

Principles of Costs Benefits Analysis

1. ***There must be a common unit of measurement.***

In order to reach a conclusion as to the desirability of a project all aspects of the project, positive and negative, must be expressed in order to a common unit; i.e., there must be a "bottom line." The most convenient and eeriest common unit is money. This means that all benefits and costs of a project should be measured in terms of their equivalent money value. A program may provide benefits which are not directly expressed in terms of dollars but there is some amount of money the recipients of the benefits would consider just as good as benefits of the project. For example, a project may provide for the elderly in an area a free monthly visit to a doctor. The value of that benefit to an elderly recipient is the minimum amount of money that that recipient would take it instead of the medical care. This could be less than the market value of the medical care which are provided. It is assumed that more esoteric benefits such as from preserving open space or historic sites have a finite equivalent money value to the public.

Not only do the benefits and costs of a project have to be expressed in terms of equivalent money value, but they have to be expressed in terms of dollars of a particular time. This is not just due to the differences in the value of dollars at different times because of inflation. A dollar available five years from now is not as good as a dollar available now. This is because a dollar available now can be invested and earn interest for five years and would be worth more than a dollar in five years. If the interest rate is r then a dollar invested for t years will grow to be $(1+r)^t$. Therefore the amount of money that would have to be deposited now so that it would grow to be one dollar t years in the future is $(1+r)^{-t}$. This called the discounted value or present value of a dollar available t years in the future.

When the dollar value of benefits at some time in the future is multiplied by the discounted value of one dollar at that time in the future the result is discounted the present value of that benefit of the project. The same thing applies to the costs. The net benefit of the projects is just the sum of the present value of the benefits which are the present value of the costs.

2. ***Cost benefits analysis valuations should represent consumers or producers valuations as revealed by their actual behavior.***

The valuation of benefits and costs should reflect the preferences that are revealed by the choices which have been made. For example, improvements in transportation often involve saving time. The question is how to measure the money value of that time saved. The value should not be merely what transportation planners think that time should be worth or even what people say their time is worth. The value of time should be that which the public reveals their time is worth through choices involving trade-offs between time and money. If people have a choice of parking close to their destination for a fee of 50 cents or parking farther away and spending 5 minutes more walking and they always choose to spend the money and save the time and effort then they have revealed that their time is more valuable to them than 10 cents per minute. If they were indifferent between the two choices they would have revealed that the value of their time to them was exactly 10 cents per minute.

The most challenging part of CBA is finding past choices which reveal the trade-offs and equivalencies in preferences. For example, the valuation of the benefit of cleaner air could be established by finding how much less people paid for housing in more polluted areas which otherwise was identical in characteristics and location to housing in less polluted areas. Generally the value of cleaner air to people as revealed by the hard market choices that seems to be less than their rhetorical valuation of clean air.

3. Benefits are Usually Measured by Market Choices

When consumers make purchases at market prices they reveal that the things they buy are at least as beneficial to them as the money they relinquish. Consumers will increase their consumption of any commodity up to the point where the benefit of an additional unit the marginal benefit is equal to the marginal cost to them of that unit, the market price. Therefore, for any consumer buying some of a commodity, the marginal benefit is equal to the market price. The marginal benefit will decline with the amount that are consumed just as the market price which has to decline to get consumers to consume a greater quantity of the commodity. The relationship between the market price and the quantity consumed is called the demand schedule. Thus the demand schedule provides the information about marginal benefit that is needed to place a money value on an increase in consumption.

There is no value of money when the product process beneficial to the consumers. Consumers always reveal that the things buy are at least as beneficial to them as the money they relinquish.

4. Gross Benefits of an Increase in Consumption is an Area under the Demand Curve

The increase in benefits resulting from an increase in consumption is the sum of the marginal benefit times each incremental increase in consumption. As the incremental increases considered are taken as smaller and smaller the sum goes to the area under the marginal benefit curve. But the marginal benefit curve is the same as the demand curve so the increase in benefits is the area under the demand curve.

When the increase in consumption is small compared to the total consumption the gross benefit is adequately approximated, as is shown in a welfare analysis, by the market value of the increased consumption; i.e., market price times the increase in consumption.

5. Analysis of a Project Should Involve a with versus without Comparison

The major concept is what the situation or effect in the study area, when there would be with and without the project.

The *impact* of a project is the difference between what the situation in the study area would be with and without the project. This that when a project is being evaluated the analysis must estimate not only what the situation would be with the project but also what it would be without the project. For example, in determining the impact of a fixed guideway rapid transit system such as the Bay Area Rapid Transit (BART) in the San Francisco Bay Area the number of rides that would have been taken on an expansion of the bus system should be deducted from the rides provided by BART and likewise the additional costs of such an expanded bus system would be deducted from the costs of BART. In other words, the alternative to the project must be explicitly specified and considered in the evaluation of the project. Note that the with-and-without comparison is not the same as a before-and-after comparison.

6. Double Counting of Benefits or Costs Must be Avoided

Sometimes an impact of a project can be measured in two or more methods. For example, when an improved highway reduces the travel time and the risk of injury the value of property in areas served by the highway will be enhanced. The increase in property values due to the project is a very good method, at least in principle, to measure the benefits of a project. But if the increased property values are included then it is unnecessary to include the value of the time and lives saved by the improvement in the highway. The property value went up because of the benefits of the time saving and the reduced risks. To include both the increase in property values and the time saving and risk reduction would involve double counting.

Decision Criteria for Projects

If the discounted present value of the benefits exceeds the discounted present value of the costs then the project is worthwhile. This is equivalent to the condition that the net benefit must be positive. Another equivalent condition is that the ratio of the present value of the benefits to the present value of the costs must be greater than one.

If there are more than one mutually exclusive projects that have positive net present value then there has to be further analysis. From the set of mutually exclusive projects the one that should be selected is the one with the highest net present value.

There is a condition, if the discounted present value of the benefit is greater then the discounted present value of the costs, then the project is worthwhile.

If the funds required to carry out all of the projects with positive net present value are less than the funds that are available this means the discount rate are used in computing the present values is too low and does not reflect the true cost of capital. The present values must be recomputed using a higher discount rate. It may take some trial and error to find a discount rate such that the funds are required for the projects with a positive net present value which is no more than the funds available. Sometimes as an alternative to this procedure, people try to select the best projects on the basis of some measure of goodness such as the internal rate of return or the benefit/cost ratio. This is not valid for various reasons.

The magnitude of the ratio of benefits to costs is to a degree arbritrary because some costs such as operating costs may be deducted from benefits and thus not be included in the cost figure. This may be done for some projects and not for others. This manipulation of the benefits and costs will not affect the net benefits and it will not raise the benefit cost ratio which is less than one to above one.

Evaluating Quantitatively whether to follow a Course of Action

You may have been intensely creative in obtaining solutions to a problem, and rigorous in your selection of the best one available. However, this solution may still not be worth implementing, as you may invest a lot of time and money in solving a problem that is not worthy of this effort.

Cost Benefit Analysis or CBA is a relatively* simple and widely used method for deciding whether to make a change. As its name suggests, you simply add up the value of the benefits of a course of action, and subtract the costs that are associated with it.

Costs are either one-off, or may be ongoing. Benefits are most frequently received over the time. We build this effect of time into our analysis by calculating a payback period. This is the time that it takes for the benefits of a change to repay its costs. Many companies look for payback on projects over a specified period of time e.g. three years.

Cost/Benefit Analysis is powerful tool which are widely used for deciding whether to make a change. To use this tool, first of all, work out how much the change will cost to make. Then calculate the benefit you will from it. Where costs or benefits are paid or received over time, work out the time it will take for the benefits to repay the costs.

Cost/Benefit Analysis can be carried out using only financial costs and financial benefits. However, You may decide to include the intangible items within the analysis. As you must evaluate a value for these, this inevitably brings an element of subjectivity into the process.

*Larger projects are evaluated using formal finance/capital budgeting, which takes into account many of the complexities which are involved with financial Decision Making.

A cost benefit analysis is done to find how well, or how poorly, a planned action will turn out. Although a cost benefit analysis can be used for almost anything, it is most generally done on financial questions. Since the cost benefit analysis relies on the addition of positive factors and the subtraction of negative ones find a net conclusion, it is also known as running the numbers.

How to Use the Tool?

In its simple form, cost-benefit analysis is carried out using only financial costs and financial benefits. For example, a simple cost benefit ratio for a road scheme would measure the cost of building the road, and subtract this from the economic benefit of improving transport links. It would not measure either the cost of environmental damage or the benefit of quicker and easier travel to work.

A more sophisticated approach to building a cost benefit models is to try to put a financial value on intangible costs and benefits. This can be highly subjective - is, for example, a historic water meadow worth $25,000, or is it worth $500,000 because if its environmental importance? What is the value of stress-free travel to work in the morning?

There are all questions that people have to answer and answers that people have to defend.

The version of the cost benefit approach we explain here is essentially simple. Where large sums of money are involved (for example, in financial market transactions), project evaluation can become an extremely complex and sophisticated art. The fundamentals of this are explained in Principles of Corporate Finance by Richard Brealey and Stewart Myers - this is something of an authority on the subject.

Here, an example of cost benefit analysis

A sales director is deciding whether to implement a new computer-based contact management and sales processing system. His department has only a few computers, and his salespeople are not computer literate. He is aware that computerized sales forces are able to contact more customers and give a higher quality of reliability and service to those customers. They are more able to meet commitments, and can work more efficiently with fulfillment and delivery staff.

His financial cost/benefit analysis is shown below:

Costs : New computer equipment:

- 10 network-ready PCs with supporting software @ $2,450 each
- 1 server @ $3,500
- 3 printers @ $1,200 each
- Cabling & Installation @ $4,600
- Sales Support Software @ $15,000

Training costs :

- Computer introduction - 8 people @ $400 each
- Keyboard skills - 8 people @ $400 each
- Sales Support System - 12 people @ $700 each

Other costs :

- Lost time: 40 man days @ $200 / day

- Lost sales through disruption: estimate: $20,000
- Lost sales through inefficiency during first months: estimate: $20,000

Total cost: $114,000

Benefits:

- Tripling of mail shot capacity: estimate: $40,000 / year
- Ability to sustain telesales campaigns: estimate: $20,000 / year
- Improved efficiency and reliability of follow-up: estimate: $50,000 / year
- Improved customer service and retention: estimate: $30,000 / year
- Improved accuracy of customer information: estimate: $10,000 / year
- More ability to manage sales effort: $30,000 / year

Total Benefit: $180,000 / year

Payback time: $114,000 / $180,000 = 0.63 of a year = approx. 8 months

Tip: The payback time is frequently known as the break even point. Sometimes this is is more important than the overall benefit of a project that can deliver, for example because the organization has had to borrow to fund a new piece of machinery. The break even point can be found graphically by plotting the costs and income on a graph of output quantity against $. Break even occurs at the point when the two lines cross to each other.

Inevitably the estimates of the benefit given by the new system are quite subjective. Despite this, the Sales Director is very likely to introduce it, given the short payback time.

Brainstorming

Brainstorming is a decision making tool which are used for generating man radical and useful ideas. It is very useful and popular tool that you can use to develop highly creative solutions to a problem.

Another option for decision-making is brainstorming. When brainstorming, group members are encouraged to generate as many ideas about a specific topic as they can. For instance, group members may use brainstorming to create as many solutions as they can in step four of the standard agenda. Group members should be encouraged to say anything that comes to mind when brainstorming. Every idea is written down and judgments about ideas that are saved until later, when the group returns to all of the ideas and selects those that are most useful.

It is specifically helpful when you need to break out of stale which established the patterns of thinking, therefore, you can develop new methods of looking at things. This can be when you need to develop new opportunities, where you want to improve the service that you offer, or when existing approaches just aren't giving you the conclusions you want. Used with your team, it helps you bring the experience of all team members into play during problem solving.

This increases the richness of solutions which are explored meaning that you can find better solutions to the problems you face, and make better decisions. It can also helps you to get buy in from team members for the solution chosen - after all, they have helped create that solution.

Brainstorming is a great way of generating the radical ideas. During the brainstorming process, there is no criticism of ideas, as free rein is given to the creativity of people. This creativity includes criticism and judgment cramp creativity.

This frequently makes group brainstorming sessions which tends to enjoyable experiences, which are great for bringing team members together.

Individual brainstorming is best for generating many ideas, but tends to be less effective at developing them. Group brainstorming tends to develop fewer ideas, but takes each idea further. Group brainstorming needs formal rules for it to work smoothly.

Brainstorming and Lateral Thinking

Brainstorming is a lateral thinking process. It asks that people come up with ideas and thoughts that seems at first to be a bit shocking or crazy. You can then change and improve them into ideas that are useful, and frequently stunningly original.

Therefore, during brainstorming sessions, there should be no criticism of ideas: You are trying to open up the possibilities and break down wrong assumptions about the limits of the problem. Judgments and analysis at this stage will stunt the idea generation.

Ideas should only be evaluated at the end of the brainstorming session that you can then explore the solutions further using conventional approaches.

Individual Brainstorming

When you brainstorm on your own that you will tend to produce a wider range of ideas than with group brainstorming - you do not have to worry about egos or opinions of other people, and can therefore be more freely creative. However, You may not develop ideas as effectively as you do not have the experience of a group to help you.

Group Brainstorming

Group brainstorming can be very effective as it uses the experience and creativity of all members of the group. When individual members reach their limit on an idea, another member's creativity and experience can take the idea to the next stage. Therefore, group brainstorming tends to develop the ideas in more depth than individual brainstorming.

Brainstorming in a group can be risky for individuals. Valuable but strange suggestions may appear stupid at first sight. Because of this, you need to chair sessions tightly so that uncreative people do not crush these ideas and leave group members feeling humiliated.

How to Use the Tool?

To use this group brainstorming effectively, do the following points:-

To run a group brainstorming session effectively, do the following:

- Define the problem that you want solved clearly, and lay out any criteria or method to be met.
- Keep the session that are focused on the problem.
- Ensure that no one criticizes or evaluates the ideas during the session. Criticism introduces an element of risk for group members when putting forward an idea. This stifles the creativity and cripples the free running nature of a good brainstorming session.
- Encourage an enthusiastic, uncritical attitude among all the members of the group. Try to get everyone to contribute and develop ideas, including the quietest members of the group.

- Let people have fun brainstorming. Encourage them to come up with as many ideas as possible, from solidly practical ones to wildly impractical ones. Welcome creativity.
- Ensure that no train of thought is followed for too long.
- Encourage the people to develop other people's ideas, or to use other ideas to create new ones.
- Appoint one person to note down ideas that come out of the session. A good method of doing this is to use a flip chart. This should be studied and evaluated after the session.

Where possible, participants in the brainstorming process should come from as wide a range of disciplines as possible. This brings a broad range of experience to the session and helps to make it more creative.

PAIRED COMPARISON ANALYSIS

Paired comparison analysis is the tool of decision making which are used for working out the relative importance of different options.

Paired Comparison Analysis helps you to work out the importance of a number of options relative to each other.

It is specifically useful where:

- **You** do not have objective data
- Priorities are ambiguous
- Priorities are competing in importance

This methods makes it easy to choose the most important problem to solve first or to select the solution that will give **you** the greatest advantage, i.e., on the basis of priority. **Paired Comparison Analysis** may also help **you** to set the Priorities.

Paired Comparison Analysis is best way of weighing up the relative importance of options. A variety of plausible options are listed. Each option is compared against each of the other options. The option with the highest score is the preferred option.

Paired Comparison Analysis helps you to work out the importance of a number of options which are related to each other. It is specifically useful where you do not have objective data to base this on.

It is also an ideal and perfect tool for comparing "apples with oranges" which are completely different options such as whether to invest in marketing, a new IT system or a new piece of machinery. These decisions are commonly much harder than comparing three possible new IT systems, for example.

This makes it easy to choose the most important problem to solve, or select the solution that will give you the greatest advantage. Paired Comparison Analysis helps you to set priorities where there are conflicting demands on your resources.

How to Use the Tool?

There are six steps to do it which are following below:-

1. List the options that you will compare. Assign a letter to each option.
2. Mark the options as row and column headings on the worksheet.
3. Note that the cells on the table where you will be comparing an option with itself have been blocked out - there will never be a difference in these cells!
4. The cells on the table where you will be duplicating a comparison are also blocked out.
5. Within the remaining cells compare the option in the row with the one in the column. For each cell, decide which of the two options is more important. Write down the letter of the more important option in the cell, and score the difference in importance from 0 (no difference) to 3 (major difference).
6. Finally, consolidate the results by adding up the total of all the values for each of the options. You may want to convert these values into a percentage of the total score.

Advantages and Disadvantages

- It is useful priorities are not clear.
- It is particular useful where you do not have objective data to base this on.
- It helps you to set priorities where there are conflicting demands on your resources.
- This makes it easy to choose the most important problem to solve, or select the solution that will give you the greatest advantages.

Steps to Conduct this Analysis

- List the options that you will compare (elements as A,B,C,D, E for example).
- Create a table 6 rows and 7 column.
- Write down option to column and row; A to row second, cell first from left and A to row first, cell second from left; B to row third, cell first from left and B to row first, cell third from left, etc.; column seventh is total point.
- Identify importance from 0 (no difference) to 3 (major difference).
- Compare element "A" to B,C,D,E and place "point" at each cell.
- Finally, consolidate the results by adding up the total of all the values for each of the options. You may want to cover these values into a percentage of the total score.

Example of Paired Comparison Analysis

As a simple example, an entrepreneur is looking at ways in which she can expand her business. She has limited resources, but also has the options she lists below:

- Expand into overseas markets
- Expand in home markets
- Improve customer service and quality

First of all, she draws up the paired comparison analysis table in fig. 1:

Figure 1: Example Paired Comparison Analysis Table (not filled in):

	Overseas Market (A)	Home Market (B)	Customer Service (C)	Quality (D)
Overseas Market (A)	Blocked Out (Step 3)			
Home Market (B)	Blocked Out (Step 4)	Blocked Out (Step 3)		

Customer Service (C)	Blocked Out (Step 4)	Blocked Out (Step 4)	Blocked Out (Step 3)	
Quality (D)	Blocked Out (Step 4)	Blocked Out (Step 4)	Blocked Out (Step 4)	Blocked Out (Step 3)

Then she compares options, writes down the letter of the most important option, and scores their difference in importance. An example of how she might do this is shown in figure 2:

Figure 2: Example Paired Comparison Analysis Table (filled in):

	Overseas Market (A)	Home Market (B)	Customer Service (C)	Quality (D)
Overseas Market (A)		A,2	C,1	A,1
Home Market (B)			C,1	B,1
Customer Service (C)				C,2
Quality (D)				

Finally she adds up the A, B, C and D values, and converts each value into a percentage of the total. This gives these totals:

- A = 3 (37.5%)
- B = 1 (12.5%)
- C = 4 (50%)
- D = 0.

Here it is most inevitable task to improve the customer service (C) and then to tackle export markets (A). Quality is not a high priority - perhaps it is good already.

This method may be conducted individually or in groups. It may include the criteria to guide the comparison or be based on intuition following an open discussion of the group. A paired choice matrix or paired comparison matrix that can be constructed to help with this type of analysis.

PARETO ANALYSIS

Pareto analysis acts a tool for decision making which re used for choosing the most important changes to make. Pareto analysis is very simple method by which you can choose the most effective changes to make.

It uses the Pareto principle – the idea that by doing 20% of work you can generate 80% of the advantage of doing the entire job. Pareto analysis is a formal method which issued for finding the changes that will give the biggest benefits. It is useful where many possible courses of action are competing for your attention.

Pareto analysis is a statistical technique in decision making which is used for selection of a limited number of methods that produce the significant overall effect. It uses the Pareto principle – the idea that by doing 20% of work you can generate 80% of the advantage of doing the entire job. Or in terms of quality improvement, a large majority of problems (80%) are produced by a few key causes (20%).

Pareto analysis is a creative way of looking at causes of problems because it helps stimulate the thinking and organize thoughts. However, it can be limited by its exclusion of possibly important problems which may be small initially, but which grow with time. It should be combined with other analytical tools such as failure mode and effects analysis and fault tree analysis for example.

Pareto analysis is a formal method which are useful where many possible courses of action are competing for your attention. In essence, the problem-solver estimates the benefit which delivered by each action, then selects a number of the most effective actions that deliver a total benefit which are reasonably close to the maximal possible one.

Pareto Analysis is a simple technique that helps you to identify the most important problem to solve.

To use it:

- List the problems you face, or the options you have available
- Group options where they are facets of the same larger problem
- Apply an appropriate score to each group

- Work on the group with the highest score

Pareto analysis not only shows you the most important problem to solve, it also gives you a score showing how severe the problem is.

*This is only one application of this important 80/20 principle. It shows the lack of symmetry that almost always appears between work put in and results achieved. This can be seen in area after area of competitive activity. The figures 80 and 20 are illustrative – for example, 13% of work could generate 92% of returns. Vilfredo Pareto was an Italian economist who noted that approximately 80% of wealth was owned by only 20% of the population. This was true in almost all the societies he studied.

Steps to Identify the Important Causes using Pareto Analysis :

- Step 1: Form a table listing the causes and their frequency as a percentage.
- Step 2: Arrange the rows in the decreasing order of importance of the causes (i.e, the most important cause first)
- Step 3: Add a cumulative percentage column to the table
- Step 4: Plot with causes on x-axis and cumulative percentage on y-axis
- Step 5: Join the above points to form a curve
- Step 6: Plot (on the same graph) a bar graph with causes on x-axis and percent frequency on y-axis
- Step 7: Draw line at 80% on y-axis which is parallel to x-axis. Then drop the line at the point of intersection with the curve on x-axis. This point on the x-axis separates the important causes (on the left) and trivial causes (on the right)
- Step 8: Review the chart to ensure that you are capturing at least 80% of the causes

The Pareto Principle states that only a "vital few" factors are responsible for producing most of the problems. This principle can be applied to quality improvement to the extent that a great majority of problems (80%) are produced by a few key causes (20%). If we correct these few key causes, we will have a greater probability of success.

How to Use the Tool?

To start using the tool, write out a list of the changes

you could make. If you have a long list, group it into related changes.

Then score the items or groups. The scoring method you use depends on the sort of problem you are trying to solve. For example, if you are trying to improve profitability, you would score options on the basis of the profit each group might generate. If you are trying to improve customer satisfaction, you might score on the basis of the number of complaints eliminated by each change.

The first change to handle is the one that has the highest score. This one will give you the biggest benefit if you solve it. The options with the lowest scores will probably not even be worth bothering with – solving these problems may cost you more than the solutions are worth.

Following are the points which are used for use this tool:-

1. Gather data on the frequency of the causes using a tally sheet.

Rank the causes from the most to the least important, and calculate the cumulative percentage (the cumulative percentage is the first percentage plus the second percentage, and so on).

Causes	Percentage of Total	Computation	Cumulative Percent
A	20%	0+20%= 20%	20%
B	18%	20%+18%=38%	38%
C	15%	38%+15%=53%	53%
D	11%	53%+11%=64%	64%

2. Draw a horizontal axis (X) that represents the different causes, ordered from the most to least frequent.

3. Draw a vertical axis (Y) with percentages from 0 to 100%

4. Construct a bar graph based on the percentage of each cause.

5. Construct a line graph of the cumulative percent.

6. Draw a line from 80% on the Y axis to the line graph, and then drop the line down to the X axis. This line separates the important causes from the trivial ones.

In the example, you can see that only 6 causes out of 20 are responsible for 80% of the problem. The other 14 causes are responsible for 20% of the problem. There is a good chance that if you focus on solving the 6 key causes, the other 14 will be solved as well.

After an analysis or ideas generating session, you will have a list of items to evaluate. If the list is a long one (say more than five or six items), try to get it down to a manageable size by putting to one side any factors you reasonably suspect are of lesser significance. Don't discard them entirely because without proper measurement you will never know for some how significant the factors are. Better just to put them to one side and return to them later if the selected alternatives don't prove successful. For the remaining factors, decide on the best manner to measure their relative significance and collect the data required. Plot the data on a histogram in descending order of importance.

Pareto analysis shows an example of laundry. This example is listed step by step development of Pareto analysis.

In this case, an analysis session was completed on the reasons why customers experienced undue delays in delivery of their goods from the time a picking slip is generated in the warehouse. This session yielded a laundry list of possible causes.

- picking errors
- missing stock
- sent to wrong address
- part-supply refused
- refused at delivery address/no receiving authority
- goods returned/exceeded use-by date
- goods returned/damaged
- goods returned/servicing or preparation not done
- goods mislaid by carrier
- delivery delayed by carrier
- goods returned/damaged in transit

To reduce the list to a manageable number of items, some less likely causes were put aside and others were aggregated to produce the following final list.

- goods returned/incorrect items
- goods returned/defective
- goods returned/wrong address

- goods not found in warehouse

A data collection program was then undertaken to find out how much time that was being taken to correct these problems for the customer.

The Pareto chart shows that the priority problem, the one causing greatest delays to customers, is incorrect goods being sent. Reducing the incidence of this problem will yield the greatest benefit to customers. After improvements have been made, another analysis can be made to determine if the problem has been reduced and confirm that "goods not found in the warehouse" is the next most important problem to address.

Setting Priorities for Action

When faced with a range of issues, it is frequently difficult to know which to work on first. To resolve this dilemna, the most useful thing to do is to apply Pareto's rule. This rule says - "eighty percent (80%) of your troubles will come from twenty per cent (20%) of your problems". In other words, problems will rarely have equal impact, so it is best to first concentrate on the most important.

The value of this rule is not that it provides a scientifically accurate estimation of the weightings which attach to a range of alternatives (which it does not), but simply that it is a reminder to always look for 'the vital few' issues, and to separate them from 'the trivial many', before attempting to solve problems. The next step is to identify which particular problems are the most important. This is done by collecting appropriate data and displaying it in the form of a histogram with each measured characteristic shown in descending order of magnitude. Such a histogram is known as a Pareto chart.

GRID ANALYSIS

Grid analysis is a useful and popular tool which is used for making a choice where many factors must .be considered.

It is particularly powerful where you have a number of good alternatives to choose from, and many various factors to take into account. This makes it a best method to use in almost any important decision where there isn't a clear and obvious preferred option.

Being able to use Grid Analysis means that you can take decisions confidently and rationally, at the time when other people might be struggling to make a decision.

It applies at immediate condition or typical circumstances. Grid analysis is also known as decision matrix analysis, Pugh matrix analysis or MAUT stands for multi-attribute utility theory which is used for making a decision.

To use the tool, lay out your options as rows on a table. Set up the columns to show your factors. Allocate weights to show the importance of each of these factors. Score each choice for each factor using numbers from 0 (poor) to 5 (very good). Multiply each score by the weight of the factor, to show its contribution to the overall selection. Finally add up the total scores for each option. Select the highest scoring option.

Grid Analysis is the simplest form of Multiple Criteria Decision Analysis (MCDA), also known as Multiple Criteria Decision Aid or Multiple Criteria Decision Management (MCDM). Sophisticated MCDA is involves highly complex modelling of different potential scenarios and advanced mathematics.

Grid Analysis helps you to decide between various options, while taking many various factors into account.

How to Use the Tool?

The methods works by getting you to list your options as rows on a table, and the factors you need to consider as columns. You then score each option/factor combination, weight this score, and add these scores up to give an overall score for the option.

In reality, the technique is quite easy to use. There are following step which are used for this tool:-

1. The first step is to list all of your options as the row labels on the table, and list the factors that you need to consider as the column headings.

2. Next, work out the relative importance of the factors in your decision. Show these as numbers from, say, 0 to 5, where 0 means that the factor is absolutely unimportant in the final decision, and 5 means that it is very important. (It's perfectly acceptable to have factors with the same importance.) We will use these to weight your preferences by the importance of the factor.

These values may be obvious. If they are not, then use a technique such as Paired Comparison Analysis to estimate them.

3. The next step is to work your way down the columns of your table, scoring each option for each of the factors in your decision.

Score each option from 0 (poor) to 5 (very good). Note that you do not have to have a different score for each option - if none of them are good for a specific factor in your decision, then all options should score 0.

4. Now multiply each of your scores from step 3 by the values for relative importance you calculated in step 2. This will give you weighted scores for each option/factor combination.

5. Finally, add up these weighted scores for each of your options. The option that scores the highest wins!

Example of Grid Analysis

A windsurfing enthusiast is about to replace his car. He needs one that not only carries a board and sails, but also that will be good for business travel. He has always loved open-topped sports cars. No car he can find is good for all three things.

His options are:

- An SUV/4x4, hard topped vehicle.
- A comfortable 'family car'.
- A station wagon/estate car.
- A convertible sports car.

Criteria that he wants to consider are:

- Cost.
- Ability to carry a sail board safely.
- Ability to store sails and equipment securely.
- Comfort over long distances.
- Fun!
- Nice look and build quality to car.

Firstly he draws up the table shown in Figure 1, and scores each option by how well it satisfies each factor:

Figure 1: Example Grid Analysis Showing Unweighted Assessment of How Each Type of Car Satisfies Each Factor

Factors:	Cost	Board	Storage	Comfort	Fun	Look	Total
Weights:							
Sports Car	1	0	0	1	3	3	
SUV/4x4	0	3	2	2	1	1	

SUV/4x4	0	3	2	2	1	1	
Family Car	2	2	1	3	0	0	
Station Wagon	2	3	3	3	0	1	

Next he decides the relative weights for each of the factors. He multiplies these by the scores already entered, and totals them. This is shown in Figure 2:

Figure 2: Example Grid Analysis Showing Weighted Assessment of How Each Type of Car Satisfies Each Factor

Factors:	**Cost**	**Board**	**Storage**	**Comfort**	**Fun**	**Look**	**Total**
Weights:	**4**	**5**	**1**	**2**	**3**	**4**	
Sports Car	4	0	0	2	9	12	**27**
SUV/4x4	0	15	2	4	3	4	**28**
Family Car	8	10	1	6	0	0	**25**
Station Wagon	8	15	3	6	0	4	**36**

This gives an interesting result: Despite its lack of fun, a station wagon may be the best choice.

If the wind-surfer still feels unhappy with the decision that maybe he has underestimated the importance of one of the factors. Perhaps he should give 'fun' a weight of 7, and buy an old station wagon to carry his board!

This is the example of wind surfing which shows the decision making by arid analysis.

DECISION THEORY

Decision theory is an interdisciplinary area of study that concerns by mathematicians, statisticians, economists, philosophers, managers, politicians, psychologists and anyone else interested in analysis of decisions and their consequences. The basic formalism of decision theory is the payoff table, which maps mutually exclusive decisions to mutually exclusive states of nature. For example, "Decision X leads to Outcome Y", "Decision Y leads to Outcome Z", and so on. When the set of outcomes corresponding to any given decision is not known, we refer to this condition as decision under uncertainty, the field of study which dominates decision theory.

Outcomes in decision theory are commonly assigned the utility values. For example, from the point of view of a military planner, the death of 1000 men on the battlefield might be assigned a negative utility of 1000, and the death of 500 a negative utility of 500. Possible outcomes in a decision theory problem may be positive, negative or both. Utility assignments can be arbitrary and based on the opinions of the decision maker — for example, the death of 1000 men might be assigned greater than twice the negative utility of the death of 500 men.

The *expected utility* of a decision is computed as the sum of the probability of each possible outcome which are multiplied by the utility of each outcome. For example, making a given decision might lead to positive utility 100 with a probability of 75%, and a negative utility of 40 with probability 25%. 75% times 100 equals positive 75. 25% times -40 equals -10. 75 minus 10 gives 65, meaning the overall expected utility of the decision is 65.

Decision theory is concerned with identifying the values, uncertainties and other issues relevant in a given decision and the resulting optional decision. It is sometimes called game theory.

Obviously, such quantitative precision is only possible in problems in which all the numbers and probabilities are known ahead of time. This is true in some gambling problems, like poker. Decision theory provides a number of suggestions for how to estimate the complex or typical probabilities under uncertainty, most of which are derived from Bayesian inference.

PROBLEMS IN DECISION THEORY

There are five categories of defining the effects of decision theory:-

1. Decision under certainty are those issues in which each alternative action concludes in one and only one outcome and where that outcome is sure to occur.

2. Decision under probabilistic uncertainty are those issues in which one of various outcomes can concludes from a given action which are depending on the state of nature, and these states occur with known probabilities. There are outcome uncertainties, and the probabilities are associated with these are known precisely.

3. Decision under probabilistic imprecision are those issues in which one of various outcomes can result from a given action depending on the state of nature, and these states occur with unknown or imprecisely specified probabilities. There are outcome uncertainties, and the probabilities are associated with the uncertainty parameters that are not all known precisely.

4. Decision under information imperfection are those issues in which one of various outcomes can concludes from a given action which are depending on the state of nature, and these states occur with imperfectly specified probabilities. There are outcome uncertainties, and the probabilities are associated with these are not all known precisely. Imperfections in knowledge of the utility of the several event outcomes may exist as well.

5. Decision under conflict and cooperation are those issues in which there is more than a single decision maker, and where the objectives and activities of one decision maker are not essentially known to all decision makers. Also, the objectives of the decision makers may differ.

TYPES OF DECISION

There are two types of decision naming reactive decisions and proactive decision. Dealing with the decision making process recommend to follow the following process:- first of all, define the problems, collect information, develop options, choose the best option, plan, execute and follow up.

Reactive Decision

Reactive decision must be carefully prepared in terms to act quite automatically when the event occurs.

A bad event with either a high or either a low probability is a **risk**. The first step is to carefully study the risks which could strike your business. Each business is exposed to particular risks which are connected with its main activity.

How to List Your Risks

In any preparation, the first step is to list your risks and their probability. To simplify, just identify **high probability** and **low probability**.

For example, with growing insecurity, a criminal attack must be graded as a high possibility for any biz involved in money business or gem trade. On the contrary, a travel agency has a low probability to be confronted with a hold up.

The second method is to estimate the impact of the event. You can distinguish the accident, the disaster and the catastrophe. With an accident, your biz will go on as usual. A disaster implies a long recovery and a catastrophe means that your business is terminated.

The notation only depends on **the impact on your own business**: For example if you head a bank, a earthquake is less harmful than a simple hold up: In general, banks have heavy walls and should not suffer to much from the effects of an earthquake!

According to the biz, the same event can be an accident or a catastrophe. For example if your tourist guide is poisoned with the food , it's for you an accident but for the food catering it could be a catastrophe because many people have certainly be poisoned too.

You have also to take in account insurances. For example, a fire which is a very stressing event should have in general a low impact because most of the biz are insured against the fire.

DECISION MAKING PROCESS

DRAWING 1

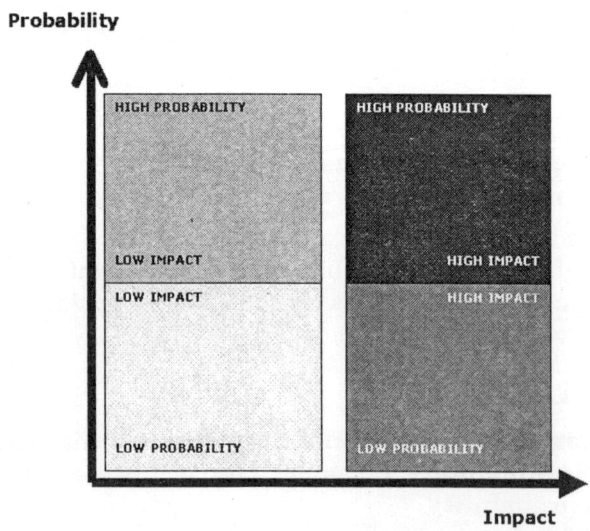

As you can see, it's an easy to use tool. **You write in each square the risks you have listed according to their probabilities and their impacts.**

Whatever their low or high probabilities, all the risks that are fully insured could be put in the left part of the drawing: low impact. However, you have to analyze: For example a burglary by night has a low impact because insurance should pay. On the contrary, a hold up causing the death of customers and employees has a high impact: Of course insurance will pay but you will nevertheless suffer of a moral prejudice and a bad impact for your image.

Proactive Decision : Proactive decision are more frequent than reactive decisions. These are the decision making process that implies a phase of preparation and phase of execution.

1. Preparation : Preparation is a must. You know the event:("Do I start a business or not") but you do not know the consequences: Is it a good decision? What are the probabilities to do well or inversely to be impoverished?

Define the Problem : In any problem, you have to establish the causes and the symptoms. Knowing the causes, you can recommend a solution just as a doctor does.

Unfortunately, most frequently there are different possible solutions such as A, B, and C. What is more you do not know the chances of success of A, B, or C!

2. Collect Information : One method for reducing uncertainty is to collect information's. For example: Will you partner with company A? This company can be good, medium or bad. For reducing this uncertainty, you can collect information's from your bank or other sources.

Unfortunately, sensible information's are not on the market place and need to enter in the domain of intelligence .

3. Asses the Consequences of Each Option : You must also intensively investigate all the consequences of the decision: Let's suppose that your decision could have three outcomes: one very good (A), one good (B) and one bad (C) with equal probabilities. In this case, your decision should have 66% of chance to be a good decision.

Now examine more carefully the possible consequences: With A, you win 100, with B you win 30 and with C you get a death penalty! In this case the consequences of C are out of proportion with the benefit that you can expect. It's why most criminal activities are risked!

4. Define your Options and the Best Alternative : Be careful about the idea to multiply the options. It could be a poor excuse for never taking any decisions. Too much options kill the decisions and risk to induce an infinite process of brainstorming.

NORMATIVE AND DESCRIPTIVE DECISION THEORY

A broad range of concept which have been developed to both describe and prescribe the process of decision making where a choice is made from a finite set of possible alternatives. Decision theory can be normative or descriptive.

Decision theory can be normative or descriptive. *Normative decision theory* defined as the theories about how we should make decisions if we want to maximize the expected utility. *Descriptive decision theory* refers to theories about how we actually make decisions. Descriptive decision theories are complex, frequently unnecessarily so, and they help teach us the methods in which human decisions systematically go wrong. This connects to the related field of heuristics and biases, which has come into great vogue in the field of economics within the last decade.

Normative decision theory describes how decisions should be made in terms to accommodate a set of axioms which are believed to be desirable; descriptive decision theory deals with how people actually make decisions; and prescriptive decision theory formulates how decisions should be made in realistic settings. Thus, this field of study involves the people from various disciplines: behavioral and social scientists and psychologists who commonly attempt to discover the elaborate descriptive models of the decision process of real humans in real settings; mathematicians and economists who are concerned with the axiomatic or normative theory of decisions; and engineers and managers who may be concerned with sophisticated prescriptive decision-making procedures.

Most of decision theory is normative or prescriptive, *i.e.*, it is concerned with determine the best way of decision to take and assuming an ideal decision maker who is fully informed which are able to find with perfect accuracy, and fully rational. The practical application of this prescriptive approach is to how people *actually* make decisions is called decision analysis, and aimed at finding tools, methodologies and software to help the people to make better decisions. The most systematic and comprehensive software tools developed in this method are called decision support systems.

Since it is obvious that people do not typically behave in optimal methods, there is also a related area of study, which is a positive or descriptive discipline are attempting to describe what people will actually do. Since the normative, optimal decision frequently creates hypothesis for testing against the actual behaviour, the two fields are closely linked with each other. Furthermore it is possible to relax the assumptions of perfect information, rationality and so forth in different methods, and produce a series of different prescriptions or predictions about behaviour, allowing for further tests of the kind of decision-making that occurs in practice.

Normative theory of decision are also known as axiomatic theory which are formalize and rationalize decision making process. This theory depends on the following assumption:-

- People make decisions without being so overwhelmed by the complexity of actual decision situations that they would necessarily use suboptimal decision strategies.
- People correctly perceive the values of the uncertainties that are associated with the outcomes of decision alternatives.
- Past preferences are valid indicators of present and future preferences.
- People make decisions that accurately reflect their true preferences over the alternative courses of action, each of which may have uncertain outcomes.
- People are able to assess decision situations correctly, and the resulting decision situation structural model is well formed and complete.
- People are able to process decision information correctly.
- People accept the axioms that are assumed to develop the various normative theories.
- Real decision situations provide people with decision alternatives that allow them to express their true preferences.

Given these necessary assumptions, there will exist departures between normative and descriptive decision theories. A principal method of those aiding others in decision making is to retain those features from the descriptive approach which enables an acceptable transition from normative approaches to prescriptive approaches. The prescriptive features should eliminate potentially undesirable features of descriptive approaches, such as flawed judgment heuristics and information processing biases, while retaining acceptable features of the normative approaches.

Determination of Utility

When choosing among alternatives, the decision maker must be able to indicate preferences among decisions that may result in diverse outcomes. In simple situations when only money is involved, an expected-value approach might be suggested, in which a larger expected amount of money is preferred to a smaller amount. However, in many situations the utility associated with money is not a linear function of the amount of money involved.

According to expected utility theory, the decision maker should seek to choose the alternative a_i which makes the resulting expected utility the largest possible. The utility u_{ij}, of choosing decision a_i and obtaining outcome event e_j, will also depend upon the specific value of the probabilistically uncertain random variable e_j as conditioned on the decision path that is selected. So, the best that the decision maker can do here is to maximize some function, such as the expected value or utility (EU), as shown below, where the maximization is carried out over all alternative decisions, and $P(e_j \mid a_i)$ is the probability that the state of nature is e_j given that alternative a_i is implemented. The notation EU$\{a_i\}$ is often used to mean the expected utility of taking action a_i. Generally, this is also called the subjective expected utility (SEU). "Subjective" denotes the fact that the probabilities may be based on subjective beliefs and the utilities may reflect personal consequences.

Decision Theory under Various Conditions

In one of the most influential textbooks in decision theory, the terms are defined as follows:

"We shall say that we are in the realm of decision making under:

(a) *Certainty,* if each action is known to lead invariably to a particular outcome the words prospect, stimulus, alternative, etc., are also used.

(b) *Risk* if each action leads to one of a set of possible particular outcomes, each conclusion occurring with a known probability. The probabilities are assumed to be known to the decision maker. For example, an action might lead to this risky outcome: a reward of $10 if a 'fair' coin comes up heads, and a loss of $5 if it comes up tails. Of course, certainty is a degenerate case of risk where the probabilities are 0 and 1.

(c) *Uncertainty,* if either action or both has as its consequence a set of possible specific outcomes, but where the probabilities of these outcomes are completely unknown or are not even meaningful."

This theory was proposed by Luce and Raiffa in 1957 in their article at p. 13.

DECISION UNDER CERTAINTY

Decision under certainty refers to the condition if an action is known to lead invariably to a specific result. It is the condition under only are event with are result of that event.

This term used in a condition when for each decision alternative, there is only one event and therefore only one outcome for each action. For example, there is only one possible event for the two possible actions: "Do nothing" at a future cost of $3.00 per unit for 10,000 units, or "rearrange" a facility at a future cost of $2.80 for the same number of units.

Note that there is only one State of Nature in the matrix because there is only one possible outcome for each action (with certainty). The decision is obviously to choose the action that will result in the most desirable outcome (least cost), that is to "rearrange.

DECISION UNDER UNCERTAINTY

Individual decision making under uncertainty can be characterized as follows:

– The decision maker has to choose one *act* from a given set of possible acts.

– A set of potential *states* is given, representing the circumstances about which there is uncertainty. It is logically necessary that one and only one of the states will occur; otherwise, the states have been erroneously specified. Eventually, the uncertainty will be resolved and one state will be realized.

When the act has been chosen and the state has been realized, the outcome is determined, as can be illustrated by the following table:

	State				
Act	s_1	...	s_j	...	s_n
a_1	$O_{1,1}$		$O_{1,j}$		$O_{1,n}$
...					
a_i	$O_{i,1}$		$O_{i,j}$		$O_{i,n}$
...					
a_m	$O_{m,1}$		$O_{m,j}$		$O_{m,n}$

For simplicity, it is assumed that there are a finite number of possible acts, denoted a_1, a_2, ..., a_i, ..., a_m, and a finite number of potential states, denoted s_1, s_2, ..., s_j, ..., s_n. In many applications, both act and state contain continuous variables, making the sets of acts and states infinite.

Acts, states and results can be complex objects but the nature of these objects are not discussed.

Everything that can affect the outcome and about which there is uncertainty, shall be made part of the state. When the act (a_i) has been chosen and the state (s_j) has become known, the outcome ($O_{i,j}$) shall follow, mechanically and with certainty.

Everything the decision maker cares about, shall be a part of the outcome. That is, if some acts or states in themselves are valued positively or negatively, the relevant aspects of the act or state shall be incorporated into the outcome. In other words, it is assumed that the decision maker has preferences over outcomes and only over outcomes.

Every combination of act and state must in principle be possible, although certain combination may lead to very bad results. The act is chosen without knowledge of which state will be realized, and this is inconsistent with some combinations being impossible.

Degrees of Uncertainty

In the concept of uncertainty, there is no total ignorance exists. It is difficult to imagine what a theory of decision making under total ignorance should look like.

Concerning degree of uncertainty, two alternatives will be discussed:

(1) The decision maker knows the set of potential states, but nothing more.

(2) The decision maker is able to assign to each potential state a precise probability.

There is uncertainty in both cases, but the decision maker knows a lot more in case (2) than in case (1).[1]

This is by no means an exhaustive list of possible degrees of uncertainty. On the one hand, there is the case of complete ignorance, that is, less knowledge than assumed in (1). On the other hand, full certainty is a possibility, amounting to more knowledge than assumed in (2). Moreover, there is a range of possibilities between (1) and (2). In such intermediate cases the decision maker knows the set of potential states and has some opinion as to which of them are more or less likely, in absolute terms or relatively to one another, without being able to express this knowledge as precise probabilities. There is an infinity of different cases falling between (1) and (2), but they are not discussed further here.[2]

Set of States

In this condition of uncertainty, states are also refers to the constraints.

When only the set of states is known, it does not make sense to put more weight on the outcomes of one state than another. For example, if one, puts greater weight on the outcome of s_1 than that of s_2, one would in a sense say that s_1 is considered more likely or probable than s_2. By assumption, this type of information is not available.

However, it is, possible to put greater weight on results that are specifically bad or good.

The following decision rule is frequently recommended in case (1): For each possible act, that is, for each line in the table in Section

1, find the worst outcome. Judge the act as if this outcome will occur and choose the act that, on this basis, is the best one.

This is often called the *maximin-rule*. One maximizes – over the set of possible acts – the minimal (worst) outcome.3 In order to apply the rule, the decision maker must be able to rank the outcomes, that is, ordinal preferences over outcomes must exist. More demanding requirements need not be imposed on the preferences.

Here, maximum refers to the maximization value of al the minimum outcomes. It is also called the condition under pessimism.

PROBABILITY

Probability refers to possibility to do something or not. Or the condition of assumption that an action may be or may not be possible to occur. As we discussed in degree to uncertainty, case 2 describe that the decision maker is able to assign to each potential state a precise probability. The states in condition of uncertainty have probabilities.

Given the assumption that there is a finite number of potential states, case (2) amounts to postulating the existence of numbers p_1, $p_2, ..., p_j, ..., p_n$, where p_j e□ 0 for all j and $p_1 + p_2 + ... + p_j + ... + p_n = 1$. Here p_j is the probability that state s_j will occur.4 The case of infinitely many states is not discussed.

In the finite case, it does not matter whether we assume p_j e□ 0 or $p_j > 0$. If $p_j = 0$, s_j is impossible and can be deleted from the set of potential states.

From where do probabilities come? In some cases, it can reasonably be claimed that there exist objectively given probabilities. This is true for controlled games of chance, where the rules of the game specify the probabilities of the outcomes. In other cases, it may be possible to base (objective) probabilities on experience, that is, probability is identified with observed frequency in (a large number of) previous cases of the same type. Frequently, however, the probabilities will contain an element of subjective judgment on part of the decision maker. Therefore, two persons who face what objectively might appear to be the same choice situation that can specify the probabilities differently.

Much can be said about probabilities and their intrinsic nature. It would lead too far to start that discussion here. For the present purpose, it suffices to assume that the decision maker is able to assign the definite probabilities to the states.

When probabilities have been introduced, an act can be identified with a lottery over outcomes. In the table of Section 1 the act *ai* will lead to the outcome *Oi*,1 with probability *p*1, *Oi*,2 with probability *p*2, ..., *Oi,j* with probability *pj*, ... and *Oi,n* with probability *pn*. Such a lottery is usually called a *prospect*. In order to be able to make rational choices, the decisions maker must have preferences prospects.

As mentioned above, the outcomes can in principle be very complex objects. For the subsequent discussion it does not really matter what the outcomes are, but it may be easier to follow the argument if attention is restricted to a simple example. Therefore, it is assumed that an outcome simply is an amount of money. Previous assumptions then imply that the decision maker is concerned only with this amount. No other aspect of the outcome is of importance, and acts and states have no (positive or negative) value in themselves.

Under these assumptions, an act can be identified with a (finite) list of possible amounts of money, with a probability assigned to each amount. Such a prospect can be denoted as follows:

$A = \{p1{:}x1; p2{:}x2; \ldots pj{:}xj; \ldots pn{:}xn\}$.

The decision maker receives the amount *xj* with probability *pj* for *j* = 1, 2, ... *n*. It is assumed that *pj* e" 0 for all *j* and *p*1 + *p*2 + ... + *pj* + ... + *pn* = 1.

Paradoxes of Uncertainty

The discussion about the distinction between uncertainty and probability has centered on two paradoxes. One of them is the paradox of ideal evidence. It was discovered by Peirce in 1932, but the formulation is very usually.

"Let *z* be a certain penny, and let *a* be the statement 'the *n*th as yet unobserved toss of *z* will yield heads'. Within the subjective theory, it may be assumed that the absolute(or prior) probability of the statement *a* is equal to ½ that is to say,

(1) P (*a*)= 1/2

Now let *e* be some *statistical evidence*; that is to say, a *statistical report* which are based upon the observation of thousands or perhaps millions of tosses of z; and let this evidence e be *ideally favorable* to the hypothesis that z is strictly symmetrical — that is a 'good' penny, with equidistribution...We then have no other option to concerning P (a,e) the probability of a, given e than to assume that

(2) P(a,e)-1/2

This means that the probability of tossing heads remains unchanged, in the light of the evidence e, for we now have

(3) P(a)= P (a,e).

But according to the subjective theory, (3) means that e is, on the whole. i.e., absolutely irrelevant information with respect to a.

Now this is a little statling; fir it means, more explicitly, that our so-called 'degree of rational belief in the hypothesis, a, ought to be completely unaffected by the accumulated evidential knowledge, e; that the absence of any statistical evidence concerning z justifies precisely the same 'degree of rational belief' as the weighty evidence of millions of observation.

This paradox was proposed to express the proper state of belief, no one number but two are requisite, the first are depending on the inferred probability, the second on the out of knowledge on which that probability in base.

The other paradox is *Ellsberg's paradox.* It concerns the following decision problem.

"imagine a bag contain 30 red balls and 60 black and yellow balls, the latter in unknown proportion...One ball is to be drawn at random from the bag the following actions are considered:

I	$100	$0	$0
II	$0	100	$0

Action I is 'a bet on red,' II is 'a bet on black.' Which do you prefer?

Now consider the following two actions, under the same circumstances:

	30	60
Red	Black	Yellow
III $100	$0	$100

IV $0 $100 $100

Action III is a 'bet on red or yellow'; IV is a ' bet on black or yellow.' Which of these do you prefer? Take your time!

A very frequent pattern of response is: action I preferred to II, and IV to III. Less frequent is: II preferred to I, and III preferred to IV." (Ellsberg [1961] 1988, p. 225)

Measures of Incompletely Known Probability

The rules that have been proposed for decision-making under uncertainty (partial probability information) all make use of some quantitative expression of partial probability information. In this section, such "measures of uncertainty" will be introduced.

There are name suggest, binary measures describes the probability values into two categories, i.e., possible and impossible values whereas multi-valued represents the numerical value to each probability value between 0 and 1.

A *binary measure* divides the probability values into two groups, possible and impossible values. In many cases, the set of possible probability values will form a single interval, such as: "The probability of a major earthquake in this area within the next 20 years in between 5 and 20 per cent."

Multi-valued measures generally take the form of a function that assigns a numerical value to each probability value between 0 and 1. this value represents the degree of reliability or plausibility of each particular probability value. Several interpretations of the measures have been used in the literature:

Second-order probability: The reliability measures may be seen as a measure of the probability that the (true) probability has a some value. We may think of this as the subjective probability that the objective probability has some value. Alternatively, we may think of it as the subjective probability, given our present state of knowledge, that our subjective probability would have had a certain value if we had "access to a certain body of information". This theory was proposed by Baron in 1987.

As was noted by Brain Skyrms, it is " hardly in dispute that people have beliefs about their beliefs. Thus, if we distinguish degrees of belief, we should not shrink from saying that people have degrees of belief about their degrees of belief. It would then be entirely natural for a degree-of-belief theory of probability to treat probabilities of probabilities," this theory was introduced by SKyrms.

Decision-making under Ignorance

By decision-making under ignorance is generally meant decision-making when it is known what the possible states of affairs are, but no information about their probabilities is available. This case is "classical ignorance" treated.

Situations are not uncommon in which information is lacking not only about the probabilities of the possible states of nature, but also about which these states of affairs are. This more severe form of ignorance about the states of nature.

Decision Rules for Classical Ignorance

The following is a variant of the umbrella example that has been used in previous sections: You have participated in a contest on a TV show, and won the big prize: The Secret Journey. You will be taken by airplane to a one week vacation on a secret place. You do not know where that place is, so for all that you know the probability of rain there may be anything from 0 to 1. Therefore, this is an example of decision-making under ignorance. As before, your decision matrix is:

	It rains	**It does not rain**
Umbrella	Dry clothes, heavy suitcase	**Dry clothes, heavy suitcase**
No umbrella	**Soaked clothes, light suitcase**	**Dry clothes, light suitcase**

Let us first see what we can do with only a preference relation (i.e., with no information about utilities). As before, your preferences are:

Dry clothes, light suitcase

is better than

Dry clothes, heavy suitcase

is better than

Soaked clothes, light suitcase

Perhaps foremost among the decision criteria proposed for decisions under ignorance is the *maximin* rule: For each alternative, we define its *security level* as the worst possible outcome with that alternative. The maximin rule urges us to choose the alternative method that has the maximal security level. In other words, *maxi*mize the *min*imal outcome. In our case, the security level of "umbrella" is "dry clothes, heavy suitcase", and the security level of "no umbrella" is "soaked clothes, light suitcase". Thus, the maximin rule urges you to bring your umbrella.

The maximin principle was first introduced by von Neumann as a strategy against an intelligent opponent. In 1950, Wald extended its use to games against nature.

The maximin rule does not differentiate between the alternatives with the same security level. A variant of it, the *lexicographic maximin*, or *leximin* rule, distinguishes between such alternatives by comparison of their second-worst outcomes. If two alternatives have the same security level, then the one with the highest second-worst outcome is chosen. If both the worst and the second-worst outcomes are on the same level, then the thirdworst outcomes are compared, etc.

The maximin and leximin rules are frequently said to represent the extreme prudence or pessimism. The other extreme is represented by the *maximax* rule: choose the alternative whose hope level (best possible outcome) is best. In this case, the *hope level* of "umbrella" is "dry clothes, heavy suitcase", and that of "no umbrella" is "dry clothes, light suitcase". A maximaxer will not bring his umbrella.

It is in general "difficult to justify the maximax principle as rational principle of decision, reflecting, as it does, wishful thinking". (Rapoport 1989, p. 57) Nevertheless, life would probably be duller if not at least some of us were maximaxers on at least some occasions.

In the condition under uncertainty, maximin rule is follow in which the final conclusion is the maximization values of all minimum conclusion but in the decision under ignorance, maximum and maximin rule maximax follows the rule which includes the final conclusion is the maximization value of the maximum outcomes.

There is an obvious requirement for a decision criterion that does not force us into the extreme pessimism of the maximin or leximin rule or into the extreme optimism of the maximax rule. For such criteria to be practicable, we need the utility of information. Let us assume that we have such information for the umbrella problem, with the following values:

It rains	It does not rain	
Umbrella	15	15
No umbrella	0	18

A middle way between maximin pessimism and maximax optimism is the *optimism-pessimism index*. (It is often called the *Hurwicz ??index*, since it was proposed by Hurwicz in a 1951 paper.

Decision under ignorance is also known as Hurwicz index, in this criteria , á is given the value of ??always lie between o and 1.

According to this decision criterion, the decision-maker is required to choose an index ??between 0 and 1, that reflects his degree of optimism or pessimism. For each alternative A, let *min*(A) be its security level, i.e. the lowest utility to which it can give rise, and let *max*(A) be the hope level, i.e., the highest utility level that it can give rise to. The ?-index of A is calculated according to the formula:

??—ÿ?*min*(A) + (1-?) —ÿ?*max*(A)

Obviously, if ??= 1, then this procedure reduces to the maximin criterion and if ??= 0, then it reduces to the maximax criterion.

As can easily be verified, in our umbrella example anyone with an index above 1/6 will bring his umbrella.

Utility information also allows for another decision criterion, namely the *minimax regret* criterion as introduced by Savage (1951, p. 59). (It has many other names, including "minimax risk", "minimax loss" and simply "minimax".)

Various Decision Rules

The decision rules discussed in this section are summarized in the following table:

Decision rule	Value information needed	Character of the rule	Valuation
maximin	preferences	pessimism	Maximization of minimum outcome
leximin	preferences	pessimism	Maximization of minimization outcome
maximax	preferences	optimism	Maximization of minimization outcome
optimism-pessimismindex		utilities	varies with index Maximization of minimization outcome
minimax regret	·utilities	cautiousness	Maximint Maximax
insufficient reason		utilities	depends onpartitioning Maximization of minimum value of regret

The major decision rules for ignorance.

In fifth decision rule, regret refers to the difference between each value of table with smallest value and then find the take the all maximum outcomes of that regret and finally takes the minimization of that maximum outcome.

For example

This is the table below shows and methods with three columns containing stable rock, geographical catas trophy and Human intrension.

	Stable rock	Geological catastrophy	Human intrusion
Method 1	1	100	100
Method 2	0	700	900

Regret table

	SR	GC	HI
	1	50	0
	0	650	800
	20	0	10
maximum	20	650	850
Minimum	0	0	0

Then the maximum outcomes are 20, 650, 800, 80 the three minimum regret value is 20, i.e., method 3 with stable rock.

DECISION UNDER UNKNOWN NON-ZERO POSSIBILITIES

In this case, we know what the possible outcomes are of the various options but all me know about their probabilities is that are non-zero.

Higher level of uncertainty is that which results from ignorance of what the possible consequences are, i.e., *decision-making under unknown possibilities*. In probabilistic language, this is the case when there is some consequence for which we do not know whether its probability, given some option, is zero or non-zero. However, this probabilistic description does not capture the gist of the matter. The characteristic feature of these cases is that we do not have a complete list of the consequences that should be taken into account.

Even if various specified versions of high-level consequence-uncertainty can be shown to be negligible, the underlying more general uncertainty may remain.

A rational decision-maker should take the issue of unknown possibilities into account in some cases, but not in others. Due to the vague and somewhat elusive nature of this type of uncertainty, we should not expect to find exact criteria for deciding when it is negligible and when it is not. The following list of four factors is meant to be a basic checklist of aspects to be taken into account in deliberations on the seriousness of unknown possibilities.

These four factors includes asymmetry of uncertainty. Novelty. Spatial and temporal limitations and last are in interference with complex systems in balance.

1. Asymmetry of uncertainty: Possibly, a raise in pensions leads in certain unknown method to a nuclear war. Possibly, not raising the pensions leads in some unknown way to a nuclear war. We have no reason why one or the other of these two causal chains should be more probable, or otherwise more worth our attention than the other. On the other hand, the introduction of a new species of earthworm is connected with much more consequence-uncertainty than the option not to introduce the new species. Such asymmetry is a necessary but insufficient condition for the issue of unknown possibilities to be non-negligible.

2. *Novelty*: Unknown possibilities come mainly from new and untested phenomena or process. The emission of a new substance into the stratosphere constitutes a qualitative novely, whereas an increase in government pensions does not.

An interesting example of the novelty factor can be found in particle of physics. Before new and more powerful particle accelerators have been built, physicists have sometimes feared that the new levels of energy may generate a new phase of matter that accretes every atom of the earth. The decision to regard these and similar fears as groundless has been based on observations showing that the earth is already under constant bombardment from outer space of particles with the same or higher energies. This theory was introduced by Ruthen in 1993.

3. *Spatial and temporal limitations*: If the effects of a proposed measure are known to be limited in space or in time, then these limitations reduce the uncertainty that are associated with the measure. The absence of such limitations contributes to the relevance of unknown possibilities in many ecological issues, such as global emissions and the spread of chemically stable pesticides.

4. *Interference with complex systems in balance*: Complex systems like ecosystems and the atmospheric system are known to have reached few type of balance, that may be impossible to restore after a major disturbance occurs. Due to this irreversibility, uncontrolled interference with such systems is connected with serious uncertainty. This same concept can be said of uncontrolled interference with economic systems. This is an argument for piecemeal rather than drastic economic reforms.

As was mentioned above, the major cases of unknown possibilities are asymmetrical in the sense that there is at least one option in which this uncertainty is avoided. Therefore, the choice of a strategy-type for the serious cases is much less abstruse than the selection of these cases:

The obvious solution is to avoid the options that are connected to the higher degrees of uncertainty.

This strategy will in many cases that take the form of *non-interference* with ecosystems and other well-functioning systems that are insufficiently understood. Such non-interference variate from general conservatism in being limited to a very special category of issues, that does not required to coincide with the concerns of political conservatism.

Case Study

Note : knowing more about "Decision Making Process and Decision Theory" reader can study documentation process of Microsoft company by visiting their site : www.members.microsoft.com

http://www.globalfuture.com/scenario2.htm

http://www.robustdecisions.com/decision-making/case-studies.php

http://www.infozee.com/channels/mba/casestudy/decision.htm

http://www.icmrindia.org/casestudies/catalogue/Human%20Resource%20and%20Organization%20Behavior/HROB053.htm

http://www.flipkart.com/clinical-decision-making-case-studies/143543983x-tox3fqovid

http://www.chemcases.com/

5

Process Analysis

This chapter include various key concepts which are shown below:-

- Systematic Approach of Process Analysis
- Business Process
- Business Process Modeling
- Business Process Integration
- Business Process Management
- Business Rules Approach
- Simulation
- ERP (Enterprise Resource Planning)
- Distribution Resource Planning (DRP)
- MRP (Material Requirements Planning)
- Manufacturing Resource Planning (MRP II)
- BOM (Bill of Materials (BOM))

SYSTEMATIC APPROACH OF PROCESS ANALYSIS

Systematic approach can be used in many areas such as system analysis, software development, web optimization, sales and training. The process typically the phases:

1. Analyze the organization's needs and identify training goals which, when reached, will equip learner's with knowledge and skills to meet the organization's needs. Usually this phase also includes identifying when training should occur and who should attend as learners.

2. Design a training system that learners and trainers can implement to meet the learning goals; typically includes identifying learning objectives (which culminate in reaching the learning goals), needed facilities, necessary funding, course content, lessons and sequence of lessons.

3. Develop a training "package" of resources and materials, including, e.g., developing audio-visuals, graphics, manuals, etc.

4. Implement the training package, including delivering the training, support group feedback, clarifying training materials, administering tests and conducting the final evaluation. This phase can include administrative activities, such as copying, scheduling facilities, taking attendance data, billing learners, etc.

5. Evaluate training, including before, during and after implementation of training.

These are five steps or approaches of process analysis including, analyze, design, develop, implement and evaluate.

BUSINESS PROCESS

Business process is collection of structured activities that produce a particular service or product.

A business process is a collection of related, structured activities or tasks that produce a specific service or product (serve a specific goal) for a particular customer or customers. There are three main types of business processes:

1. *Management processes*, the processes that govern the operation of a system. Typical management processes include "Corporate Governance" and "Strategic Management".

2. *Operational processes*, processes that constitute the core business and create the primary value stream. Typical operational processes are Purchasing, Manufacturing, Marketing, and Sales.

3. *Supporting processes*, which support the core processes. Examples include Accounting, Recruitment, Technical support.

A business process can be categorized into various sub-processes, which have their own attributes, but also contribute to achieving the goal of the super-process. The analysis of business processes typically includes the mapping of processes and sub-processes down to activity level. A business process model is a model of one or more business processes, and defines the methods in which operations are carried out to accomplish the intended objectives of an organization. Such a model remains an abstraction and depends on the intended use of the model. It can describe the workflow or the integration between business processes. It can be constructed in multiple levels.

A workflow is a depiction of a sequence of operations, declared as work of a person, work of a simple or complex mechanism, work of a group of persons, work of an organization of staff, or machines. Workflow may be seen as any abstraction of real work, segregated in workshare, work split or whatever types of ordering. For control purposes, workflow may be a view on real work under a chosen aspect.

BUSINESS PROCESS MODELING

It addresses the process aspects of a business architecture which are leading to an all encompassing enterprise architecture.

Business process modeling (BPM) in systems engineering and software engineering is the activity of representing processes of an enterprise, therefore, the current process may be analyzed and improved in future. BPM is typically performed by business analysts and managers who are seeking to improve process efficiency and quality. The process improvements identified by BPM may or may not require Information Technology involvement, although that is a common driver for the need to model a business process, by creating a process master.

Change management programs are typically involved to put the improved business processes into practice. With advances in technology from large platform vendors, the vision of BPM models becoming fully executable (and capable of simulations and round-trip engineering) is coming closer to reality every day.

Business process modeling plays an important role in the business process management (BPM) discipline. Since both business process modeling and business process management share the same abbreviation (BPM), these activities are sometimes confused with each other.

The graphical representation of business process information has proven effective for presenting it to business stakeholders, including business analysts and system developers. Visual modeling languages used to represent business processes include Business

Process Modeling Notation (BPMN) and the Unified Modeling Language (UML).

Business Process Modeling Tools

Business process modeling tools provide the business users with the ability to model their business processes, implement and execute those models, and refine the models based on as-executed data. As a conclusion, business process modeling tools can provide the transparency into business processes, as well as the centralization of corporate business process models and execution metrics.

BUSINESS PROCESS INTEGRATION

A business model, which may be considered an elaboration of a business process model, typically shows business data and business organizations as well as business processes. By showing business processes and their information flows a business model allows business stakeholders to define, understand, and validate their business enterprise. The data model part of the business model shows how business information is stored, which is useful for developing software code.

Business model is created after conducting an interview, which is the part of business analysis process.

BUSINESS PROCESS MANAGEMENT

Business process management is abbreviated as BPM. This process is used to manage the various business process. It acts as field of management.

Business process management (BPM) is a field of management which are focused on aligning organizations with the wants and needs of clients. It is a holistic management approach that promotes business effectiveness and efficiency while striving for innovation, flexibility and integration with technology. Business process management attempts to continuously improve processes. Therefore, it could be described as a "process optimization process".

A business process is "a collection of related, structured activities that produce a service or product that meet the needs of a client." These processes are typical to any organization as they generate revenue and frequently represent a significant proportion of costs. BPM articles and pundits often discuss BPM from one of two viewpoints: people and technology.

BPM can be used to understand the organizations through expanded views that would not otherwise be available to organize and present. These views prefers to the relationships of processes to each other which, when included in the process model, provide for advanced reporting and analysis that would not otherwise be available. BPM is regarded by some as the backbone of enterprise content management.

Life-cycle of BPM

The activities which constitute business process management can be described in the form of BPM life cycle that is processed into five steps:

1. Design,
2. Modeling,
3. Execution,
4. Monitoring, and
5. Optimization.

The description of these steps are shown below:

Step 1 : Design : Process Design encompasses both the identification of existing processes and the design of "to-be" processes. Areas of focus this step include: representation of the process flow, the actors within it, alerts & notifications, escalations, Standard Operating Procedures, Service Level Agreements, and task hand-over mechanisms.

Good design reduces the number of problems over the lifetime of the process. Whether or not existing processes are considered, the aim of this step is to ensure that a correct and efficient theoretical design is prepared.

The proposed improvement could be in human to human, human to system, and system to system workflows, and might target regulatory, market, or competitive challenges faced by the businesses.

Step 2 : Modeling : Modeling takes the theoretical design and introduces all the combinations of variables, for instance, changes in the cost of materials or increased rent, that determine how the process might operate under different circumstances. It also involves running "what-if analysis" on the processes: "What if I have 75% of resources to do the same task?" "What if I want to do the same job for 80% of the current cost?"

Step 3 : Execution : One of the methods to automate processes is to develop or purchase an application that executes the required steps of the process; however, in practice, these applications rarely execute all the steps of the process accurately or completely. Another approach is to use a combination of software and human intervention; however this approach is more complex, making the documentation process difficult.

As a conclusion of to these problems, software has been developed that enables the full business process (as developed in the process design activity) to be defined in a computer language which can be directly executed by the computer. The system will either use services in connected applications to perform business operations (e.g. calculating a repayment plan for a loan) or, when a step is too complex to automate, will ask for human input. Compared to either of the previous approaches, directly executing a process definition can be more straightforward and therefore easier to improve. However, automating a process definition needs flexible and comprehensive infrastructure, which typically rules out implementing these systems in a legacy IT environment.

Business rules have been used by systems to provide definitions for governing behavior, and a business rule engine can be used to drive process execution and resolution.

Step 4 : Monitoring : Monitoring encompasses the tracking of individual processes, therefore, the information on their state can be easily seen, and statistics on the performance of one or more processes can be provided. An example of the tracking is being able to determine the state of a customer order (e.g. ordered arrived, awaiting delivery, invoice paid) so that problems in its operation can be identified and corrected.

In addition, this information can be used to work with customers and suppliers to improve their connected processes. Examples of the statistics are the generation of measures on how quickly a customer order is processed or how many orders were processed in the last month. These measures tend to fit into three categories: cycle time, defect rate and productivity.

The degree of monitoring depends on what information the business wants to evaluate and analyze and how business wants it to be monitored, in real-time or ad-hoc. Here, business activity monitoring (BAM) extends and expands the monitoring tools in generally provided by BPMS.

Process mining is a mixture of methods and tools which are related to process monitoring. The objective of process mining is to analyze the event logs which are extracted through process monitoring and to compare them with an 'a priori' process model. Process mining allows process analysts to detect discrepancies between the actual process execution and the a priori model as well as to analyze bottlenecks.

Step : 5 Optimization : Process optimization includes the retrieving process performance information from modeling or monitoring phase; identifying the potential or actual bottlenecks and the potential opportunities for cost savings or other improvements; and then, applying those enhancements in the design of the process. Overall, this creates greater business value.

All these five steps are useful to manage the business processes.

BUSINESS RULES APPROACH

Every business has their own rules and regulations which are followed by the members of these business to achieve the peak of the success.

Business rules are the abstractions of the policies and practices of a business organization. The Business Rules Approach is a development methodology where rules are in a form that is used by, but does not have to be embedded in business process management systems.

The Business Rules Approach formalizes an enterprise's critical business rules in a language that managers and technologists understand. Business rules create an unambiguous statement of what a business does with information to decide a proposition. The formal specification becomes information for process and rules engines to run.

Advantages of Business Rules

The adoption of business rules adds another tier to systems that automate business processes. Compared to traditional systems, this approach has the following major advantages,

- lowers the cost incurred in the modification of business logic
- shortens development time
- rules are externalized and easily shared among multiple applications
- changes can be made faster and with less risk

Business rules represent a natural step in the application of computer technology aimed at enhancing productivity in the workplace. Automated business processes that have business logic embedded inside often take substantial time to change, and such changes can be prone to errors. And in a world where the life cycle of business models has greatly shortened, it has become increasingly critical to be able to adapt to changes in external environments promptly. These needs are addressed by a business rules approach.

There is rule engine which acts as system software that executed due or more business rules in a runtime production environment. These rules might come from legal regulation.

Rule engine software is usually provided as a component of a business rule management system which, among other functions, provides the ability to: register, define, classify, and manage all the rules, verify consistency of rules definitions ("Gold-level customers are eligible for free shipping when order quantity > 10" and "maximum order quantity for Gold-level customers = 10"), define the relationships between different rules, and relate some of these rules to IT applications that are affected or need to enforce one or more of the rules.

Business rules can be expressed in a same manner to conventional programming languages or in languages resembling natural ones. In some commercial BRMS's rules can also be expressed in user-friendly rule forms such as decision tables and decision trees. Provided with appropriate interface to design or edit the decision tables or trees, it is possible for business users to check or change rules directly, with minimal IT involvement.

When rules are expressed in a some manner to a natural language, it is essential to first define a vocabulary to be used, which contains words and expressions that correspond to business objects and conditions and operations involving them. To make the rules executable by a rule engine, it is also essential to implement the operations and conditions in a programming language. With a defined and implemented vocabulary, it is relatively easy to write rules in a BRMS. Changes can also be made quickly as long as they can be expressed in the existing vocabulary. If not, the vocabulary must be expanded accordingly.

Rules can also be modeled, with the business user taking the part of mapping their business logic and IT being responsible for integration of data as well as integration of the generated code into the target application. Business rules are also key to the Enterprise Decision Management approach to decision automation.

SIMULATION

Simulation is the imitation of some real thing, state of affairs, or process. The act or method of simulating something that usually entails representing some key characteristics or behaviours of a selected physical or abstract system.

The process of simulation is used in various contexts, including the modeling of natural systems or human systems in order to gain insight into their functioning. Other contexts include simulation of technology for performance optimization, safety engineering, testing, training and education. Simulation can be used to show the eventual real effects of alternative conditions and courses of action.

Key issues in simulation include acquisition of valid source information about the relevent selection of key characteristics and behaviours, the use of simplifying approximations and assumptions within the simulation, and fidelity and validity of the simulation outcomes.

ERP (ENTERPRISE RESOURCE PLANNING)

Enterprise resource planning (ERP) is a company-wide computer software system which are used to manage and coordinate all the resources, information, and functions of a business from shared data stores.

An ERP system typically has modular hardware and software units and "services" that communicate on a local area network. The modular design allows a business to add or reconfigure modules (perhaps from different vendors) while preserving data integrity in one shared database that may be centralized or distributed

Ideally, ERP delivers a single database that contains all data for the software modules, which would include:

1. Customer relationship management Sales and marketing, commissions, service, customer contact and call center support

2. Financials General ledger, cash management, accounts payable, accounts receivable, fixed assets

3. Manufacturing Engineering, bills of material, scheduling, capacity, workflow management, quality control, cost management, manufacturing process, manufacturing projects, manufacturing flow

4. Data warehouse and various self-service interfaces for customers, suppliers, and employees

5. Access control - user privilege as per authority levels for process execution

6. Supply chain management Order to cash, inventory, order entry, purchasing, product configurator, supply chain planning, supplier scheduling, inspection of goods, claim processing, commission calculation

7. Customization - to meet the extension, addition, change in process flow

8. Project management Costing, billing, time and expense, performance units, activity management

9. Human resources Human resources, payroll, training, time and attendance, rostering, benefits

ERP is a term originally derived from manufacturing resource planning (II) that followed material requirements planning.

To implement ERP systems, companies frequently seek the help of an ERP vendor.

Implementation of ERP

1. Identifying the data to be migrated
2. Determining the timing of data migration
3. Generating the data templates
4. Freezing the tools for data migration
5. Deciding on migration related setups
6. Deciding on data archiving

ERP implementation is considerably more difficult (and politically charged) in organizations structured into nearly independent business units, each responsible for their own profit and loss, because they will each have several processes, business rules, data semantics, authorization hierarchies and decision centers. Solutions that include requirements coordination which are negotiated by local change management professionals or, if this is not possible, federated implementation using loosely integrated instances (e.g. linked via Master Data Management) specifically configured and/or customized to meet local needs.

DISTRIBUTION RESOURCE PLANNING (DRP)

Distribution Resource Planning (DRP) is a method used in business administration for planning orders within a supply chain. DRP enables the user to set some inventory control parameters (like a safety stock) and formulated the time-phased inventory requirements.

DRP uses several variables:

- the backordered demand at the end of a period.
- the on-hand inventory at the end of a period.
- the recommended order quantity at the beginning of a period.
- the constrained quantity of product available at the beginning of a period.
- the required quantity of product needed at the beginning of a period.

DRP needs the following information:

- the scheduled receipts at the beginning of a period.
- the on-hand inventory at the beginning of a period.
- the safety stock requirement for a period.
- the demand in a future period.

MRP (MATERIAL REQUIREMENTS PLANNING)

Material Requirements Planning (MRP) is a software based production planning and inventory control system which are used to manage manufacturing processes. Although it is not common nowadays, it is possible to conduct MRP by hand as well.

An MRP system is intended to simultaneously has three objectives involving:

- Ensure materials and products are available for production and delivery to customers.
- Maintain the lowest possible level of inventory.
- Plan manufacturing activities, delivery schedules and purchasing activities.

The major problem with MRP systems is the integrity of the data. If there are any errors in the inventory data, the bill of materials which are commonly referred to as 'BOM' data, or the master production schedule, then the outputted data will also be incorrect. Most vendors of this type of system recommend at least 99% data integrity for the system to give useful results.

Another major problem with MRP systems is the requirement that the user specify how long it will take a factory to make a product from its component parts (assuming they are all available). Additionally, the system design also assumes that this "lead time" in manufacturing will be the same each time the item is made, without regard to quantity being made, or other items being made simultaneously in the factory.

MANUFACTURING RESOURCE PLANNING (MRP II)

This is not exclusively a software function, but a marriage of people skills, dedication to data base accuracy, and computer resources. It is a total company management concept for using human resources more productively.

The MRP II system integrates these modules together so that they use common data and freely exchange information, in a model of how a manufacturing enterprise should and can operate. Therefore, the MRP II approach is much different from the "point solution" approach, where individual systems are deployed to help a company plan, control or manage a specific activity. MRP II is by definition fully integrated or at least fully interfaced.

Benefits of MRP II:-

MRP II systems can provide:

- Productive relationships with suppliers
- Improved scheduling
- Better control of inventories

For Design / Engineering:

- Improved design control

For Financial and Costing:

- Accurate inventory records
- Timely and valid cost and profitability information
- Improved cash flow through quicker deliveries
- Reduced working capital for inventory

BOM (BILL OF MATERIALS (BOM))

Bill of materials (BOM) is a list of the raw materials, sub-assemblies, intermediate assemblies, sub-components, components, parts and the quantities of each needed to manufacture an end item (final product) . It may be used for communication between manufacturing partners, or confined to a single manufacturing plant.

A BOM can define products as they are designed, as they are ordered, as they are built, or as they are maintained. The several types of BOMs depend on the business need and use for which they are intended. In process industries, the BOM is also referred as the formula, recipe, or ingredients list. In electronics, the BOM represents the list of components which are used on the printed wiring board or printed circuit board. Once the design of the circuit is completed, the BOM list is passed on to the PCB layout engineer as well as component engineer who will procure the components required for the design.

BOMs are hierarchical in nature with the top level representing the finished product which may be a sub-assembly or a completed item. BOMs that describe the sub-assemblies are referred to as modular BOMs.

Format of BOM

There are three format of BOM which includes the single level BOM, indented BOM and Modular BOM.

A BOM can be displayed in the following formats:

- A single-level BOM that displays the assembly or sub-assembly with only one level of children. Thus it displays the components which are directly needed to make the assembly or sub-assembly.
- An indented BOM that displays the highest-level item closest

to the left margin and the components which are used in that item indented more to the right.

- Modular (planning) BOM

A BOM can also be visually represented by a product structure tree, although they are rarely used in the workplace.

Capacity Planning

It is the process of evaluating the production capacity which are needed by an organization to accept the varying demands for its products.

Capacity planning is the process of determining the production capacity which are needed by an organization to meet changing demands for its products. In the context of capacity planning, "capacity" is the maximum amount of work that an organization is capable of completing in a given period of time.

A discrepancy between the capacity of an organization and the demands of its customers concludes in inefficiency, either in under-utilized resources or unfulfilled customers. The objectives capacity planning is to minimize this discrepancy. Demand for an organization's capacity varies are based on changes in production output, such as increasing or decreasing the production quantity of an existing product, or producing new products. Better utilization of existing capacity can be accomplished through improvements in overall equipment effectiveness (OEE). Capacity can be increased through introducing new techniques, equipment and materials, increasing the number of workers or machines, increasing the number of shifts, or acquiring additional production facilities.

Capacity is formulated: (number of machines or workers) × (number of shifts) × (utilization) × (efficiency).

The broad classes of capacity planning are lead strategy, lag strategy, and match strategy.

- *Lead strategy* is adding capacity in anticipation of an increase in demand. Lead strategy is an aggressive strategy with the goal of luring customers that are away from competitors of the company. The possible disadvantage to this strategy is that it frequently includes in excess inventory, which is costly and often wasteful.
- *Lag strategy* is defined as to adding capacity only after the organization is running at full capacity or beyond due to

increase in demand. This is a more conservative strategy. It decreases the risk of waste, but it may result in the loss of possible customers.

- *Match strategy* is adding capacity in small amounts in response to changing demand in the market. This is a more moderate strategy.

Advancements in Cross-Platform

Whether it's about maximizing throughput, minimizing response time, maximizing availability, or minimizing costs, a thorough capacity planning exercise requires the evaluation of alternative configurations. A change in configuration might be as simple as moving a heavily used file to a less active disk controller or adding a CPU. A good capacity planning tool makes it quick and easy to evaluate such alternatives. One configuration alternative that deserves consideration is a change in processor architecture. TeamQuest's capacity planning tool, TeamQuest Model, has been enhanced to simplify predicting the affect on performance of using different processor types. This paper shows how new capabilities in TeamQuest Model streamline the process of predicting the effect of cross-platform migrations, making it easy for people to evaluate alternative vendor configurations.

How Cloud Computing will Change Capacity Management

Capacity management is a critical part of ensuring that your company is getting the performance and functionality it needs from computation resources. It ensures that the required IT resources are available to conduct day-to-day business and also ensures that just enough money is being spent to do so, not more, or less. As the resources available to IT evolve — cloud computing, virtualization, and other innovations — the requirements and benefits of capacity management will also change.

Capacity planning: From buckets to rivers : When dealing with a constrained set of resources found in the traditional, in-house data center, capacity management can be metaphorically viewed as making sure you have a big enough bucket to hold all of the water the business needs to slake its thirst. There are boundaries on this pool of resources because the IT department must own each computational resource: hardware, software, and the people used to deliver and manage it. Capacity management under this "bucket" approach tends to center on predicting peak usage needs and ensuring that in-house data centers can meet those demands.

Years ago, grid or utility computing promised to offer an alternative to this physical limit; instead of a bucket, IT resources would be like a fast flowing river that limitless cycles could be drawn from. For various reasons — such as low bandwidth to remote grids, the high cost of entry, and the batch-job nature of most grid offers — grid and utility computing didn't go mainstream in initial efforts.

Slipping in under the moniker "cloud computing," some of the aspirational benefits of utility computing are once again making the rounds in IT departments. The same challenges that muddled utility computing efforts must be addressed. Hopefully better networks and a bias for application-based instead of job-based computing will cause greater uptake.

Case Study

Note : knowing more about "Process Analysis" reader can study documentation process of Microsoft company by visiting their site : www.members.microsoft.com

http://www.allacademic.com/meta/p_mla_apa_research_citation/0/9/5/2/3/p95234_index.html

http://college.cengage.com/business/resources/casestudies/students/overview.htm

http://www.soamag.com/I23/1108-4.asp

https://store.darden.virginia.edu/business-case-study/operations-business-math-process-analysis-level-one-problems-2546

http://www.klocwork.com/resources/case-studies.asp

http://ocw.utokyo.ac.jp/wpcontent/uploads/lecturenotes_eng/Eco_01/BusinessAdministration1_03.pdf

6

Project Management

This chapter includes the key concepts which are shown below:-

- Introduction
- Approaches of Project Management
- Traditional Approach
- PRINCE2
- Process-based Management
- Stages of Project Development
- Critical Chain Project Management
- Project Control Systems
- Critical Chain Analysis
- Risk Assessment

INTRODUCTION

A project means to achieve a path and goal of an organization but it has specific time period to complete it with in the limit.

A project is a finite endeavor that have specific start and completion dates which is undertaken to meet the particular goals and objectives, usually to bring about beneficial change or added value. This finite characteristic of projects stands in contrast to processes, or operations—which is repetitive, permanent or semi-permanent functional work to produce the products or services. In practice, the management of these two systems is frequently found to be quite different, and as such requires the development of distinct technical skills and the adoption of separate management.

Each management has their own objectives, goals, achievements and features to peak the success of their own business.

Project management is the discipline of planning, organizing and managing all the resources to bring about the successful completion of specific goals and objectives of project. It is often closely related to and sometimes conflated with Program management.

The primary challenge of project management is to achieve all of the project goals and objectives while honoring the preconceived project constraints. Typical constraints are scope, time and budget. The secondary—and more ambitious—challenge is to optimize the allocation and integration of inputs that are necessary to meet the pre-defined objectives.

The major issue of project management to get all the objectives and goals while the project constraints are honored. These constrains includes, scope, time and budget.

APPROACHES OF PROJECT MANAGEMENT

Project management have various approaches to arrange all the project activities. There are several approaches that can be taken to managing the all project activities which include the agile, interactive, incremental, and phased approaches.

Regardless of the approach employed, careful consideration needs to be given to clarify surrounding project objectives, goals, and importantly, the roles and responsibilities of all participants and stakeholders.

TRADITIONAL APPROACH

Each approach of project management have their own step to achieve all the project activities. This approach have five components which includes the initiation, planning and design, executing, monitoring and controlling and completion stage.

A traditional phased approach identifies a sequence of steps to be completed. In this "traditional approach", we can distinguish 5 components of a project (4 stages plus control) in the development of a project:

Here, Ist stage is project initiation stage where the project begins, IInd stage is planning or design stage where planning should be done and design should be made to develop a project. IIIrd stage is executing which refers to the project execution or production stage.

For particular projects, the project plan should undergo the Resource Leveling, and the longest sequence of resource-constrained tasks is known as the critical chain. In multi-project environments, resource leveling should be performed across all the projects. However, it is frequently enough to identify (or simply select) a single "drum" resource—a resource that acts as a constraint across the projects—and stagger projects which are based on the availability of that single resource.

The major objective of CCPM is to increase the rate of throughput or completion rates. CCPM is the application of TOC.

Extreme Project Management

Here, extreme refers to the extreme programming which are used for development of software and scrum techniques.

In critical studies of Project Management, it has been noted that several of these fundamentally PERT-based models are not well suited for the multi-project company in environment today's. Most of them are aimed at very large-scale, one-time, non-routine projects, and now-a-days all kinds of management are expressed in terms of projects.

Using complex models for "projects" (or rather "tasks") spanning a few weeks has been proven to cause unnecessary costs and low maneuverability in various cases. Instead, project management experts tries to identify the various "lightweight" models, such as Agile Project Management methods including Extreme Programming for software development and Scrum techniques.

The generalization of Extreme Programming to the other kinds of projects is extreme project management, which may be used in combination with the process modeling and management principles of human interaction management.

Event Chain Methodology

Event chain methodology is the next advance way of critical path method and critical chain project management. Event chain methodology is an uncertainty modeling and schedule network analysis technique that is focused on identifying and managing events and event chains that affect the project schedules. Event chain methodology helps to mitigate the negative impact of psychological heuristics and biases, as well as to allow for easy modeling of uncertainties in the project schedules.

There are some principle or which chain methodology based, these principle includes probabilistic moment of risk, event chains, critical events or event chains, project tracking with events and event chain visualization.

- Probabilistic moment of risk includes an activity or task in most real life processes which is not a continuous uniform process. These tasks are affected by external events, which can occur at certain point in the middle of the task.
- Event chains: Events can cause other events, which will create event chains. These event chains can significantly affect the course of the project. Quantitative analysis is used to determine a cumulative effect of these event chains on the project schedule.
- Critical events or event chains: The single events or the event chains that have the most potential to affect the projects are the "critical events" or "critical chains of events." They can be determined by the analysis.
- Project tracking with events: If a project is partially completed and data about the project duration, cost, and events are occurred is available, it is possible to refine the information about the future potential events and helps to forecast the future project performance.
- Event chain visualization: Events and event chains can be visualized using event chain diagrams on a Gantt chart.

PRINCE2

Prince 2 is also a structured approaches of project management which was proposed in 1996.

PRINCE2 is a structured approach to project management, released in 1996 as a generic project management method. It combined the original PRINCE methodology with IBM's MITP (managing the implementation of the total project) methodology.

PRINCE2 provides a way for managing all the projects within a clearly defined framework. PRINCE2 describes the procedures to coordinate the people and performed activities in a project, how to design and supervise the project, and what to do if the project has to be adjusted if it doesn't develop as planned.

Prince 2 is a process model which have various operations that are performed in it.

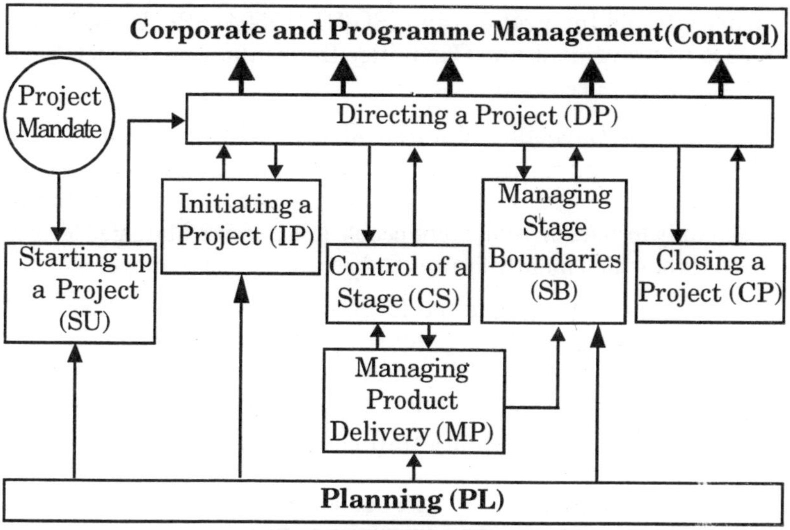

Fig. 1. PRINCE2 model

In this method each process is specified with its key inputs and outputs and with specific goals and activities which are to be carried out, and gives an automatic control of any deviations from the plan. Divided into manageable stages, the method enables an efficient control of resources. On the basis of close monitoring the project can be carried out in a controlled and organized way.

Above fig. 1 shows all the flow of prince2 process model. This model consists of various levels or stages including Directing a project (DP), starting a stage (CS). Managing stage boundaries (SB), closing a project (CP), managing product delivery (MP) and last one is planning (PL).

PRINCE2 provides a general language for all participants in the project. The various management roles and responsibilities involved in a project are fully described and are adaptable to suit the complexity of the project and skills of the organization.

PROCESS-BASED MANAGEMENT

Process based management is usually based on maturity model like CMMI → capability maturity model integration and SPICE → software process improvement and capability determination.

Also furthering the concept of project control is the incorporation of process-based management. This area has been driven by the use of Maturity models such as the CMMI (Capability Maturity Model Integration) and ISO/IEC15504 (SPICE - Software Process Improvement and Capability Determination), which have been far more successful.

CMMI → Capability Maturity Model — Integrated managed, defined, quantitatively managed and fifth is optimizing. Each level has their own focus areas, process areas and also have conclusion. Initial level mainly focuses on competent people and heroics. Managed level is second level which mainly focuses on basic of project management.

The focus area of defined level is process standardized and quantitative managed level is fourth in numbering which focuses on quantitative management, and the last level, i.e., fifth level is optimizing which focuses on improvement of continuous process.

Capability Maturity Model

Level	Focus	Process areas	Result
I initial	Competent people and Heroics		Low productivity and Quality.
II Managed	Basic Project Management	Requirements management Project planning Project monitoring and Control Supplier agreement Management. Measurement and analysis Process and product quality assurance Configuration management	Greater then I stage

III Defined	Process Standardization	Requirement development Technical solution Product integration Verification Validation Organizational process focus Organizational process definition Organizational training Integrated project Management. Risk management Decision analysis and resolution	Greater then IInd stage managed
IV Quantitatively Managed	Quantitative management	Organizational process performance Quantitative project management	Greater then IIIrd stage defined
V Optimizing	Continuous Process Improvement	Organizational innovation and deployment Casual analysis and resolution	It has much highest productivity and quality.

Agile Project Management approaches are based on the principles of human interaction management which are founded on a process view of human collaboration. This contrasts sharply with traditional approach. In the agile software development or flexible product development approach, the project is seen as a series of relatively small tasks conceived and executed as the situation demands in an adaptive manner, rather than as a completely pre-planned process.

STAGES OF PROJECT DEVELOPMENT

Project development includes several stages, these are

generally as four stages but these are extended from four to five stages including control system.

Traditionally, project development includes a number of elements: four to five stages, and a control system. Regardless of the methodology used, the project development process will have the same major stages: including initiating, planning, executing, monitoring and controlling and closing.

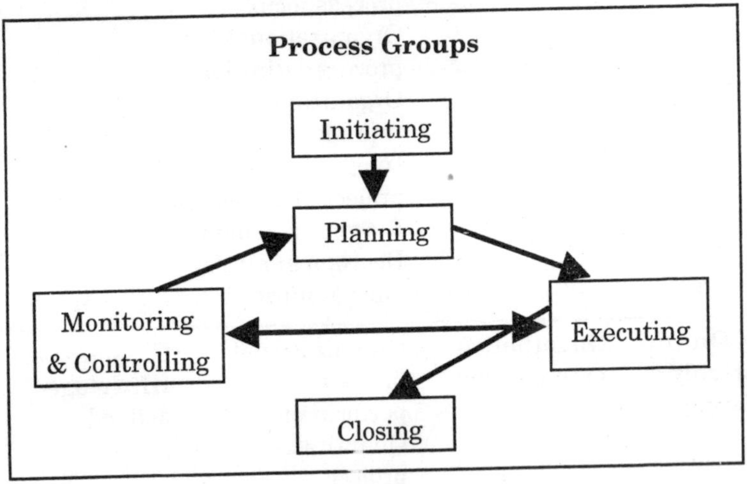

These are the process groups.

The project development stages are :

I. initiation,

II. planning or development,

III. production or execution,

IV. monitoring and controlling, and

V. closing.

I stage: Initiation

The initiation stage determines the nature and scope of the development. If this stage is not work properly, it is unlikely that the project will be successful in meeting the needs of the business. The key project controls needed here are an understanding of the business environment and making sure that all the necessary controls are incorporated into the project. Any deficiencies should be reported and a recommendation should be made to fix them.

Includes the scope of develop charter and develop preliminary scope statement. Following figures shows the initiating process groups processes.

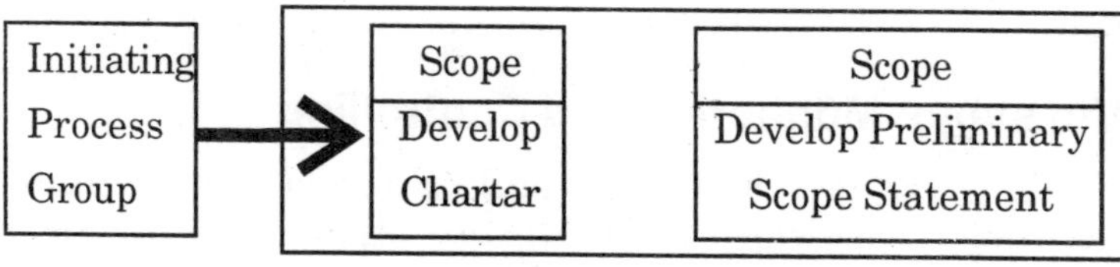

The initiation stage should include a cohesive plan that encompasses the following areas:

The initiation stage should include a cohesive plan that encompasses the following areas:

- Study analyzing the business needs in measurable goals.
- Review of the current operations.
- Conceptual design of the operation of the final product.
- Equipment and contracting requirements including an assessment of 'long-lead' items.
- Financial analysis of the costs and benefits including a budget.
- Stakeholder analysis, including users, and support personnel for the project.
- Project charter including costs, tasks, deliverables, and schedule.

IInd stage: Planning and Design

Planning and design is the second stage of project development. Figure of planning and design.

Political and social suitable of the project should be considered first.

IIIrd stage: Executing

It is the third stage of project development. It is next stage to planning and design stage. Figure of executing a project

Executing consists of the processes which are used to complete the work or tasks which are defined in the project management plan to accomplish the requirements of project. Execution process involves the coordinating people and resources, as well as integrating and performing the activities of the project in accordance with the project management plan. The deliverables are produced as outputs from the processes performed as defined in the project management plan.

IVth stage: Monitoring and Controlling

It is the fourth stage of project development next to the executing stage, which allows the execution of project. Figure of monitoring and controlling

Monitoring and Controlling consists of those processes performed to observe project execution, therefore, potential problems can be identified in a timely manner and corrective action that can be taken, when necessary, to control the execution of the project. The key benefit is that the project performance is observed and measured regularly to identify the variances from the project management plan.

Monitoring and controlling includes various features which are following below:-

- Measuring the ongoing project activities such as *where we are*;
- Monitoring the project variables like cost, effort, ... which are against the project management plan and the project performance baseline (*where we should be*);
- Identify corrective actions to properly address issues and risks (*How can we get on track again*);
- Influencing the factors that could circumvent integrated change control so only approved changes are implemented

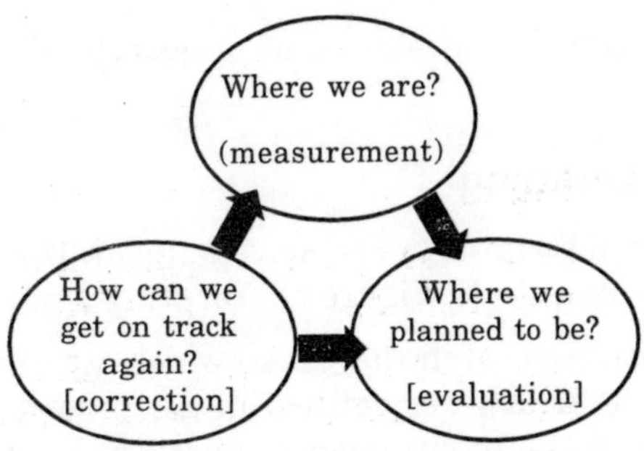

In this stage, auditors should pay attention to how effectively and quickly user problems are resolved.

In multi-phase projects, the Monitoring and Controlling process also provides the feedback between project phases, in terms to implement the corrective or preventive actions to bring the project into compliance with the project management plan.

Project Maintenance is an ongoing process, and it includes: Continuing support of end users; Correction of errors; and Updates of the software over time.

When changes are introduced to the project the viability of the project has to be assessed again. It is important not to lose sight of the initial goals and targets of the projects. When the changes accumulate, the forecasted end result may not justify the proposed investment.

IVth stage is monitoring and controlling which refers to the stage of monitoring as well as controlling the project.

Vth stage is closing usually refers to the completion of project, i.e., trermination.

Typical development phases of a project

- Project initiation stage;
- Project planning or design stage;
- Project execution or production stage;
- Project monitoring and controlling systems;
- Project completion stage.

Not all the projects will visit every stage as projects can be terminated before they reach at the completion stage. Some projects don't have planning and/or monitoring stages. Some projects will go through steps 2, 3 and 4 multiple times.

Many industries utilize the variations on these stages. For example, in bricks and mortar architectural design, projects typically progress through stages like Pre-Planning, Conceptual Design, Schematic Design, Design Development, Construction Drawings (or Contract Documents), and Construction Administration. In software development, this approach is frequently known as the waterfall model, i.e., one series of tasks after another in linear sequence. In software development many organizations have adapted the Rational Unified Process (RUP) to fit this methodology, although RUP does not need or explicitly recommend this practice. Waterfall development can work for small tightly defined projects, but it is not suited for larger projects that are undefined or unknowable scope. The Cone of Uncertainty explains some of this as the planning that are made on the initial phase of the project which suffers from a high degree of uncertainty. This becomes especially true as software development is often the realization of a new or novel product, this way has been broadly that is accepted as ineffective for software projects where requirements are largely unknowable up front and susceptible to change. While the names may vary from industry to industry, the actual stages typically follow the common steps to the problem solving — "defining the problem, weighing options, choosing a path, implementation and evaluation."

CRITICAL CHAIN PROJECT MANAGEMENT

Critical chain project management is usually abbreviated as CCPM, it is also a type of management which have some specific goals, objectives, achievements and features of their own.

Critical Chain Project Management (CCPM) is a method of planning and managing the projects that puts more emphasis on the resources which are required to execute the project tasks. It is an application of the Theory of Constraints (TOC) to projects. The aim is to increase the rate of through or completion rates of projects in an organization. Applying the first three of the five focusing steps of TOC is the system constraint for all projects which is known as resources. To exploit the constraint, tasks on the critical chain are given priority over all other activities. Finally, projects are planned and managed to ensure that the critical chain tasks are ready to start as soon as the needed resources are available, subordinating all other resources to the critical chain.

Over the course of any construction project, the work scope changes. Change is a normal and expected part of the construction process. Changes can be the result of necessary design modifications, differing site conditions, material availability, contractor-requested changes, value engineering and impacts from third parties, to name a few. Beyond executing the change in the field, the change normally needs to be documented to show what was actually constructed. This is referred to as Change Management. Hence, the owner usually requires a final record to show all changes or, more specifically, any change that modifies the tangible portions of the finished work. The record is made on the contract documents – usually, but not necessarily limited to, the design drawings. The end product of this effort is what the industry terms as-built drawings, or more simply, "asbuilts." The requirement for providing them is a norm in construction contracts.

Vth stage: Closing

It is the fifth stage of project development which is the next stage to monitoring and controlling. This stage is the steps to terminate the project.

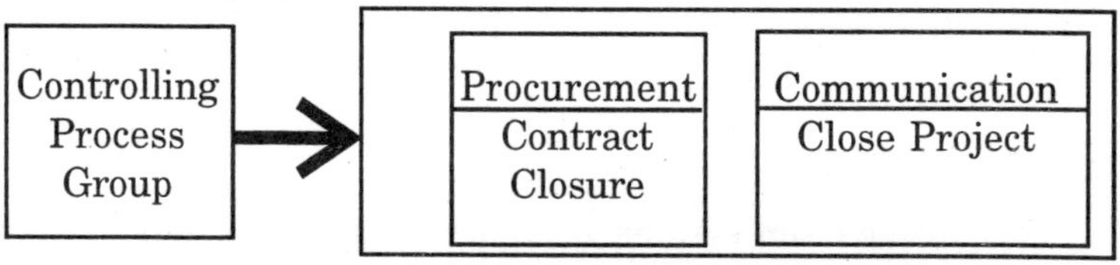

The process of closing includes the formal acceptance of the project and the ending thereof. Administrative activities include the archiving of the files and documenting the lessons which are learned. Closing phase consist of two parts, i.e., close project and contract closure. Contract closure is the part of procurement and close project is the part of communication.

- Close project is to finalize all activities across all of the process groups to formally close the project or a project phase
- Contract closure is necessary for completing and settling each contract, including the resolution of any open items, and closing each contract applicable to the project or a project phase.

PROJECT CONTROL SYSTEMS

Control is major part of the completing a project, without controlling the process must be destroyed.

Project control is that element of a project that keeps it on-track, on-time and within budget. Project control starts early in the project with planning and ends late in the project with post-implementation review, having a thorough involvement of each step in the process. Each project should be assessed for the appropriate level of control needed too much control is too time consuming, too little control is very risky. If project control is not implemented correctly, the cost to the business should be clarified in terms of errors, fixes, and additional audit fees.

Control systems are needed for cost, risk, quality, communication, time, change, procurement, and human resources. In addition, auditors should consider how important the projects are to the financial statements, how reliant the stakeholders are on controls, and how many controls exist. Auditors should review the development process and procedures for how they are implemented. The process of development and the quality of the final product may also be assessed if needed or requested. A business may want the auditing firm to be involved throughout the process to catch problems earlier on so that they can be fixed more easily. An auditor can serve as a controls consultant as part of the development team or as an independent auditor as part of an audit.

Formal System Development

Businesses sometimes use formal systems development processes. These help to assure that systems are developed successfully. A formal process is more effective in creating strong controls, and auditors should review this process to confirm that it is well designed and is followed in practice. A good formal systems development plan outlines the following features:-

- Procedures describing the process
- Standards for new systems
- Project management policies for timing and budgeting
- A strategy to align development with the organization's broader objectives

CRITICAL CHAIN ANALYSIS

Critical chain is used as an alternative to critical path analysis.

Critical Chain Project Management (CCPM) is a way of planning and managing the projects that puts the main emphasis on the resources which are required to execute the project tasks. It was developed by Eliyahu M. Goldratt. This is in contrast to the more traditional Critical Path and PERT methods, which emphasize the task order and rigid scheduling. A Critical Chain project network will tend to keep the resources levelly loaded, but will need them to be flexible in their start times and to quickly switch between tasks and task chains to keep the whole project on schedule.

Historical Development

Developed by Eliyahu M. Goldratt, Critical Chain Project Management is based on the methods and algorithms are derived from his Theory of Constraints. The idea of CCPM was introduced in 1997 in his book, *Critical Chain*. Application of CCPM has been credited with achieving projects 10% to 50% faster and/or cheaper than the traditional methods (i.e. CPM, PERT, Gantt, etc.) developed from 1910 to 1950's.

From numerous studies by Standish Group and others references as of 1998 for traditional project management methods, only 44% of projects are typically finish on time, projects usually complete at 222% of the duration originally planned, 189% of the original budgeted cost, 70% of projects fall short of their planned scope (technical content delivered), and 30% are cancelled before completion.

These traditional statistics are mostly avoided through CCPM. Typically, CCPM case studies report 95% on-time and on-budget completion when CCPM is applied correctly. Mabin and Balderstone, in their meta-analysis of seventy-eight published case studies, found that implementing Critical Chain resulted in mean reduction in lead-times of 69%, mean reduction of cycle-times of 66%, mean improvement in due date performance of 60%, mean reduction in inventory levels of 50% and mean increases in revenue / throughput of 68%.

In project management, the critical chain is the sequence of both precedence- and resource-dependent terminal elements that prevents a project from being completed in a shorter time, given finite resources. If resources are always available in unlimited quantities, then critical chain of a project's is identical to its critical path.

As we studied above in this topic tat critical chain is used as an alternative to critical path analysis. The main features that distinguish the crtical chain from critical path are described below:-

1. *The use of (often implicit) resource dependencies*. Implicit means that they are not included in the project network but have to be identified by looking at the resource requirements.
2. *Lack of search for an optimum solution*. This means that a "good enough" solution is enough because:

1. As far as is known, there is no analytical method of finding an absolute optimum (*i.e.* having the overall shortest critical chain).

2. The inherent uncertainty in estimates is much greater than the difference between the optimum and near-optimum ("good enough" solutions).
3. *The identification and insertion of buffers*:
   - project buffer
   - feeding buffers
   - resource buffers.
4. Monitoring project progress and health by monitoring the consumption rate of the buffers rather than individual task performance to schedule.

CCPM aggregates the large amounts of safety time added to many subprojects on project buffers to project due-date performance and to avoid wasting this safety time through bad multitasking.

Critical chain project management uses buffer management instead of earned the value management to assess the performance of a project. Some project managers feels that the earned value management technique is misleading, because it does not distinguish the progress on the project constraint (*i.e.* on the critical chain) from progress on non-constraints (*i.e.* on other paths). Event chain methodology can be used to determine a size of project, feeding, and resource buffers.

Even chain methodology have some features naming planning execution and monitoring: methodology can be used to find the size of project feeding and resource buffers.

Planning → planning is first step of CCPM of methodology. A project plan is created in much the same manner as with critical path. The plan is worked backward from a completion date with each task starting as late as possible. Two durations are entered for each task: a "best guess," or 50% probability duration, and a "safe" duration, which should have higher probability of completion (perhaps 90% or 95%, depending on the amount of risk that the organization can accept).

Resources are then assigned to each task, and the plan is resource leveled that are using the 50% estimates. The longest sequence of resource-leveled tasks that lead from beginning to end of the project is then identified as the critical chain. The justification for using the 50% estimates is that half of the tasks will finish early and half will finish late, so that the variance over the course of the project should be zero.

Recognizing that tasks are more likely to take more rather than less time due to Parkinson's law, Student syndrome, or other reasons, "buffers" are used to establish dates for deliverables and for monitoring project schedule and financial performance. The "extra" duration of each task on the critical chain—the difference between the "safe" durations and the 50% durations—is gathered together in a buffer at the end of the project. In the same way, buffers are gathered at the end of each sequence of tasks that feed into the critical chain.

Execution

Execution is the second stage of methodology of event chain. The process of execution is applied after the plan is to be made.

When the plan is complete and the project ready to kick off, the project network is fixed and the buffers size is "locked" (i.e. their planned duration may not be altered during the project), because they are used to monitor project schedule and financial performance.

Because task duration have been planned at the 50% probability duration, there is a pressure on the resources to complete critical chain tasks as quickly as possible.

With no slack in the duration of individual tasks, the resources on the critical chain are exploited by ensuring that they work on the critical chain task and nothing else; bad multitasking is eliminated. An analogy is drawn in the literature with a relay race. The critical chain is the race, and the resources on the critical chain are the runners. When they are running their "leg" of the project, they should be focused on completing the assigned task as quickly as possible, with no distractions or multitasking. In some case studies, actual batons are reportedly hung by the desks of people when they are working on critical chain tasks so that others know not to interrupt. The goal, here, is to overcome the tendency to delay work or to do extra work when there seems to be time.

Monitoring

Monitoring is the third stage of event chain methodology. This process continues whenever it checks the execution of process is to be done perfectly or not.

In some ways, monitoring is the greatest advantage of the Critical Chain method. Because individual tasks will vary in duration from the 50% estimate, there is no point in trying to force every task to complete "on time;" estimates can never be perfect. Instead, we monitor the buffers that were created during the planning stage. A fever chart or similar graph can be easily created and posted to show the consumption of buffer as a function of project completion. If the rate of buffer consumption is low, the project is on target. If the rate of consumption is such that there is likely to be little or no buffer at the end of the project, then corrective actions or recovery plans must be developed to recover the loss. When the buffer consumption rate exceeds some critical value (roughly: the rate where all of the buffer may be expected to be consumed *before* the end of the project, resulting in late completion), then those alternative plans need to be implemented.

RISK ASSESSMENT

This topic is earlier discussed in chapter 1 introduction. It is the step of risk management process.

Risk assessment is a step in a risk management process. Risk assessment is the determination of quantitative or qualitative value of risk which are related to a concrete situation and a recognized threat are also called hazard. *Quantitative risk assessment* needs the calculations of two components of risk: R, the magnitude of the potential loss L, and the probability p, that the loss will occur.

There are some evaluations are to be done with the help of formula which are described below:-

Risk assessment consists in an objective evaluation of risk in which assumptions and uncertainties are clearly considered and presented. Part of the difficulty of risk management is that measurement of both of the quantities in which risk assessment is concerned - potential loss and probability of occurrence - can be very difficult to measure. The chance of error in the measurement of these two concepts is large. A risk with a large potential loss and a low probability of occurring is often treated differently from one with a low potential loss and a high likelihood of occurring. In theory, both are of nearly equal priority in dealing with first, but in practice it can be very difficult to manage when faced with the scarcity of resources, especially time, in which to conduct the risk management process. Expressed mathematically,

$$R_i = L_i p(L_i)$$

$$R_{total} = \sum_i L_i p(L_i)$$

Above formula is the mathematical formulation of risk assessment

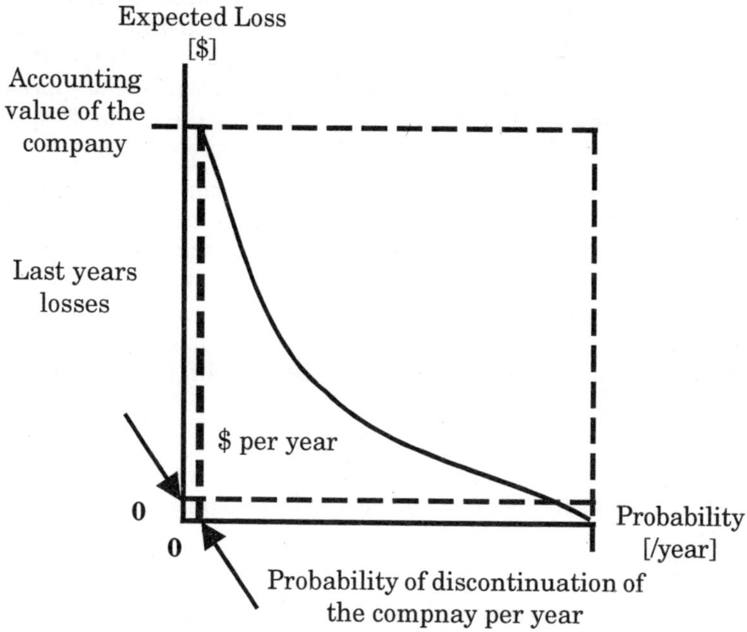

Figure : financial view point of risk assessment

Methods of Determining Risk

There are three steps of determining that how risk developed. These step including hazard identification, Does response analysis and exposure quantification.

1. Hazard Identification, aims to determine the qualitative nature of the potential adverse consequences of the contaminant (chemical, radiation, noise, etc.) and the strength of the evidence it can have that effect. This is done, for chemical hazards, by drawing from the results of the sciences of toxicology and epidemiology. For other kinds of hazard, engineering or other disciplines are involved.

2. Dose-Response Analysis, is determining the relationship between dose and the probability or the incidence of effect (dose-response assessment). The complexity of this step in many contexts derives mainly from the need to extrapolate results from experimental animals (e.g. mouse, rat) to humans, and/or from high to lower doses. In addition, the differences between individuals due to genetics or other factors mean that the hazard may be higher for particular groups, called susceptible populations. An alternative to dose-response estimation is to determine an effect unlikely to yield observable effects, that is, a no effect concentration. In developing such a dose, to account for the largely unknown effects of animal to human extrapolations, increased variability in humans, or missing data, a prudent approach is often adopted by including safety factors in the estimate of the "safe" dose, typically a factor of 10 for each unknown step.

3. Exposure Quantification, aims to determine the amount of a contaminant (dose) that individuals and populations will receive. This is done by examining the results of the discipline of exposure assessment. As different location, lifestyles and other factors likely influence the amount of contaminant that is received, a range or distribution of possible values is generated in this step. Particular care is taken to determine the exposure of the susceptible population(s).

The conclusions of these three steps are then combine to produce an estimate of risk. Because of the different sees capabilities and exposures this risk will vary within a population.

Case Study

Note : knowing more about "Project Management" reader can study documentation process of Microsoft company by visiting their site : www.members.microsoft.com

http://www.icmrindia.org/casestudies/Case_Studies.asp?cat=Project%20Management

http://infogoal.com/pmc/pmcprj.htm

http://www.mpmm.com/project-management-case-studies.php

http://www.pmi.org/BusinessSolutions/Pages/Case-Study-Library.aspx

http://www.flipkart.com/project-management-case-studies-harold/0471751677-1xw3fsvtbb

http://www.infibeam.com/Books/info/Harold-Kerzner/Project-Management-Case-Studies/0471751677.html

http://www.projectsmart.co.uk/case-studies.html

7

Process Performance and Quality Management

This chapter includes various key concepts which are shown below:-

- Introduction
- Total Quality Management
- Customer Satisfaction
- Process Control
- Control Chart
- Process Capability
- Quality Engineering
- Six Sigma
- Quality Improvement
- Quality Standards
- Quality Terms
- Quality Assurance
- Quality Audit
- Quality Control
- Quality Management System
- Quality Management System Processes
- Non-conformity

INTRODUCTION

This introduction includes the introduction about process performance as well as quality management.

Process performance only applies to a particular batch of material. It is only used when process control can not be evaluated. Whereas quality management is mainly focus not only on product quality but also the means to achieve it.

TOTAL QUALITY MANAGEMENT

Total quality management is abbreviated as TQM which acts a business management strategy.

The influence of quality thinking has spread to non-traditional applications outside of walls of manufacturing, extending into service sectors and into areas such as sales, marketing and customer service.

Total Quality Management (TQM) is a business management strategy which are aimed at embedding the awareness of quality in all organizational processes. TQM has been broadly used in manufacturing, education, hospitals, call centers, government, and service industries, as well as NASA space and science programs.

Total Quality Management is the organization-wide management of quality. Management consists of planning, organizing, directing, control, and assurance. These are also the features of management . Total quality is called *total* because it consists of two qualities: *quality* of return to satisfy the needs of the shareholders, or *quality* of products.

According to the international organization for standardization (ISD):

"TQM is a management approach for an organization, centered on quality that are based on the participation of all its members and aiming at long-term success through customer satisfaction, and benefits to all members of the organization and to society." ISO 8402:1994

One major objective of TQM is to reduce variation from every process so that greater consistency of effort is obtained.

TQM requires that the company maintain this quality standard in all the aspects of its business. This requires ensuring that things which are done right the first time and that defects and waste are eliminated from operations. Total quality management has not been independent of its environment. TQM is usually associated with management accounting system includes timely, flexible, externally focused information, close interactions between advanced technology and strategy.

CUSTOMER SATISFACTION

In a business term customer satisfaction is a measure of how products and services supplied by a company meet or fulfill the customer expectation. It is seen as a key performance indicator within business and is part of the four perspectives of a Balanced Scorecard.

Customer satisfaction is must for a particular company it supports the status of company. Process Performance attempts to answer the question: does this sample from the process meet customer requirements? It differs from Process Capability in that Process Performance that only applies to a specific batch of material. Samples from the batch may need to be quite large to be representative of the variation in the batch.

Process Performance is only used when process control cannot be evaluated. An example of process performance is for a short pre-production run.

Process Performance commonly used sample sigma in its calculation; Process capability uses the process sigma value which are determined from either the Moving Range , Range , or Sigma control charts.

The calculated Process Performance and Process Capability indices will likely be quite similar when the process is in statistical control.

Process performance includes process capabilities and six sigma process, both the process are described in this chapter.

Quality management can be considered to have three further main components: quality control, quality assurance and quality improvement. These are described in this chapter. Quality management is mainly focused on product quality, and also the means to achieve it. Therefore, quality management uses quality assurance and control of processes as well as products to achieve more consistent quality.

Quality management is a recent phenomenon. Advanced civilizations that supported the arts and crafts which are allowed clients to choose goods providing higher quality standards than normal goods. In societies, where art and craft (and craftsmanship) were valued, one of the responsibilities of a master craftsman (and similarly for artists) was to lead their studio, train and supervise the work of their craftsmen and apprentices. The master craftsman set standards, reviewed the work of others and ordered the rework and revision as necessary. One of the limitations of the craft approach was that relatively few goods could be produced, on the other hand an advantage was that each item produced could be individually shaped to suit the client. This craft based approach to quality and the practices used were the major inputs when quality management was created as a management science.

Customer recognized the quality of any product that it is an important attribute in product or services.

Suppliers recognize that the quality can be an important differentiator between their own offerings and those of competitors including quality differentiation is also called the quality gap. In the past two decades this quality gap has been broadly reduced between competitive products and services. This is partly due to the contracting which is called outsourcing of manufacture to countries like India and China, as well internationalization of trade and competition.

There are a huge number of books are available on quality. In recent times, some themes have become more significant including quality culture, the importance of knowledge management, and the role of leadership in promoting and achieving high quality. Disciplines like systems thinking are bringing more holistic approaches to quality so that people, process and products are considered together rather than independent factors in quality management.

influence of quality thinking has spread to non-traditional application outside of manufacturing which are extending into service sectors and into areas including sales, marketing and customer service.

In a competitive marketplace where businesses compete for customers, customer satisfaction is seen as a key differentiator and increasingly has become a key element of business strategy. There is empirical concept that provides the benefits of customer satisfaction for firms.

How to Measure Customer Satisfaction

Customer satisfaction is an ambiguous and abstract concept and the actual manifestation of the state of satisfaction will change from person to person and product/service to product/service. The state of satisfaction mainly depends on a number of both psychological and physical variables which correlate with satisfaction behaviors such as return and recommend rate. The level of satisfaction can also change which are depending on other options the customer may have and other products against which the customer can compare products of the organization.

Organizations are mostly interested in retaining existing customers while targeting non-customers; measuring customer satisfaction provides an indication of how successful the organization is at giving the products and services to the marketplace.

Because satisfaction is usually a psychological state the care should be taken in the effort of quantitative measurement, although a large quantity of research in this area has recently been developed. Work done by Berry (Bart Allen) and Brodeur between 1990 and 1998 defined ten 'Quality Values' which influence the satisfaction behavior, further expanded by Berry in 2002 and known as the ten domains of satisfaction. These ten domains of satisfaction include: Quality, Value, Timeliness, Efficiency, Ease of Access, Environment, Inter-departmental Teamwork, Front line Service Behaviors, Commitment to the Customer and Innovation. These factors are emphasized for continuous improvement and organizational change measurement and are most frequently utilized to develop the architecture for satisfaction measurement as an integrated model. Work done by Parasuraman, Zeithaml and Berry (Leonard L) between 1985 and 1988 provides the basis for the measurement of customer satisfaction with a service by using the gap between the customer's expectation of performance and their perceived experience of performance. The common measures of customer satisfaction include the survey with a set of statements using a likert technique or scale. The customers are as lead to determine expectation of performance of the organization being measured.

PROCESS CONTROL

process control is the term which are used to control the processing, generally these are the disciplines of statistics and engineering.

Process control is a statistics and engineering discipline that deals with architectures, mechanisms, and algorithms for controlling the output of a specific process.

For example, heating up the temperature in a room is a process that has the specific, desired outcome to reach and maintain a defined temperature (e.g. 20°C), kept constant over time. Here, the temperature is the **controlled variable**. At the same time, it is the **input variable** since it is measured by a thermometer and used to decide whether to heat or not to heat. The desired temperature (20°C) is the **setpoint**. The state of the heater (e.g. the setting of the valve allowing hot water to flow through it) is called the **manipulated variable** since it is subject to control actions.

In practice, process control systems can be characterized by three form which are following forms:

- Batch – Some applications require that specific quantities of raw materials be combined in specific manner for specific durations to produce an intermediate or end result. One example is the production of adhesives and glues, which normally require the mixing of raw materials in a heated vessel for a period of time to form a quantity of end product. Other important examples are the production of food, beverages and medicine. Batch processes are generally used to produce a relatively low to intermediate quantity of product per year (a few pounds to millions of pounds).
- Continuous – Often, a physical system is represented though variables that are smooth and uninterrupted in time. The control of the water temperature in a heating jacket, for example, is an example of continuous process control. Some important continuous processes are the production of fuels, chemicals and plastics. Continuous processes, in manufacturing, are used to produce very large quantities of product per year(millions to billions of pounds).
- Discrete form was found in many manufacturing, motion and packaging applications. Robotic assembly, such as that found in automotive production, can be characterized as discrete process control. Most discrete manufacturing involves the production of discrete pieces of product, such as metal stamping.

Statistical Process Control

It is an effective method of monitoring a process through the use of control charts. Much of its power lies in the ability to monitor both process center and its variation about that center. By collecting data from samples at various points within the process, variations in the process that may affect the quality of the end product or service can be detected and corrected, thus reducing waste as well as the likelihood that problems will be passed on to the customer. It has an emphasis on early detection and prevention of problems.

CONTROL CHART

The **control chart** are also known as the *Shewhart chart* or *process-behaviour chart*, in statistical process control is a tool that are used to determine whether a manufacturing or business process is in a state of statistical control or not.

If the chart indicates that the process is currently under the control then it can be used with confidence to predict the future performance of the process. If the chart indicates that the process being monitored is not in control, the pattern it reveals can help to determine the source of variation which to be eliminated to bring the process back into control. A control chart is a particular kind of run chart that allows the significant change to be differentiated from the natural variability of the process.

The control charts like flow chart, are to analysis are already discussed in chapter 4 namely decision making process and decision theory.

This is key to the effective process control and improvement. On a practical level the control chart can be seen as part of an objective disciplined approach that facilitates the decision as to whether process performance that warrants the attention or not. Control chart consists of following features:-

- Points representing measurements of a quality characteristic in samples taken from the process at different times [the data]
- A center line, drawn at the process characteristic mean, which is calculated from the data
- Upper and lower control limits (sometimes called "natural process limits") that indicate the threshold at which the process output is considered statistically 'unlikely'.

Other features including:-

- Upper and lower warning limits, drawn as separate lines, typically two standard deviations above and below the center line
- Division into zones, with the addition of rules that are governing the frequencies of observations in each zone
- Annotation with events of interest, as evaluated by the Quality Engineer in charge of quality of the process.

Usage of Chart

If the process is in control, all points will plot within the control limits. Any observations outside the limits, or systematic patterns within, suggest the introduction of a new (and likely unanticipated) source of variation are known as a special-cause variation. Since increased variation means increased quality costs, a control chart "signaling" the presence of a special-cause requires immediate investigation.

The goal of control charts is to allow the simple detection of events that are indicative of actual process change. This simple decision can be difficult where the process characteristic is continuously varying; the control chart provides statistically objective criteria of change. When change is detected and considered as good its cause should be identified and possibly become the new method of working, where the change is bad then its cause should be identified and eliminated.

Performance of Control Charts

When a point falls outside of the limits that are established for a given control chart, those are responsible for the underlying the process are expected to evaluate whether a special cause has occurred. If one has, then that cause should be eliminated if possible. It is known that even when a process is *in control* that is, no special causes are present in the system, there is approximately a 0.27% probability of a point exceeding *3-sigma* control limits. Since the control limits are evaluated each time a point is added to the chart, it readily follows that *every* control chart will eventually signal the possible presence of a special cause, even though one may not have actually occurred. For a Shewhart control chart using *3-sigma* limits, this *false alarm* occurs on average once every 1/0.0027 or 370.4

observations. So that, the *in-control the average run length* (or in-control ARL) of a Shewhart chart is 370.4.

Meanwhile, if a special cause does occur, it may not be of appropriate or suitable magnitude for the chart to produce an immediate *alarm condition*. If a special cause occurs, one can describe that cause by measuring the change in the mean and/or variance of the process in question. When those changes are quantified, it is possible to determine the out-of-control ARL for the chart.

PROCESS CAPABILITY

Process is mixture of tools, materials methods and people engaged in producing a measurable output.

The **Process Capability** is a measurable property of a process to the specification, that are expressed as a process capability index (e.g., C_{pk} or C_{pm}) or as a process performance index (e.g., P_{pk} or P_{pm}). The output of this measurement is generally illustrated by a histogram and calculations that are predict how many parts will be produced out of specification.

Process capability is also refers to the capability of a process to meet its purpose as managed by management and process definition structures of an organization. Process capability are of two types: 1) Measure the variability of a process, and 2) Compare that variability with a proposed specification.

Measure the Process

The input of a process generally has at least one or more measurable characteristics that are used to specify the outputs. These can be analyzed statistically, where the output data shows a normal distribution the process can be described by the process mean (average) and the standard deviation.

A process needs to be established with appropriate process controls in place. A control chart analysis is used to evaluate whether the process is "in statistical control". If the process is not in statistical control then capability has no meaning. Therefore, the process capability involves only common cause variation and not special cause variation.

Capability Study

The ability of a process to meet specifications can be expressed as a single number using a process capability index or it can be assessed using control charts. Either case requires running the process to obtain enough measurable output so that engineering is confident that the process is stable and so that the process mean and variability can be reliably estimated. Statistical process control defines techniques to properly differentiate between stable processes, processes that are drifting (experiencing a long-term change in the mean of the output), and processes that are growing more variable. Process capability indices are only meaningful for processes that are stable (in a state of statistical control).

The input of a process is expected to meet all the customer requirements that extent to which the process can meet these expectations.

For Information Technology, ISO 15504 specifies a process capability measurement framework for assessing the process capability. This measurement framework consists of 5.5+0.5 levels of process capability from none (Capability Level 0) to optimizing all the processes (CL 5). The measurement framework has been generalized, therefore, it can be applied to non IT processes. There are currently two process reference models covering software and systems. The Capability Maturity Model in its latest version (CMMI continuous) also follows this approach.

QUALITY ENGINEERING

Quality Engineering is a quarterly academic journal which are focusing on quality control and quality assurance management via use of physical technology, standards information, and statistical tools. The journal is co-published between American Society for Quality and Marcel Dekker, Inc.

SIX SIGMA

Six Sigma is a business management strategy which are initially implemented by Motorola, that today enjoys widespread application in many sectors of industry.

Six Sigma seeks to improve the quality of process outputs by identifying and removing the causes of defects or errors and variability in manufacturing and business processes. It uses a set of quality management methods, including statistical methods, and creates a special infrastructure of people within the organization

("Black Belts","Green Belts", etc.) who are experts in these methods. Each Six Sigma project carried out within an organization which follows a defined sequence of steps and has quantified are financial targets including cost reduction or profit increase.

Six Sigma was originally developed as a set of practices are designed to improve manufacturing processes and eliminate defects. In Six Sigma process a defect is defined as anything that could lead to customer dissatisfaction. Six sigma is derived from a field of statistics which are known as process capability studies. It refers to the ability of manufacturing processes to produce a very high proportion of output with in specification. The goal of six sigma is to improve all processes to that level of quality or better.

Like its predecessors, Six Sigma asserts that –

- Achieving sustained quality improvement needs the commitment from the whole organization, particularly from top-level management.
- Continuous efforts to achieve stable and predictable process results (i.e. reduce process variation) are of vital importance to business success.
- Manufacturing and business processes have the characteristics that can be measured, analyzed, improved and controlled.

Features that set Six Sigma apart from previous quality improvement initiatives include –

- A special infrastructure of "Champions," "Master Black Belts," "Black Belts," etc. to lead and implement the Six Sigma approach.
- A clear focus on achieving the measurable and quantifiable financial returns from any Six Sigma project.
- A clear commitment to making decisions on the basis of verifiable data, rather than assumptions and guesswork.
- An increased emphasis on strong and passionate management leadership and support.

Six Sigma projects follow the two project methodologies where are inspired by Deming's Plan-Do-Check-Act Cycle. These methodologies comprise of five phases each and are known by the acronyms DMAIC and DMADV.

- DMAIC is used for projects aimed at improving an existing business process.

- DMADV is used for projects aimed at creating new product or process designs.

DMAIC

DMAIC stands for define measure, analyze, improve, control. There are five phases in DMAIC project.

The five phases in the DMAIC project methodology are:

- *Define* high-level project goals and the current process.
- *Measure* the key aspects of the current process and collect relevant data.
- *Analyze* the data to verify cause-and-effect of relationships. Determine what the relationships are, and attempt to ensure that all factors have been considered.
- *Improve* or optimize the process which are based upon data analysis using various methods like Design of experiments.
- *Control* to ensure that any deviations from target are corrected before they conclude in defects. Set up pilot runs to establish the process capability, move on to production, set up control mechanisms and continuously monitor the process.

DMADV

DMADV stands for define, measure, analyze, design and verity. These are five phases in DMADV project.

The five phases in the DMADV project methodology are:

- *Define* design goals that are consistent with customer demands and the enterprise strategy.
- *Measure* and identify CTQs (characteristics that are Critical *To Qu*ality), product capabilities, production process capability, and risks.
- *Analyze* to develop and design alternatives, create a high-level design and evaluate the design capability to select the best and suitable design.
- *Design* details, optimize the design, and plan for design verification. This phase may require the simulations.
- *Verify* the design, set up pilot runs, implement the production process and hand it over to the process owners.

DMADV is also known as DFSS, an abbreviation of "Design For Six Sigma".

Implementation Roles

One of the key innovations of Six Sigma is the professionalizing of quality management functions. Prior to Six Sigma, quality management in practice was largely relegated to the production floor and to statisticians in a separate quality department. Six Sigma borrows the martial arts ranking terminology to define a hierarchy (and career path) that cuts across all business functions and a promotion path which are straight into the executive suite.

The term "six sigma process" comes from the notion that if one has six standard deviations between the process mean and the nearest specification limit, as shown in the graphic, there will be practically no items that fail to meet that specifications. Which is based on the calculation method that are employed in process capability studies.

Six Sigma has made a huge impact on industry and is widely employed as a business strategy for achieving and sustaining the operational and service excellence. However, there have also been different criticisms of Six Sigma.

QUALITY IMPROVEMENT

Quality improvement includes various improvements like product improvement, process improvements and people based improvement:-

There are many methods for quality improvement. These cover product improvement, process improvement and people based improvement. In the following list are methods of quality management and techniques that incorporate and drive quality improvement—

1. ISO 9004:2000 — Guidelines for performance improvement.
2. ISO 15504-4: 2005 — Information technology — Process assessment — Part 4: Guidance on use for process improvement and process capability determination.
3. QFD — It should for Quality Function Deployment which are also known as the House of Quality approach.
4. Kaizen —Japanese for change for the better; the common English usage is continual improvement.

5. Zero Defect Program — It was created by NEC Corporation of Japan which are based upon Statistical Process Control and one of the inputs for the inventors of Six Sigma.
6. Six Sigma — It is denoted by 6ó, Six Sigma combines the established methods such as Statistical Process Control, Design of Experiments and FMEA in an overall framework.
7. PDCA — Plan, Do, Check, Act cycle for quality control purposes. (Six Sigma's DMAIC method previously described (Design, Measure, Analyze, Improve, Control) may be viewed as a particular implementation of this.)
8. Quality circle — It refers to a group (people oriented) approach to improvement.
9. Taguchi methods — This methods refers to the statistical oriented methods including Quality robustness, Quality loss function and Target specifications.
10. The Toyota Production System — reworked in the west into Lean Manufacturing.
11. Kansei Engineering — It is an approach that focuses on capturing the customer emotional feedback about products to drive improvement.
12. TQM — Total Quality Management is a management strategy which are aimed at embedding awareness of quality in all organizational processes. First promoted in Japan with the Deming prize which was adopted and adapted in USA as the Malcolm Baldrige National Quality Award and in Europe as the European Foundation for Quality Management award (each with their own variations).
13. TRIZ — meaning "Theory of inventive problem solving"
14. BPR — Stands for Business process reengineering which is a management approach aiming at 'clean slate' improvements (That is, ignoring existing practices).

There has been well publicized failures of BPR, as well as Six Sigma. Therefore, enterprises need to consider carefully which quality improvement methods to adopt, and certainly should not adopt all those listed here.

Some of the common differentiators between success and failure of a project include commitment, knowledge and expertise to guide improvement, scope of change/improvement desired (Big Bang type changes tends to fail more frequently compared to smaller changes) and adaption to enterprise cultures. For example, quality circles do not work well in every enterprise (and are even discouraged by some managers), and relatively few TQM-participating enterprises have won the national quality awards.

Proponents of these above approach have sought to improve them as well as apply them to enterprise types which are not originally targeted. Six Sigma was designed for manufacturing but has spread to service enterprises. Each of these approaches and methods has met with success but also with failures.

Improvements that change the culture take longer as they have to overcome the greater resistance to change. It is easier and frequently more effective to work within the existing cultural boundaries and make small improvements (that is **Kaizen**) than to make major transformational changes. Use of Kaizen in Japan was a major reason for the creation of Japanese industrial and economic strength.

It is essential not to underestimate the people factors, such as culture, in selecting a quality improvement approach. Any improvement or change that takes time to implement, gain acceptance and stabilize as accepted practice. Improvement must allow the pauses between implementing new changes, therefore, the change is stabilized and assessed as a real improvement, before the next improvement is made, hence continual improvement, not continuous improvement.

QUALITY STANDARDS

Each business, company and also an organization have their own quality standards. These standards are created by the ISO, i.e., international organization for standardization.

The International Organization for Standardization (ISO) created the Quality Management System (QMS) standards in 1987. They were the ISO 9000:1987 series of standards comprising ISO 9001:1987, ISO 9002:1987 and ISO 9003:1987; which were applicable in various types of industries, based on the type of activity or process: designing, production or service delivery. Each standard has the level of their own which contains the versions.

The standards are reviewed every few years by the International Organization for Standardization. The version in 1994 was called the ISO 9000:1994 series; comprising of the ISO 9001:1994, 9002:1994 and 9003:1994 versions.

The last major revision was in the year 2000 and the series was called ISO 9000:2000 series. The ISO 9002 and 9003 standards were integrated into one single certifiable standard: ISO 9001:2000. After December 2003, organizations holding ISO 9002 or 9003 standards had to complete a transition to the new standard.

ISO released a minor revision, ISO 9001:2008 on 14 October 2008. It contains no new requirements. Many of the changes were to improve consistency in grammar, facilitating translation of the standard into other languages for use by over 950,000 certified organisations in the 175 countries (as at Dec 2007) that use the standard.

The ISO 9004:2000 document gives guidelines for performance improvement over and above the basic standard (ISO 9001:2000). This standard provides a measurement framework for improved quality management, similar to and based upon the measurement framework for process assessment. Quality Management System standards created by ISO are meant to certify the processes and the system of an organization, not the product or service itself. ISO 9000 standards do not certify the quality of the product or service.

In 2005 the International Organization for Standardization released a standard, ISO 22000, meant for the food industry. This standard covers the values and principles of ISO 9000 and the HACCP standards. It gives one single integrated standard for the food industry and is expected to become more popular in the coming years in such industry.

ISO has also released standards for other industries. For example Technical Standard TS 16949 defines requirements in addition to those in ISO 9001:2008 specifically for the automotive industry.

ISO has a number of standards that support quality management. One group describes processes (including ISO 12207 & ISO 15288) and another describes process assessment and improvement ISO 15504.

QUALITY TERMS

- Quality Improvement can be distinguished from Quality Control in that Quality Improvement is the purposeful change of a process to improve the reliability of achieving an outcome.

- Quality Control is the ongoing effort to maintain the integrity of a process to maintain the reliability of achieving an outcome.
- Quality Assurance is the planned or systematic actions necessary to provide enough confidence that a product or service will satisfy the given requirements for quality.

These are three terms of quality which are included in quality management system.

QUALITY ASSURANCE

Quality assurance is abbreviated as **QA** which refers to planned and systematic production processes that provide confidence in suitability of a product for its intended purpose. Refer to the definition by Merriam-Webster for further information. It is a set of activities intended to ensure that products (goods and/or services) satisfy customer requirements in a systematic, reliable fashion. QA cannot absolutely guarantee the production of *quality* products, unfortunately, but makes this more likely.

Two key principles characterise the QA: "fit for purpose" refers to the product that should be appropriate for the intended purpose and "right first time" refers to the mistakes should be eliminated. QA includes regulation of the quality of raw materials, assemblies, products and components; services related to production; and management, production and inspection processes.

It is inevitable to realize also that *quality* is determined by the intended users, clients or customers, not by society in general: it is not the same as 'expensive' or 'high quality'. Even goods with low prices can be considered quality items if they meet a market need.

Quality Assurance versus Quality Control

Quality control emphasize the testing of products to uncover the defects, and reporting to management who make the decision to allow or deny the release. Whereas quality assurance attempts to improve and stabilize production, and that are with associated processes, to avoid, or at least minimize all the issues that led to the defects in the first place. To prevent mistakes from arising, several QA methodologies are used. However, QA does not necessarily eliminate the need for QC: some product parameters are so critical that testing is still necessary. QC activities are treated as an integral part of the overall QA processes.

Deep analysis of QA practices and premises are used about them is the most essential inspection control of all in cases, where, despite statistical quality control methods or quality improvements are implemented with sales decrease.

The major problem which leads to a decrease in sales was that the specifications did not include the most important factor, "What the specifications have to state in order to satisfy the customer requirements?".

The major characteristics, ignored during the search to improve manufacture and overall business performance were:

- Reliability
- Maintainability
- Safety
- Strength

QUALITY AUDIT

Quality audit is the phenomenon of systematic examination of a quality system which are carried out by an internal or external quality auditor or an audit team. It is an important part of quality management system of organization and is a key element in the ISO quality system standard, ISO 9001.

Quality audits are generally performed at predefined time intervals and ensure that the institution has clearly-defined internal quality monitoring procedures which are linked to effective action.

Audits are necessary management tool which is to be used for verifying the objective evidence of processes, to assess how successfully processes have been implemented, for judging the effectiveness of achieving any defined target levels, to provide the evidence which are concerning with the reduction and elimination of problem areas. For the benefit of the organisation, quality auditing should not only report non-conformances and corrective actions, but also highlight areas of good practice. In this way, other departments may share information and amend their working practices as a conclusion, also contributing to continual improvement.

Quality audits are typically performed at predefined time intervals and ensure that the institution has clearly-defined internal quality monitoring procedures are linked to effective action. This can help to determine if the organization complies with the defined quality system processes and can involve procedural or results-based assessment criteria.

Audits can also be used for safety purposes. Auditing is one of the most powerful safety monitoring techniques and 'an effective way to avoid complacency and highlight slowly deteriorating conditions', especially when the auditing focuses not just on compliance but effectiveness.

QUALITY CONTROL

Quality control is the discipline of engineering and manufacturing which directly deals with assurance and failure testing in design and production of products or services, to meet or exceed the customer requirements.

A valuable process to perform on a whole consumer product is *failure testing* (also known as stress testing), the operation of a product until it fails, often under stresses such as increasing vibration, temperature and humidity. This exposes many unanticipated weaknesses in a product, and the data is used to drive engineering and manufacturing process improvements.

QUALITY MANAGEMENT SYSTEM

Quality management system consists of 5 elements naming Organizational Structure, Responsibilities. Procedures, Processes and Resources also.

QUALITY MANAGEMENT SYSTEM PROCESSES

A Quality Management System process is a business excellence which forms an element of the Quality Management System (QMS) of an organisation. The ISO9001:2000 standard requires organisations which are seeking compliance or certification to define the processes which form the QMS and the sequence and interaction of these processes.

NON-CONFORMITY

In quality management, a **nonconformity** is also known as a **defect** which is a deviation from a specification, a standard, or an expectation. Nonconformities are classified as either critical, major, or minor.

ISO 9126 distinguishes between a defect and a nonconformity, a defect being the non-fulfillment of intended the usage requirements, whereas a nonconformity is the non-fulfillment of specified requirements. A similar distinction is made between validation and verification.

There are three types of non-conformity such as minor non-conformity, major conformity and critical non-conformity.

Minor nonconformity - Any nonconformity which does not adversely affect the airworthiness, performance, durability, interchangeability, reliability, maintainability, effective use or operation, weight or appearance (where a factor), health or safety. Multiple minor nonconformities when considered collectively may raise the category to a major or critical nonconformity.

Major nonconformity - Any nonconformity other than critical, which may result in failure or materially reduce the usability of the product for the intended purpose (i.e. effective use or operation, weight or appearance (where a factor), health or safety) and which can not be completely eliminated by rework or reduced to a minor nonconformity by an approved repair.

Critical nonconformity - Any nonconformity which may result in hazardous or unsafe conditions for individuals that are using, maintaining or depending upon the product or prevent the performance of a essential agency mission.

Case Study

Note : knowing more about "Process Performance and Quality Management t" reader can study documentation process of Microsoft company by visiting their site : www.members.microsoft.com

http://www.wbdg.org/references/casestudies.php

http://www.tmforum.org/CaseStudiesBusiness/Proactive Performance/39443/article.html

http://www.springerlink.com/content/k0340x222253w383/

http://www.matrikon.co.za/training/webcasts/186/index.aspx

http://www.icmrindia.org/casestudies/Management.asp?area=Quality%20Management

http://www.nwlink.com/~Donclark/perform/casesty.html

http://www.tqmcasestudies.com/

http://www.asq.org/government/why-quality/case-studies.html

http://www.essays.se/about/Total+quality+management+case+studies/

8

Supply Chain Strategy

This chapter includes the key concept which are shown below:-

- Introduction
- Problems in Supply Chain Management
- Functions and Approaches in SCM
- Decision for SCM
- Customer Relationship
- Approaches in Supply Chain Modeling
- Strategic Supply Chain Management
- Operational Supply Chain Management
- Supply Chain in Business Process Integration
- Theories of Supply Chain Management
- Supply Chain Sustainability
- Consignment
- Supply Chain Performance
- Supply Chain Dynamics

INTRODUCTION

You have heard the concept of supply chain strategy. Used informally, it is frequently confused with supply chain management, where supply chain operations are controlled to reduce costs. Supply chain strategy defines that how the supply chain should operate in order to compete. Supply chain strategy is an iterative process that evaluates the cost benefit trade-offs of operational components. Business strategy involves leveraging the core competencies of the organization to achieve a defined high-level goal or objective. It also includes the analytic and decision-making process surrounding what to offer (e.g., products and services), when to offer (timing, business cycles, etc), and where to offer (e.g., markets and segments) as a competitive plan. While the business strategy constitutes the overall direction that an organization wishes to go, the supply chain strategy constitutes the actual operations of that organization and the extended supply chain to meet a specific supply chain objective.

A supply chain can be defined as a network of autonomous or semiautonomous business entities which are collectively responsible for procurement, manufacturing and distribution activities that are associated with one or more families of related products. Different entities in a supply chain operate subject to several sets of constraints and objectives. However, these entities are highly interdependent when it comes to improving the performance of the supply chain in terms of objectives such as on-time delivery, quality assurance, and cost minimization.

The term supply chain "refers to the network of autonomous or semiautonomous business entities. These entities are much responsible for manufacturing and distribution activities of the related products.

As a conclusion, performance of any entity in a supply chain depends on the performance of others, and their willingness and ability to coordinate all the activities within the supply chain. A global economy and increase in customer expectations regarding to the cost and service have influenced the manufacturers to strive to improve all the processes within their supply chains, which are frequently referred to as supply chain re-engineering this theory was introduced by (Swaminathan, on 1996). For example, Hewlett Packard's Vancouver division reduced inventory costs by approximately 18 % for HP Deskjet printers through delayed product differentiation (Billington, 1994). Similarly, National Semiconductor has managed to reduce delivery time, increase sales and reduce distribution cost through effective supply chain re-engineering (Henko_, 1994).

Supply chain re-engineering efforts have potential to impact the performance of supply chains in a great manner. Frequently they are undertaken with only a probabilistic view of the future, and it is necessary to perform a detailed risk analysis before adopting a new process. In addition, many times these re-engineering efforts are made under politically and emotionally charged circumstances. As a conclusion, decision support tools can analyze several alternatives that can be very useful in impartially quantifying gains and helping the organization to make the right decision. This concept was proposed by Feigin, An, Connors, and Crawford in 1996. In most organizations, re-engineering decisions are usually based on either qualitative analysis such as bench marking or on customized simulation analysis. This is due to the complex interactions between different entities and the multi tiered structure of supply chains make it typical to utilize the closed form of analytical solutions. Bench marking solutions provide insights into current trends but are not prescriptive. This leaves simulation as the only viable platform for detailed analysis for alternative solutions. However, there are two major problems with building customized simulation models: (1) they take a long time to develop and, (2) they are most specific and have limited reuse. The objective is to provide a flexible and re-usable modeling and simulation framework that enables the rapid development of customized decision support tools for supply chain management.

It is necessary to understand important issues (decision trade-off) and common processes in different types of supply chains to develop a generic, modular and reusable frame work.

These supply chain differs in order to the centers of decision-making in supply chain and relationship with suppliers. Decision-making process and decision theory are also described in chapter 4 of this book. The decision-making was decentralized, and different organization including operating under various different individual environment were part of some supply chain.

Despite these differences, we found that there are a number of processes which are common to these supply chains. We have identified these processes and have developed a library of software components for modeling them. The library consists of two main categories- structural elements and control elements. Structural elements (like retailer, distribution center, manufacturer, supplier and transportation vehicles) are used to model the production and transportation of products are those elements which control elements and those elements which are used to specify different control policies are related to information, demand, supply and material flow that govern product flow within the supply chain.

Given this base of primitives, an executable simulation model of a given supply chain model is constructed by instantiating and relating appropriate structural and control elements. Our framework allows the development of models to address various issues which are related to configuration, coordination and contracts. Configuration deals with issues that are related to the network structure of a supply chain which are based on factors such as leadtime, transportation cost and currency fluctuations; Coordination deals with routine activities in a supply chain such as materials flow, distribution, inventory control and information exchange; Contracts control the material flow over a longer horizon that are based on factors such as supplier reliability, number of suppliers, quantity discounts, demand forecast mechanisms and flexibility to change the commitments.

We model the structural elements as heterogeneous agents which utilize the control elements in terms of communicate and control flow of product within the supply chain. Our approach emphasize the models that capture the locality that typically exists with the respect to the preview, operating constraints and objectives of individual supply chain entities.

A typical supply chain faces the uncertainty in order to supply, demand and process. Our framework reduces the effort that are involved in modeling several alternatives and measuring their performance through simulation under different assumptions about uncertainties. This eases the ability of decision makers to quantitatively assess the risk and benefits that are associated with various supply chain re-engineering alternatives. In this concept, we describe the framework in its current state and provide examples to demonstrate how issues relevant to supply chain management can be analyzed using it.

Organization Challenges

The company and its organizational culture play an important role in developing and executing a supply chain strategy. The following are some common organizational challenges which are found in many companies:

1. **Lack of ownership** – many supply chain processes and value levers do not have an owner in the traditional sense
2. **"Tower of Babel" problem** – most organizations across the enterprise do not speak a common supply chain language

3. **Organizational focus** – some managers are functional or process oriented and do not understand the value levers' multiple drivers model

4. **Extending the Supply Chain** – most supply chain initiatives involve external parties (trading partners) which makes strong collaboration a requirement

As supply chain have moved from a cost focus to a customer focus and now currently to a strategic focus, the need to think strategically about the supply chain has never been more important.

The success of a strategy is only as good as the ability of company to fully and properly execute it. A great supply chain strategy, linked with operational excellence that can provide success for not only the company in question but also its partners and customers.

Executing a supply chain strategy means dealing with many different entities, both internally and externally. Just as it is difficult to align the supply chain strategy with the business strategy, it is equally important to execute in a way that are consistent with these various groups or stakeholders. The objectives of supply chain components and those that you deal with must be similar and conducted at the same speed. Your organization may be able to move at speeds other supply chain entities are unable to maintain, resulting in misalignment and poor efficiencies. And some of your supply chain partners may not have the resources to commit to realizing these goals. Good communication can keep the extended supply chain in sync.

PROBLEMS IN SUPPLY CHAIN MANAGEMENT

Supply chain management has various problems which includes:-

- *Distribution Network Configuration:* Number, location and network missions of suppliers, production facilities, distribution centers, warehouses, cross-docks and customers.
- *Distribution Strategy:* Including questions of operating control (centralized, decentralized or shared); delivery scheme (e.g., direct shipment, pool point shipping, Cross docking, DSD (direct store delivery), closed loop shipping); mode of transportation (e.g., motor carrier, including truckload, LTL, parcel; railroad; intermodal, including TOFC and COFC; ocean freight;

airfreight); replenishment strategy (e.g., pull, push or hybrid); and transportation control (e.g., owner-operated, private carrier, common carrier, contract carrier, or 3PL). Trade-Offs in Logistical Activities

The above activities must be coordinated well together in terms to achieve the least total logistics cost. Trade-offs exist that increase the total cost if only one of the activities is optimized. For example, full truckload (FTL) rates are more economical on a cost per pallet basis than less than truckload (LTL) shipments. However, If a full truckload of a product is ordered to reduce the transportation costs there will be an increase in inventory holding costs which may increase total logistics costs. Therefore, it is imperative to take a systems approach when planning logistical activities. These trade-offs are key to developing the most efficient and most effective Logistics and SCM strategy.

How to Develop Supply Chain Strategy

There are various steps of developing supply chain strategy including understanding business strategy, assess the extended supply chain.

Step I: Understand the Business Strategy

The first step is for supply chain executives to clearly understand how the enterprise chooses to compete. This is important not only for the obvious reason of working off the "same play book," but also for the reason that it forces the supply chain operation to see itself as a customer facing entity that are serving the competitive goals of the enterprise—not merely an operational department. Supply chain strategy is not simply a linear derivative of the business strategy. At best, supply chain strategy can be the enabler of the business strategy. If the business strategy is to be the low cost provider, the supply chain strategy should support this. And just like when developing a business strategy, look to your core competencies, focus, and means of differentiation when developing a supply chain strategy. Being able to strategically source parts at an attractive price may support both your supply chain strategy and business strategy, but only if you have the capabilities to do so effectively. Look to your supply chain competencies and leverage what you do well. You may want to focus on a particular market or segment in which to gain supply chain efficiencies. Or you may want to differentiate your organization operationally by providing lower costs to customers or providing services that other industry players are unable to do.

Step II: Assess the Extended Supply Chain

The next step is to conduct a detailed, realistic assessment of the capabilities that are exist within the organization and even the extended supply chain. Begin by closely scrutinizing the assets of organization and evaluate how well they support the strategy. Old machinery and disparate systems may mean high operational overhead and costly process inefficiencies and redundancies – clearly not supportive of a low cost provider strategy. A formal supply chain assessment by a non-biased outside party may assist you in better understanding your operational strengths and opportunities for improvement. Look for a firm that can provide you with operational benchmarks both inside and outside of your industry in terms to gauge core competencies. Once the assessment is complete, assemble a team to review and prioritize recommendations, validate the opportunities, define the risks, and the requirements for implementation. Ultimately, if there is a disparity between the supply chain strategy and the operational assets, you may have to make capital investments. Of course, the other alternative is to change your assumptions and alter your strategy all together!

Goals of Supply Chain Strategy

There are three types of goals in supply chain strategy naming strategic goal, tactical goal and operational goal as well.

That being said, most companies have a business strategy, but are unlikely to have overtly that are designed a supply chain strategy. So, why is a supply chain strategy so important? Well, one good reason is to operationalize and support your business strategy. At some point, a business strategy must be executed and typically this is done through the operational components of a company. Supply chain strategy also focuses on driving down operational costs and maximizing efficiencies. For example, an organization may choose a strategy directed at supplier management as a way to remain competitive. By providing a clear purpose, the organization keeps sight of the strategy and is able to devise tactical steps to achieve these goals. Another reason for having a supply chain strategy is to establish how you work with your supply chain partners, including suppliers, distributors, customers, and even your customers'

customers. As the marketplace becomes more competitive, it is critical to reinforce existing relationships and work together. And for all these reasons, a well executed supply chain strategy results in value creation for the organization. These goals sometimes acts as levels of supply chain activities. These levels are described below:-

Strategic Levels

Following are the strategic levels.

- Aligning overall organizational strategy with supply strategy
- Information Technology infrastructure which is used to support supply chain operations
- Product life cycle management, so that new and existing products that can be optimally integrated into the supply chain and capacity management
- Strategic network optimisation, including the number, location, and size of warehousing, distribution centers, and facilities
- Where-to-make and what-to-make-or-buy decisions
- Strategic partnership with suppliers, distributors, and customers that are creating the communication channels for critical information and operational improvements such as cross docking, direct shipping, and third-party logistics

Tactical Levels

Following are the tactical levels:-

- [Benchmarking] of all operations against competitors and implementation of best practices throughout the enterprise.
- Focus on customer demand.
- Inventory decisions, including quantity, location, and quality of inventory.
- Milestone payments
- Production decisions, including contracting, scheduling, and planning process definition.
- Sourcing contracts and other purchasing decisions.
- Transportation strategy, including frequency, routes, and contracting.

Operational Levels

There are also have some operational levels inclulding:-

- Demand planning and forecasting, coordinating the demand forecast of all customers and sharing the forecast with all suppliers.
- Daily production and distribution planning, including all nodes in the supply chain.
- Inbound operations, including transportation from suppliers and receiving inventory.
- Outbound operations, including all fulfillment activities, warehousing and transportation to customers.
- Order promising, accounting for all constraints in the supply chain, including all suppliers, manufacturing facilities, distribution centers, and other customers.
- Production scheduling for each manufacturing facility in the supply chain.
- Production operations, including the consumption of materials and flow of finished goods.
- Sourcing planning, including current inventory and forecast demand, in collaboration with all suppliers.

A supply chain strategy should always support the intent of the business strategy and it is precisely because of these different "levels" of the enterprise at which strategies necessarily must be developed, that companies so often have major gaps between their highest level business strategy and their supply chain strategy. There are some additional risks associated with developing these separately, which include:

- Developing a supply chain strategy without a true understanding of the business case and value propositions – the costs and benefits are not known
- Utilizing different or new resources in the operational model development that weren't exposed to the original business strategy thinking, thereby diluting and weakening the supply chain strategy
- Confusing or conflicting communications to the organization where objectives may be contradictory.

These two problems are distribution network configuration and also there is distribution strategy. Distribution network configuration includes number and network location as well as production facilities and distribution strategy includes questions of operating control as well as delivery scheme.

- Information: Integration of and other processes through the supply chain to share valuable information, including demand signals, forecasts, inventory, transportation, and potential collaboration etc.
- Inventory Management: Quantity and location of inventory including raw materials, work-in-progress (WIP) and finished goods.
- Cash-Flow: Arranging the payment terms and the methodologies for exchanging the funds across all the entities within the supply chain.

Supply chain execution is managing and coordinating the movement of materials, information and funds across the supply chain. The flow is bi-directional.

FUNCTIONS AND APPROACHES IN SCM

Supply chain management is a cross-function approach to manage the movement of raw materials into an organization, some aspects of the internal processing of materials into finished goods, and then the movement of finished goods out of the organization toward the end-consumer. As organizations strive to focus on core competencies and becoming more flexible, they have reduced their ownership of raw materials sources and distribution channels. These functions are increasingly being outsourced to other entities that can perform the activities which are better or more cost effectively. The effect is to increase the number of organizations which are involved in satisfying the customer demand, while reducing management control of daily logistics operations. Less control and more supply chain partners led to the creation of supply chain management concepts. The purpose of supply chain management is to improve the trust and collaboration among supply chain partners, thus improving inventory visibility and improving inventory velocity.

Several models have been proposed for understanding the activities which are needed to manage the material movements across the organizational and functional boundaries. SCOR is a supply chain management model promoted by the Supply Chain Council. Another model is the SCM Model proposed by the Global Supply Chain Forum (GSCF). Supply chain activities can be grouped into strategic, tactical, and operational levels of activities. These three levels of supply chain activities are also described above in pervious topic.

DECISION FOR SCM

Each process is done after making some decision. These decision are also categorized in supply chain management.

We classify the decisions for supply chain management into two broad categories — strategic and operational. As the term implies, strategic decisions are made typically over a longer time horizon, i.e., for long term period. These are closely linked to the corporate strategy they are sometimes the corporate strategy, and guide supply chain policies from a design perspective. On the other hand, operational decisions are made typically short term, and mainly focus on activities over a day-to-day basis. The effort in these type of decisions is to effectively and efficiently manage the product flow in the "strategically" planned supply chain.

There are four major decision areas in supply chain management: 1) location, 2) production, 3) inventory, and 4) transportation (distribution), and there are both strategic and operational elements in each of these decision areas. These four decision including both strategic and operational decision.

1. Location Decisions

The geographic placement of production facilities, stocking points, and sourcing points is the natural first step in creating a supply chain. The location of facilities includes the a commitment of resources to a long-term plan. Once the size, number, and location of these are determined, so are the possible paths or ways by which the product flows through to the final customer. These decisions are of great significance to a firm since they represent the basic strategy for accessing the customer markets, and will have a considerable impact on revenue, cost, and level of service. These decisions should be determined by an optimization routine that considers production costs, taxes, duties and duty drawback, tariffs, local content, distribution costs, production limitations, etc. Although location decisions are primarily strategic, they also have implications on an operational level. It supports operational level but strategic decision.

2. Production Decisions

The strategic decisions include what products to produce, and which plants to produce them in, allocation of suppliers to plants, plants to DC's, and DC's to customer markets. As before, these decisions have a great impact on the revenues, costs and customer service levels of the firm. These decisions assume the existence of the facilities, but determine the exact path(s) through which a product flows to and from these facilities. Another typical issue is the capacity of the manufacturing facilities—and this issue largely depends on the degree of vertical integration within the firm. Operational decisions focus on detailed production scheduling. These decisions include the construction of the master production schedules, scheduling production on machines, and equipment maintenance. Other considerations include workload balancing, and quality control measures at a production facility. Production decision supports operational decision.

3. Inventory Decisions

These refer to means by which inventories are managed. Inventories exist at every stage of the supply chain as either the raw materials, semi-finished or finished goods. They can also be in-process between locations. Their primary goals to buffer against any uncertainty that might exist in the supply chain. Since holding of inventories can cost anywhere between 20 to 40 percent of their value, their efficient management is critical in supply chain operations. It is strategic in the sense that top management sets goals. Inventory decision supports strategic level or decision.

However, most researchers have approached the management of inventory from an operational perspective. These include deployment strategies (push versus pull), control policies — the determination of the optimal levels of order quantities and reorder points, and setting safety stock levels, at each stocking location. These levels are critical, since they are primary determinants of customer service levels.

4. Transportation Decisions

The mode choice aspect of these decisions are the more strategic ones. These are closely linked to the inventory decisions, since the best choice of mode is frequently found by trading-off the cost of using the specific mode of transport with the indirect cost of inventory associated with that mode. While air shipments may be fast, reliable, and warrant lesser safety stocks, they are expensive. Meanwhile shipping by sea or rail may be much cheaper, but they necessitate holding relatively large amounts of inventory to buffer against the inherent uncertainty associated with them. Therefore, customer service levels, and geographic location play vital roles in such decisions. Since transportation is more than 30 percent of the logistics costs, operating efficiently makes good economic sense. Shipment sizes (consolidated bulk shipments versus Lot-for-Lot), routing and scheduling of equipment are key in effective management of transport strategy of the firm. This decision supports strategic decision mode and closely attached with inventory decision.

CUSTOMER RELATIONSHIP

Customer relationship are at heat of every business or organization, how the people who keep your company afloat are treated. Because loyalty and trust are built, dealing with those who treat us well is something we look forward to and appreciate.

Customer relationship management (**CRM**) consists of the processes a company uses to track and organize its contacts with its current and prospective customers. CRM software is used to support these processes; information about customers and customer interactions can be entered, stored and accessed by employees in various company departments. Typical CRM goals are to improve all the services which are provided to customers, and to use customer contact information for targeted marketing.

From the outside, customers interacting with a company perceive the business as a single entity, despite frequently interacting with a number of employees in several roles and departments. CRM is a combination of policies, processes, and strategies implemented by an organization to unify its customer interactions and gives a means to track the customer information. It includes the use of technology in attracting new and profitable customers, while forming tighter bonds or linkages with existing ones.

CRM is the mixture of strategies, process and policies which are implemented by a company to make their customer intreractions.

While the term CRM usually refers to a software-based approach which are used to handling customer relationships, most CRM software vendors stress that a successful CRM effort that requires a holistic approach. CRM initiatives often fail because implementation was limited to software installation, without giving the context, support and understanding for employees to learn, and take full advantage of the information systems. CRM can be implemented without major investments in software, but software is frequently essential to explore the full benefits or advantages of a CRM strategy.

Other problems occur when failing to think of sales as the output of a process that itself needs to be studied and taken into account when planning automation.

Aspects of CRM

CRM includes many aspects which relate directly to one another:

- Front office operations includes direct interaction with customers, e.g. face to face meetings, phone calls, e-mail, online services etc.
- Back office operations includes operations that ultimately affect the activities of the front office (e.g., billing, maintenance, planning, marketing, advertising, finance, manufacturing, etc.)
- Business relationships includes the interaction with other companies and partners, such as suppliers/vendors and retail outlets/distributors, industry networks (lobbying groups, trade associations). This external network supports front and back office activities.
- Analysis includes the concept that key CRM data can be analyzed in terms to plan the target-marketing campaigns, conceive business strategies, and judge the success of CRM activities (e.g., market share, number and types of customers, revenue, profitability).

Proponents of CRM software claim that it doesn't only allow more effective methods of managing customer relationships, but also more customer-centric method of doing business.

APPROACHES IN SUPPLY CHAIN MODELING

Clearly, each of the above two levels of decisions needs various perspective. For the most the strategic decisions are, global or "all encompassing" in that they try to integrate different aspects of the supply chain. Consequently, the models that describe these decisions are huge, and needs a considerable amount of data. frequently due to the enormity of data requirements, and the broad scope of decisions, these models provide approximate solutions to the decisions they describe. The operational decisions, meanwhile, address the day to day operation of the supply chain. Therefore, the models that describe them are frequently very specific in nature. Because of their narrow perspective, these models frequently consider the great detail and provide very good, if not optimal, solutions to the operational decisions.

To facilitate a concise review of the literature, and at the same time that are attempting to accommodate the above polarity in modeling, we divide the modeling approaches into three areas — Network Design, "Rough Cut" methods, and simulation based methods. For the most part, the network design methods, provide normative models for the more strategic decisions. These models typically cover the four major decision areas described earlier, and focus more on the design aspect of the supply chain; the establishment of the network and the associated flows on them. On the other hand, "Rough cut" methods, provide the guiding policies for the operational decisions. These models typically assume a "single site" (i.e., ignore the network) and add supply chain characteristics to it, such as explicitly considering the site's relation to the others in the network. Simulation methods is a method by which a comprehensive supply chain model can be analyzed, considering both strategic and operational elements. However, as with all simulation models, one can only determine the effectiveness of a pre-specified policy rather than develop new ones. It is the traditional question of "What If?" versus "What's Best?". Now we discussed about these models in descriptive text.

Network Design Model

Network design gives the normative models for the more strategic decision. These normative models are also described in chapter 4 namely decision making process and decision theory.

As the name suggest, network design, these methods evaluate the location of production stocking and sourcing facilities and paths the product which take through them.

These methods tends to be large scale, and used commonly at the inception of the supply chain. The earliest work in this area, although the term "supply chain" was not in vogue which was proposed by Geoffrion and Graves in 1974. They introduce a multicommodity logistics network design model for optimizing annualized finished product flows from plants to the DC's to the final customers. Geoffrion and Powers in 1993 later give a review of the evolution of distribution strategies over the past twenty years that are describing how the descendants of the above model can accommodate more echelons and cross commodity detail.

In 1985 Cohen and Lee develop a conceptual framework for manufacturing the strategy analysis, where they describe a series of stochastic sub-models, that considers the annualized product flows from raw material vendors through intermediate plants and distribution echelons to the final customers. They use heuristic methods to link and optimize these sub-models. They later give an integrated and readable exposition of their models and methods by Cohen and Lee in 1988.

In 1989 Cohen and Lee present a normative model for resource deployment in a global manufacturing and distribution network. Global after-tax profit (profit-local taxes) is maximized through the design of facility network and control of material flows within the network. The cost structure consists of variable and fixed costs for material procurement, production, distribution and transportation. They validate the model by applying it to analyze the global manufacturing strategies of a personal computer manufacturer.

Clearly, these network-design based methods add the value to the firm in that they lay down the manufacturing and distribution strategies far into the future. It is imperative that firms at one time or another make such integrated decisions, encompassing production, location, inventory, and transportation, and such models are therefore indispensable. Although the above review shows considerable potential for these models as strategic determinants in the future, they are not without their shortcomings. Their very nature forces these problems to be of a very large scale. They are frequently difficult to solve to optimality. Furthermore, most of the models in this category are largely deterministic and static in nature. Additionally, those that consider stochastic elements are very restrictive in nature. In sum, there does not seem to yet be a comprehensive model that is representative of the true nature of material flows in the supply chain.

Rough Cut Methods

These models form the bulk of the supply chain literature, and typically deal with the more operational or tactical decisions. Most of the integrative research (from a supply chain context) in the literature seem to take on an inventory management perspective. In fact, the term "Supply Chain" first appears in the literature as an inventory management approach. The thrust of the rough cut models is the development of inventory control policies, considering several levels or echelons together. These models have come to be known as "multi-level" or "multi-echelon" inventory control models.

Although current research in multi-echelon are based on supply chain inventory problems that shows considerable promise in reducing inventories with increased customer service, the studies have various notable limitations. (1) First, these studies largely ignore the production side of the supply chain. Their starting point in most cases is a finished goods stockpile, and policies are given to manage these goods effectively. Since production is a natural part of the supply chain, there seems to be a need with models that include the production component in them. (2) Second, even on the distribution side, almost all published research assumes an arborescence structure, i. e. each site receives re-supply from only one higher level site but can distribute to various lower levels. (3) Third, researchers have largely focused on the inventory system only. In logistics-system theory, transportation and inventory are primary components of the order fulfillment process in order to cost and service levels. Therefore, companies must consider important interrelationships among transportation, inventory and customer service in determining their policies. Fourth, most of the models under the "inventory theoretic" paradigm are very restrictive in nature, i.e., mostly they restrict themselves to certain well known forms of demand or lead time or both, often quite contrary to what is observed.

STRATEGIC SUPPLY CHAIN MANAGEMENT

Supply chain management operates at three levels; strategic, tactical and operational. At the strategic level, company management makes high level strategic supply chain decisions that are relevant to whole organization. The decisions that are made with regards to the supply chain should reflect the overall corporate strategy that the organization is following. These three levels are also discussed in this chapter. The strategic supply process that management has to decide upon will cover the breath of the supply chain. These includes product development, customers, manufacturing, vendors and logistics.

Product Development

Senior Management has to define a strategic direction when considering the products that the company should manufacture and offer to their customers. As product cycles mature or products sales decline, management has to make strategic decisions to create and introduce new versions of existing products into the marketplace, rationalize the current product offering or whether develop a new range of products and services. These strategic decisions may include the requirement to acquire another company or sell existing businesses. However, when making these strategic product development decisions, the overall goals and objectives of the firm should be the determining factor.

Customers

At the strategic level, a company has to identify the nature of customers for its products and services. When company management makes strategic decisions on the products to manufacture, they requires to then identify the key customer segments where company marketing and advertising will be targeted.

Manufacturing

At the strategic level, manufacturing decisions define the manufacturing infrastructure and technology that is needed. Based on high level forecasting and sales estimates, the company management has to make strategic decisions on how products will be manufactured. The decisions can require new manufacturing facilities that are to be built or to increase the production at exiting facilities. However, if the overall company objectives include moving manufacturing overseas, then the decisions may lean towards using subcontracting and third party logistics. As environmental issues influence the corporate policy to a greater extent, this may influence the strategic supply chain decisions with regards to manufacturing.

Suppliers

Company management has to decide on the strategic supply chain policies with regards to suppliers. Reducing the purchasing spend for a company can directly relate to an increase in profit and strategically, there are a number of decisions that can be made to develop that result. Leveraging the total purchases of company over many businesses can allow the company management to select strategic global suppliers who offer the greatest discounts. But these decisions have to correspond with the overall company objectives. If a company has adopted policies on quality, then strategic decisions on suppliers will have to fall within the overall company objective.

Logistics

As well as strategic decisions on manufacturing locations, the logistics function is key to the success of the supply chain. Order fulfillment is an important part of the supply chain and company management need to make strategic decisions on the logistics network. The design and operation of the network has a significant influence on the performance of the supply chain. Strategic decisions are needed on warehouses, distribution centers which transportation modes should be used. If the overall company objectives identify the use of more third party subcontracting, the company may strategically decide to use third party logistics companies in the supply chain.

Strategic decisions evaluates the overall direction of supply chain of company. These decisions can be refined, as required, to the particular requirements of the company at the lower levels which allow for tactical and operational supply chain decisions to be made. These levels of decisions are also described previously in this chapter.

OPERATIONAL SUPPLY CHAIN MANAGEMENT

Operational supply chain decisions are made hundreds of times each day in a company. These are the decisions that are made at business locations that affect how products are developed, sold, moved and manufactured.

Operational decisions are made with awareness of the strategic and tactical decisions that have been adopted within a company. These higher level decisions are made to create a framework within the company's supply chain operate and to the best competitive advantage. The day to day operational supply chain decisions ensure that the products efficiently move along the supply chain achieving the maximum cost benefit. A number of examples of operational decisions can be identified in manufacturing, supplier relationships and logistics.

Manufacturing

Companies make tactical decisions with regards to manufacturing, such as the adoption of kanban and just-in-time. However, if the local manufacturing site is unable to rely on some supplier delivery times, the just-in-time method may not be appropriate for certain product lines. The local plant management may make an operational decision to keep some items in stock to ensure that production is not halted. This inventory will increase costs, but a greater cost would be incurred if the production line was brought to a standstill due to a lack of items from a supplier.

Suppliers

Global suppliers and negotiated contracts are decisions made at a company level to take advantage or benefits of global buying power of the company. This offers considerable cost savings, but local sites may have to make operational decisions with suppliers to ensure an efficient supply chain. In some instances local negotiations with global suppliers are required to ensure quality of the product. For example, in some countries the quality of the product produced by a supplier is not at the same level as other countries. The local management would have to make an operational decision to negotiate with the supplier for them to create a product with a higher quality to ensure the quality of the finished product.

Logistics

Strategic and tactical supply chain decisions in the logistics process frequently focus on the use of third party logistics companies (3PL). Many companies have identified the cost benefits of these 3PL companies and have integrated them into their supply chain. However, in some instances these 3PL companies may not operate in all regions where the company needs logistics. In those cases the local management has to make operational decisions on leasing local warehousing and negotiating with regional logistics companies.

SUPPLY CHAIN IN BUSINESS PROCESS INTEGRATION

Successful SCM needs a change from managing individual functions to integrating activities into key supply chain processes. An example scenario: the purchasing department places orders as requirements become appropriate. Marketing, responding to customer demand, communicates with several distributors and retailers as it attempts to satisfy this demand. Shared information between supply chain partners can only be fully leveraged through process integration.

Supply chain business process integration involves the collaborative work between buyers and suppliers, joint product development, common systems and shared information. In 2000, according to Lambert and Cooper operating an integrated supply chain needs continuous information flow. However, in many companies, management has reached the conclusion that optimizing the product flows that cannot be accomplished without implementing a process approach to the business. The key supply chain processes stated by Lambert in 2004 are:

- Customer relationship management
- Customer service management
- Demand management
- Order fulfillment
- Manufacturing flow management
- Supplier relationship management
- Product development and commercialization
- Returns management

THEORIES OF SUPPLY CHAIN MANAGEMENT

Currently there exists a gap in the literature which are available in the area of supply chain management studies, on providing theoretical support for explaining the existence and the boundaries of supply chain management. Few authors such as Halldorsson, et al. (2003), Ketchen and Hult (2006) and Lavassani, et al. (2008[b]) had tried to give the theoretical foundations for various concepts that are related to supply chain with employing the organizational theories. These theories includes:

- Agency theory (AT)
- Institutional theory (InT)
- Knowledge-based view (KBV)
- Network Perspective (NP)
- Resource-based view (RBV)
- Transaction Cost Analysis (TCA)
- Strategic Choice Theory (SCT)
- Systems Theory (ST)

These theories are included in the supply chain management.

SUPPLY CHAIN SUSTAINABILITY

Supply chain sustainability is a business issue that are affecting supply chain or logistics network of an organization in order to risks and wastage of costs. Sustainability in the supply chain is the increasingly seen among high level executives as necessary to delivering long-term profitability and has replaced monitory cost, value and speed.

Many companies are limited to measuring the sustainability of their own business operations and are unable to extend this evaluation to their suppliers and customers. This makes determining their true environmental costs highly challenging and reduces their ability to remove waste from the supply chains.

One of the key requirements of successful sustainable supply chains is collaboration. The practice of collaboration such as sharing distribution to reduce waste by ensuring that half-empty vehicles do not get sent out and that deliveries to the same address are on the same truck — is not widespread because many companies fear a loss of commercial control by working with others. Investment in alternative modes of transportation — such as use of canals and airships — can play an important role in helping companies reduce the cost and environmental impact of their deliveries.

There are three terms of sustainability including tiers 1 consists of getting the basic rights, tier 2 consists of learning to think sustainably and third tier consists of the science of sustainability.

CONSIGNMENT

Consignment is act of consigning, which is placing a person or thing in the hand of another, but retaining ownership until the goods are sold or person is transferred. This may be done for shipping, or for sale in a short.

Features of Consignment

Following are the features of consignment which includes:-

1. The relation between the two parties is that of consignor and consignee and not that of buyer and seller
2. The consignor is entitled to receive all the expenses in connection with consignment
3. The consignee is not responsible for damage of goods during transport or any other procedure.
4. Goods are sold at the risk of consignor. The profit or loss belongs to consignor only.

SUPPLY CHAIN PERFORMANCE

One of the objective of developing an integrated framework is to provide an ability to simultaneously observe global and local performance of supply chain.

Supply chain performance measures can be classified broadly into two categories: qualitative measures such as customer satisfaction and product quality and quantitative measures such as order-to-delivery lead time, supply chain response time, flexibility, resource utilization, delivery performance, etc. In our study, we consider only the quantitative performance measures. Improving supply chain performance requires a multi-dimensional strategy that addresses how the organization will service diverse customer needs. While the performance measurements may be similar, the specific performance goals of each segment may be quite different.

Quantitative metrics of supply chain performance can be classified into two broad categories: Non-financial and financial.

In this framework, we separate local performance (PMI) from the global performance measures (GPM). A global performance measure may be an appropriate yard stick for an intra organizational supply chain whereas local performance becomes a mean are for inter organizational supply chain.

Supply chain performance measures can be classified into two broad categories. Qualitative performance measures such as customer satisfaction, integration of information and material flow and, effective risk management. Quantitative performance measures relate are to the cost minimization, profit maximization, fill-rate maximization, customer response time minimization, supplier reliability and lead time minimization. In this framework, we consider only quantitative performance measures. We provide the capability for analysts to monitor the suitable performance measures (either local or global or both) which are depending on the situation or circumstances. It should be noted that there is a very strong link between goals of the agent in terms of the performance measures PMi and priorities Qi of an agent. These priorities determine the sequence in which incoming messages are selected and in some sense drive the simulation.

SUPPLY CHAIN DYNAMICS

Supply chain dynamics can become complicated or typical to model because of the presence of heterogeneous entities, multiple performance measures and complex interaction effects. The variety of supply chains poses a limitation on reusability of processes across them. For example, a supply chain could be highly centralized and have most of the entities belonging to the same organization (like IBM integrated supply chain) or could be highly decentralized with all the entities being separate organizations (like a grocery supply chain). As a inclusion, it is a difficult process to develop a set of generic processes that capture the dynamics of supply chains across a wide spectrum. In this section, we present a classification of library of software components which enables modeling and analysis of a large variety of problems though it is not exhaustive by any means.

There are two types of elements of supply chain library, i.e., structural elements and control elements.

Structural elements (modeled as agents) are included in actual production and transportation of products and Control elements that helps in coordinating the flow of products in an efficient way with the use of messages. Structural elements correspond to agents and control elements correspond to the control policies in our framework. Structural elements are further categorized into two basic sets of elements namely, Production and Transportation elements. Control elements are categorized into Inventory Control, Demand Control, Supply Control, Flow Control and Information Control elements.

Structural Elements

As indicated earlier, structural elements are involved in production and transportation of products. Strategic placement of these elements includes major issues that are related to supply chain configuration.

1. Production Agents—Production agents use inventory control elements for managing their inventory, contracts with downstream entities for supply control, flow control elements for loading and unloading products, forecast elements for propagating demand forecasts to the downstream entity and may use information control elements with other entities in the supply chain. Production agents includes retailer, distribution center, manufacturing plant, external suppliers.

- Retailer: A retailer is where customers buy products. The main focus here is on reducing the cycle time for the delivery of a customer order and minimizing stock-outs.
- Distribution Center: A distribution center included in receiving products from the manufacturing plant and either storing them or sending them right away to the retailer. Here, the main focus is to reduce the inventory carried and maximize throughput.
- Manufacturing Plant: A manufacturing plant is an agent where components are assembled and a product is manufactured. In general, orders come from the distribution center but they could also come from the retailer (when there is a cross-dock or the supply chain does not have a distribution center).
- External Suppliers: An external supplier agent models external suppliers. These suppliers could be a manufacturing plant or assembly plant or could have their own supply chain for production. However, we model all these conditions through a single agent because the parent organization has no direct control on their internal operations.

2. Transportation Agent—This type of agent includes only transportation vehicles.

Transportation Vehicles: Transportation vehicles move product from one production agent to another. Each vehicle has associated with the characteristics in order of capacity and relative speed. Vehicles use flow control elements in terms to load and unload the products as well as to evaluate the route. The route taken by the vehicle depends on the state of the vehicle which contains information on destination of products that have been loaded. Using distance to the next destination from the current destination, the time required to reach the next destination is obtained. At that time, products destined for that production agent are unloaded and other products may get loaded.

Control Elements

Control elements facilitate the production and transportation of products within the supply chain. Choice of appropriate control elements is the goal of problems that arerelated to supply chain contracts and supply chain coordination. Here is a brief description of control elements currently defined.

1. Inventory Control—Inventory control elements are an integral part of any supply chain. They control the flow of materials within the supply chain. They are mainly of two types - Centralized and Decentralized control. Inventory includes both centralized and decentralized control.

Centralized Control: These elements controls the inventory at a specific production element while taking into account the inventory levels in the supply chain as a whole.

Decentralized Control: These elements control inventory at a specific production element by considering all the inventory levels at that entity in the supply chain.

2. Demand Control—The demand process within a supply chain is sustained through actual and forecasts these are modeled as messages in our framework. Orders contain information on — types of products which are being ordered, the number of products that are needed, the destination where the product has to be supplied, and the due date of the order. Two important demand control elements are: Marketing elements and forecast element.

- Marketing Element: One of the important aspects of product management is how well the product is marketed to consumers. There are no methods which are used to increase the demand for a specific product. These include advertisements, discounts, coupons and seasonal sale. It provides a process that can trigger additional demand for products.

- Forecast Element: Forecast evaluate the concept that determine how forecasts are generated within the supply chain and how they are evolve over time. In a \Push" system, forecast evolution plays a very important role because manufacturing decisions are based on demand forecasts. In a \Pull" system, products are built-to-order still forecast accuracy plays an important role in materials procurement and capacity planning.

3. Supply Control—Supply Control elements dictate the terms and condition that are used for delivery of the material once orders have been placed. Contractual agreements are the only form of supply control element that we have identified. Contracts contain information on the price of the material, length of the contract, volume to be purchased over the contract period, penalty for defaulting, leadtime to get the product once the final order has been placed, the amount of flexibility that the buyer has in order to updating the demand forecasts over time which are frequently referred to as flexibility which are offered by the supplier) and types of information control that could be used. Supply contracts may variate in characteristics and rigidity that are depending on whether supplier of the product belongs to the same organization or not. Transfer pricing mechanisms are employed while dealing with internal suppliers (this could be thought of as a form of centralized supply control).

4. Flow Control—Flow control elements coordinate the flow of products between production and transportation elements. Two types of flow control elements are: loading element and routing element.

- Loading Element: Loading Elements control the way in which the transportation elements are loaded and unloaded. This control is variation based on the type of the production element where products are loaded or unloaded.
- Routing Element: Routing elements control the services in which products are delivered by the transportation element. The route are taken by the transportation vehicle which depends to a great extent on the destination of products that it is carrying. So, the routing is dynamic in that sense. The route

can be decided in a centralized or a decentralized manner which depending on how much information is available about destination of other transportation elements.

5. Information Control—Information control elements are necessary for coordination within the supply chain. Two types of information flow are: directly accessible information and periodic information.

- Directly Accessible Information: Directly accessible information transfer refers to the instantaneous propagation of information. For example this could be information on inventory levels,
- Periodic: Periodic information updates may be sent by various production and transportation elements which are used to indicate the changes in business strategy, price increase, introduction of new services or features in the products, introduction of new production elements, etc.

Case Study

Note : knowing more about "Supply Chain Strategy" reader can study documentation process of Microsoft company by visiting their site : www.members.microsoft.com

http://www.icmrindia.org/casestudies/Case_Studies.asp?cat=Supply%20chain%20Management

http://logistics.about.com/od/supplychaincasestudies/Supply_Chain_Case_Studies.htm

http://www.establishinc.com/cs_supply_chain.asp

http://www.infosys.com/supply-chain/case-studies/default.asp

http://cscmp.org/resources/casestudy.asp

http://www.ilog.com/products/supplychain/casestudies/

http://www.scdigest.com/TypeList.php?colid=CASESTUDY

http://www.smithweb.com/sw/en/about-smith/case-studies/smith-service-supply-chain-strategies

9

Inventory Management

This chapter includes the key concepts which are shown below:-

- Inventory Basics
- Types of Inventory
- EOQ
- Inventory Control System
- Distressed Inventory
- Inventory Credit
- Objective of Inventory Management
- Importance of Inventory Management
- Techniques of Inventory Management
- How to Improve Inventory Turnover
- Techniques of Inventory Control

INVENTORY BASICS

Inventory is financial as well as counting terms which refers to the goods and materials which are available in stock by a business.

Inventory is a list for goods and materials, or those goods and materials themselves which are held available in stock by a business. It is also used for a list of the contents of a household and for a list for testamentary purposes of the possessions of someone who has died. In accounting, inventory is considered an asset.

The raw materials, work-in-process goods and completely finished goods that are considered to be the portion of assets of a business that are ready or will be ready for sale. Inventory represents one of the most important assets that most of the businesses possess, because the turnover of inventory represents one of the primary sources of revenue generation and subsequent earnings for shareholders/owners of the company.

Possessing a high amount of inventory for long periods of time is not usually good for a business because of inventory storage, obsolescence and spoilage costs. However, possessing too little inventory isn't good either, because the business runs the risk of losing out on potential sales and potential market share as well.

Form business's point of view, inventory refers to the asset of an organization which are ready for sale. Inventory is the total amount of goods and materials contained in a store or factory at any given time.

The word 'inventory' can refer to both the total amount of goods and the act of counting them. Many companies take an inventory of their supplies on a regular basis in terms to avoid running out of popular items. Others take an inventory to insure the number of items ordered matches the actual number of items which are counted physically.

Store owners need to know the precise number of items on their shelves and storage areas in terms to place the orders or control loses whereas factory mangers need to know how many units of their products are available for customer orders.

There are three basic reasons for keeping an inventory:

1. Time — The time lags present in the supply chain, from supplier to user at every stage, requires that you maintain some amount of inventory to use in this "lead time"
2. Uncertainty — Inventories are maintained as buffers to meet the uncertainties in demand, supply and movements of goods.
3. Economies of scale — Ideal condition of "one unit at a time at a place where user needs it, when he needs it" principle tends to incur lots of costs in terms of logistics. So bulk buying, movement and storing brings in economies of scale, thus inventory.

All these stock reasons can apply to any owner or product stage. Buffer stock is held in individual workstations against the possibility that the upstream workstation may be a little delayed in long setup or change-over time. This stock is then used while that change-over is happening.

Where these stocks contain the same or similar items it is frequently the work practice to hold all these stocks which are mixed together before or after the sub-process to which they relate. This 'reduces' the costs. Because they are mixed-up together there is no visual reminder to operators of the adjacent sub-processes or line management of the stock which is due to a particular cause and should be a specific responsibility of an individual with inevitable consequences. Some plants have centralized stock holding across sub-processes which makes the situation even more acute.

Inventory management forecasts and strategies, such as a just-in-time inventory system, can help to minimize the inventory costs because goods are created or received as inventory only when needed.

TYPES OF INVENTORY

As we discussed above the inventory. Now we studied about the inventory and their types also.

Inventory is defined as a stock or store of goods. These goods are maintained on hand at or near location of a business so that the firm may meet the demand and fulfill its reason for existence. If the firm is a retail establishment, a customer may look elsewhere to have his or her needs which are satisfied if the firm does not have the necessary item in stock when the customer arrives. If the firm is a manufacturer, it must maintain some inventory of raw materials and work-in-process in terms to keep the factory running. In addition, it must maintain some supply of finished goods in order to meet all the demand.

There are four categorized of inventory including raw material, work in-process, finished goods and MRO goods.

1. Raw Materials

Raw materials are inventory items that are used in conversion process of the manufacturer to produce the components, subassemblies, or finished products. These inventory items may be commodities or extracted materials that the firm or its subsidiary has produced or extracted. They also may be objects or elements that the firm has purchased from outside the organization. Even if the item is partially assembled or is considered as a finished good to the supplier, the purchaser may classify it as a raw material if his or her firm had no input into its production. Typically, raw materials are the commodities such as ore, grain, minerals, petroleum, chemicals, paper, wood, paint, steel, and food items. However, items such as nuts and bolts, ball bearings, key stock, casters, seats, wheels, and even engines may be regarded as the raw materials if they are purchased from outside the firm.

The bill-of-materials file in a material requirements planning system (MRP) or a manufacturing resource planning (MRP II) system utilizes a tool which are known as a product structure tree which is used to clarify the relationship among its inventory items and provide a basis for filling out, or "exploding," the master production schedule.

Generally, raw materials are used in the manufacture of components. These components are then incorporated into the final product or become part of a subassembly. Then subassemblies are used to manufacture or assemble the final product. A part that goes into making another part is known as a component, while the part it goes into is known as its parent. Any item that does not have a component is regarded as a raw material or purchased item. From the product structure tree it is apparent that the rolling cart's raw materials are steel, bars, wheels, ball bearings, axles, and caster frames.

Raw materials are inventory items which are used in the formation of components. Raw materials are the initial stage of manufacturing the components.

2. Work-in-Process

Work in process refers to the stage between initial to final. This inventory means the manufacturing of components are in processing. This inventory is abbreviated as WIP.

Work-in-process (WIP) is made up of all the materials, parts or components, assemblies, and subassemblies that are being processed or are waiting to be processed within the system. This is usually includes all material—from raw material that has been released for initial processing up to the material that has been completely processed and is awaiting final inspection and acceptance before inclusion in finished goods.

Any item that has a parent but is not a raw material which is considered to be work-in-process. A glance at the rolling cart product structure tree example reveals that work-in-process in this situation consists of tops, leg assemblies, frames, legs, and casters. Actually, the leg assembly and casters are labeled as subassemblies because the leg assembly consists of legs and casters and the casters are assembled from wheels, ball bearings, axles, and caster frames.

3. Finished Goods

This is the third type of inventory. This stage occurs when raw materials are processed.

Raw materials

Finished goods

work in

process

It is the part which is ready for customer order.

A finished good is a completed or finished part that is ready for a customer order. Therefore, finished goods inventory is the stock of completed products. These goods have been inspected and have passed for final inspection requirements, therefore, they can be transferred out of work-in-process and into finished goods inventory. From this point, finished goods can be sold directly to their final user, sold to retailers, sold to wholesalers, sent to distribution centers, or held in anticipation of a customer order.

Any item that does not have a parent can be classified as a finished good. By looking at the rolling cart product structure tree example one can determine that the finished good in this case is a cart.

Inventories can be further classified according to the purpose they serve. These types of inventory include transit inventory, buffer inventory, anticipation inventory, decoupling inventory, cycle inventory, and MRO goods inventory. Some of these also are know by other names, such as speculative inventory, safety inventory, and seasonal inventory.

Inventories can also categorized according to their aims and objectives by which they serve. These types are described below:-

(a)*Transit Inventory*: This concludes from the requirement of items or materials. It is also known as pipe line inventories.

Transit inventories result from the need to transport items or material from one location to another, and from the fact that there is some transportation time are involved in getting from one location to another. Sometimes this inventory is referred to as pipeline inventory. Merchandise shipped by truck or rail can sometimes take days or even weeks to go from a regional warehouse to a retail facility. Some large firms, such as automobile manufacturers, employ freight consolidators to pool their transit inventories coming from various locations into one shipping source in terms to take the advantage of economies of scale. Of course, this can broadly increase the transit time for these inventories, hence an increase in the size of the inventory in transit.

(b)*Buffer inventory*:- This is a type of inventory which used for safety that's why this is also known as safety stock. This refers to the inventory which are used to protect a company or a business from uncertainties of supply and demand. It increase the level of customer service of a firm as their level is increase.

As previously stated, inventory is sometimes used to protect against the uncertainties of supply and demand, as well as unpredictable events such as poor delivery reliability or poor quality of products of a supplier. These inventory cushions are frequently referred to as safety stock. Safety stock or buffer inventory is any amount which are held on hand that is over and above that currently needed to meet demand. Generally, the higher the level of buffer inventory, the better customer service of the firm. This occurs because of the firm suffers fewer "stock-outs" when a customer's order cannot be immediately filled from existing inventory and has less requirements to backorder the item, make the customer wait until the next order cycle, or even worse, cause the customer to leave empty-handed to find another supplier. Obviously, the better the customer service the greater the likelihood of customer satisfaction.

(c)*Anticipation Inventory*: It is the type of inventory which are used by the retailers, this inventory allow them to build-up the inventory when demands tends to be low, therefore, when demand meets the increased inventory will be slowly depleted and firm doesn't have to react by increasing production time.

Some oftentimes, firms will purchase and hold inventory which is in excess of their current requirements in anticipation of a possible future event. Such events may include a price increase, a seasonal increase in demand, or even an impending labor strike. This trick is usually used by the retailers, who routinely build up inventory months before the demand for their products will be unusually high (i.e., at Halloween, Christmas, or the back-to-school season). For manufacturers, anticipation inventory allows them to build up the inventory when demand is low and also keeping workers busy during slack times therefore, when demand picks up the increased inventory will be slowly depleted and the firm does not have to react by increasing production time along with the subsequent increase in hiring, training, and other associated labor costs. Therefore, the firm has avoided both excessive overtime due to increased demand and hiring costs due to increased demand. It also has avoided layoff costs which are associated with the production cut-backs, or worse, the idling or shutting down of facilities. This process is sometimes called "smoothing" because it smoothes the peaks and valleys in demand, allowing the firm to maintain a constant level of output and a stable workforce.

(d)*Decoupling Inventory*:- This is the inventory which are used by a firm between various stages in its manufacturing system, then is the requirement of less coordination is need to keep the system running smoothly.

Very rarely, if ever, will one see a production facility where every machine in the process produces at exactly the same rate. In fact, one machine may process parts various times faster than the machines in front of or behind it. Yet, if one walks through the plant it may seem that all machines are running smoothly at the same time. It also could be possible that while passing through the plant, one notices the different machines are under repair or are undergoing some form of preventive maintenance. Even so, this does not seem to interrupt the flow of work-in-process through the system. The reason for this is the existence of an inventory of parts between machines, a decoupling inventory that serves as a shock absorber, cushioning the system against production irregularities. As such it "decouples" or disengages the plant's dependence upon the sequential requirements of the system (i.e., one machine feeds parts to the next machine).

The more inventory a firm carries as a decoupling inventory between the various stages in its manufacturing system or even distribution system, the less coordination is required to keep the system running smoothly. Naturally, logic would dictate that an infinite amount of decoupling inventory would not keep the system running in peak form. A balance can be reached that will allow the plant to run relatively smoothly without maintaining an absurd level of inventory. The cost of efficiency must be weighed against the cost of carrying excess inventory, therefore, there is an optimum balance between inventory level and coordination within the system.

(e) *Cycle Inventory*:- This type of inventory are also known as lot size inventory, which includes the concept that the total cost tends to be minimized when two costs are equal, and when lot size decrease increase whenever more orders are required to meet all the value of demands.

Those who are familiar with the concept of economic order quantity (EOQ) know that the EOQ is an attempt to balance the inventory which are holding or carrying costs with the costs incurred from ordering or setting up machinery. When large quantities are ordered or produced, inventory holding costs are increased, but ordering/setup costs decrease. Conversely, when lot sizes decrease, inventory holding/carrying costs decrease, but the cost of ordering/ setup increases since more orders/setups are required to meet demand. When the two costs are equal (holding/carrying costs and ordering/setup costs) the total cost (the sum of the two costs) is minimized. Cycle inventories, sometimes called lot-size inventories which are resulted from this process. Usually, excess material is ordered and, consequently, held in inventory in an effort to reach this minimization point. Hence, cycle inventory results from ordering in batches or lot sizes rather than ordering material strictly as needed.

(f) *Theoretical Inventory*:- it is type of inventory which acts as average inventory from a given throughput which are assuming that no WIP item had to wait in a buffer. It is the inventory where inflow, outflow, processing rates were all equal at any measure of the inventory which represents the minimum inventory which are needed for goods to flow through the system without waiting.

The theoretical inventory is defined as the minimum output of inventory which are necessary to generate a process throughout (R), expressed as:-

Theoretical Inventory = Throughput × Theoretical Flow Time

$$I_{th} = R \times T_{th}$$

In this equation, theoretical flow time equals the sum of all activity times not including wait time need to process one unit. So that, WIP will equal theoretical inventory whenever actual process flow time equals to theoretical flow time.

Inventory exists in various categories as a conclusion of its position in the production process (raw material, work-in-process, and finished goods) and according to the function, that it serves within the system transit inventory, buffer inventory, anticipation inventory, decoupling inventory, cycle inventory, and MRO goods inventory. As such, the purpose of each seems to be that of maintaining a high level of customer service or part of an attempt to minimize the overall consists costs.

4. MRO goods Inventory

This is fourth type of inventory which includes the term maintenance, repair and operating supplies refers to the MRO goods. These three goods are consumed as the conclusion of production process but not the final decision, i.e., finished goods.

Maintenance, repair, and operating supplies, or MRO goods, are items that are used to support and maintain the production process and its infrastructure. These goods are commonly consumed as a result of the production process but are not directly a part of the finished product. Examples of MRO goods include oils, lubricants, coolants, janitorial supplies, uniforms, gloves, packing material, tools, nuts, bolts, screws, shim stock, and key stock. Even office supplies such as staples, pens and pencils, copier paper, and toner are considered part of MRO goods inventory.

EOQ

EOQ stands for economic order quality is the level of inventory that minimize the total inventory which are used for holding costs and ordering costs.

Economic order quantity is the stage of inventory which are used to minimizes the total inventory for holding costs and ordering costs. The framework that are used to determine this order quantity is also known as Wilson EOQ Model. The model was developed by F. W. Harris in 1913. But still R. H. Wilson is given credit for his early in-depth analysis this model.

Various Assumptions of this Model includes

1. The ordering cost is constant.
2. The rate of demand is constant
3. The lead time is fixed

4. The purchase price of the item is constant, i.e., no discount is available
5. The replenishment is made instantaneously, the whole batch is delivered at once.

EOQ is the quantity to order, so that ordering cost + carrying cost finds its minimum. A common misunderstanding is that formula which tries to find when these are equal.

Used Variables

- Q = order quantity
- Q^* = optimal order quantity
- D = annual demand quantity of the product
- P = purchase cost per unit
- C = fixed cost per order (*not* per unit, in addition to unit cost)
- H = annual holding cost per unit (also known as carrying cost) (warehouse space, refrigeration, insurance, etc. usually not related to the unit cost)

Total Cost Function

The single-item EOQ formula finds the minimum point of the following cost function: Total cost refers to the sum of purchase cost, ordering cost and holding. These three costs are described below:-

Total Cost (TC) = purchase cost + ordering cost + holding cost

- Purchase cost: This is the variable cost of goods: purchase unit price (P) × annual demand quantity (D). This is P×D

- Ordering cost: This is the cost of placing orders: each order has a fixed cost C, and we need to order D/Q times per year. This is C × D/Q

- Holding cost: the average quantity in stock (between fully replenished and empty) is Q/2, so this cost is H × Q/2

$$TC = PD + \frac{CD}{Q} + \frac{HQ}{2}.$$

Here, PD refers to purchase cost,
CD/Q refers to the ordering cost, and
HQ/2 refers to the holding costs.

To determine the minimum point of the total cost curve, set its derivative equal to zero:

$$\frac{dTC(Q)}{dQ} = \frac{d}{dQ}\left(PD + \frac{CD}{Q} + \frac{HQ}{2}\right) = 0.$$

Here, d refers to the derivatives

The result of this derivation is:

$$-\frac{CD}{Q^2} + \frac{H}{2} = 0.$$

Solving for Q gives Q* (the optimal order quantity): $\frac{H}{2} = \frac{CD}{Q^2}$

$$Q^2 = \frac{2CD}{H}$$

Therefore: $Q^* = \sqrt{\frac{2CD}{H}}.$

Note that interestingly, Q* is independent of P, it is a function of only C, D, H.

Extensions in EOQ

Several extensions can be made to the EOQ model, including backordering costs and multiple items. Additionally, the ***economic order interval*** can be evaluated from the EOQ and the ***economic production quantity*** model which determines the optimal production quantity that can be used to evaluated in a same manner.

INVENTORY CONTROL SYSTEM

Inventory control system includes the maintenance of information of all the activities which occurs in a firm that ensure the delivering of goods to the customer.

Inventory control systems maintain information about activities within firms that ensure the delivery of products to customers. The subsystems that perform these functions include sales, manufacturing, warehousing, ordering, and receiving. In different firms the activities which are associated with each of these areas may not be strictly contained within separate subsystems, but these functions must be performed in series in terms to have a well-run inventory control system.

In today's business environment, even small and mid-sized businesses have come to rely on computerized inventory management systems. Certainly, there are plenty of small retail outlets, manufacturers, and other businesses that continue to rely on manual means of inventory tracking. Indeed, for some small businesses, like convenience stores, shoe stores, or nurseries, purchase of an electronic inventory tracking system might constitute a wasteful use of financial resources. But for other firms operating in industries that feature the high volume turnover of raw materials and/or finished products, computerized tracking systems that have emerged as a key component of business strategies that are aimed at increasing productivity and maintaining competitiveness. Moreover, the recent development of powerful computer programs are capable of addressing a wide range of record keeping needs that including the inventory management—in one integrated system which have also contributed to the growing popularity of electronic inventory control options.

Given such developments, it is little wonder that business experts commonly cite the inventory management as a vital or necessary element that can spell the difference between success and failure in keenly competitive business of today world.

Future of Inventory Control System

In the latter part of the 1990s, many businesses invested heavily in integrated order and inventory systems that are designed to keep inventories at a minimum and replenish stock quickly. But business owners have a range of system integration options from which to choose and based on their needs and financial liquidity.

At the same time, these integrated systems have increased in popularity, business observers have suggested that "stand-alone" systems are falling into disfavor. A 1996 study by the International Mass Retail Association (IMRA), for example, concluded that stand alone Warehouse Management System (WMS) packages acquired to perform the individual functions will soon become obsolete because they do not integrate well with other systems.

Another development of which small business vendors should be aware is a recent trend wherein powerful retailers ask their suppliers to implement vendor-managed inventory systems. These arrangements place the responsibility for inventory management squarely on the shoulders of the vendors. Under such an agreement, the vendors creates warehouse or point of sale information from the retailer and use that information to make the inventory restocking decisions.

Warehouse Layout and Operation

The key of a firm is to getting productivity gains from inventory management which is placing real-time intelligent information processing in the warehouse.

Real-time processing in the warehouse uses combinations of hardware including material handling and data collection technologies. But according to these executives, the intelligent part of the system is sophisticated software which automates and controls all aspects of warehouse operations.

Another important component of good inventory management is the creation and maintenance of a sensible, effective warehousing design. A well-organized, user-friendly warehouse layout can be of enormous benefit to the small business owners, especially if they are involved in processing large volumes of goods and materials. Conversely, an inefficient warehouse system can cost businesses dearly in order to of efficiency, customer service, and, ultimately, profitability.

Various business utilizes warehouse storage system that can take to help ensure that they get the most out of their facilities. It recommended that companies utilize the various tools which are described below:-

1. *Stock locator database*—"The stock locator database required for proactive decision making will be an adjunct of the inventory file in a state-of-the-art space management system. A running record will be maintained of the stock number, lot number, and number of pallet loads in each storage location. Grid coordinates of the reserve area, including individual rack tier positions, must therefore be established, and the pallet load capacity of all storage locations must be incorporated into the database."

2. *Grid coordinate numbering system*—Warehouse numbering system should be developed in conjunction with the storage layout, and should be user-friendly so that workers can quickly locate currently stocked items and open storage spaces alike.

3. *Communication systems*—Again, this can be a valuable investment if the business's warehouse requirements are significant.

Such facilities frequently utilize fork lift machinery that can be used more effectively if their operators are not required to periodically return to a central assignment area. Current technology makes it possible for the warehouse computer system to interact with terminal displays or other communications devices on the fork lifts themselves. "Task assignment can then be made by visual display or printout, and task completion can be confirmed by scanning, keyboard entry, or voice recognition, " this concept was observed in *Transportation and Distribution.*

4. *Maximization of storage capacity*—Warehouses that adhere to rigid the "storage by incoming lot size" storage arrangements do not always make the best use of their space. Instead, businesses should settle on a strategy that eases the traffic congestion and best eases problems which are associated with ongoing turnover in inventory.

Some companies choose to outsource their warehouse functions. "This allows a company that isn't as confident in running their own warehousing operations to concentrate on their core business and let the experts worry about keeping track of their inventory, This concept Bergin. Third-party inventory control operations can provides all the companies with an array of valuable information that includes the analysis of products and spare parts, evaluations of their time sensitivity, and information on vendors. Of course, businesses weighing whether to outsource such a key component of their operation need to consider the expense of such a course of action, as well as their feelings about relinquishing that level of control.

DISTRESSED INVENTORY

Distressed inventory is the inventory in which the potential of this inventory is to be sold at a regular cost. This is also known as expired stock.

Also known as distressed or expired stock, distressed inventory is the inventory whose potential is to be sold at a normal ***cost*** that has or will soon pass. In some of the industries it could also mean that the stock is or will soon be impossible to sell. Examples of distressed inventory include products that have reached its ***expiry date***, or has reached a date in advance of expiry at which the planned market will no longer purchase it (e.g. 3 months left to expiry), clothing that is defective or out of ***fashion***, and old newspapers or magazines. It also includes the computer or consumer-electronic equipment that is obsolescent or discontinued and whose manufacturer is unable to support it. One current example of distressed inventory is the ***VHS*** format.

INVENTORY CREDIT

Inventory credit is defined as the use of stock or inventory to raise the status of finance of an organization or firm.

Inventory credit refers to the use of stock, or inventory, as ***collateral*** to raise the finance. Where banks may be reluctant to accept the traditional collateral, for example in ***developing countries*** where ***land title*** may be lacking, inventory credit is a potentially the important method of overcoming the financing constraints. Obtaining finance against stocks of a vast variety of products that are held in a ***bonded warehouse*** which is common in much of the world. For example, it is used with parmesan cheese in Italy. Inventory credit on the basis of stored agricultural produce is vastly used in Latin American countries and in some Asian countries. A precondition for such credit is that banks must be confident that the stored product will be available if they need to call on the collateral; this implies the existence of a reliable network of certified warehouses. Banks also face the problems in valuing the inventory. The possibility of sudden falls in commodity prices means that they are generally reluctant to lend more than about 60% of the value of the inventory at the time of the loan.

OBJECTIVE OF INVENTORY MANAGEMENT

Its objective is to minimize the cost of inventory at stock and maximize the wealth of owner of the company or organization.

One of the largest costs to any business is that of inventory or stock at hand. Whether a manufacturer, retailer or distributor, the amount of inventory held directly impacts your bottom line in more number of methods than you can imagine. Having too much cash tied up by not stocking up on items that customers need, can have a major impact on your business.

A product that is in excessive demand is commonly extremely typical to manage. Supplying the right amount of products implies that an accurate demand forecast is essential. This impacts the entire supply chain. A similar situation exists at the warehouse level and even the manufacturer end.

Continuous replenishment in a warehouse can become a mammoth task if consumer response is not studied accurately. To facilitate the efficient consumer response are based on consumer demands, warehouse data, sales forecasts, and inventory planning, it becomes imperative that such companies consider the inventory management seriously. Making accurate demand and supply predictions is an ideal situation that anyone in the supply chain management arena could dream off.

Inventory management can remove the barriers between manufacturer and retailers and establish a closer relationship between them. Ideally inventory management should be easy as the main objective is to reduce all the inventories. If items wanted are not at hand or even if merchandize wanted is reordered frequently, sales will be lost to competitors. Precise control of inventory is a vital ingredient for a successful company.

The 3 main objectives in inventory management are:

- Improved customer service
- Reduced inventory investment
- Increased productivity

Benefits of inventory management applications includes:

- Complete control of inventory.
- Complete information about the value of the inventory
- Complete visibility on Quantities on hand, Quantities committed and Quantities sold
- Increased sales
- Frequent analysis of purchases, sales and inventory records.
- Knowledge of the exact size of merchandizing inventory
- Response time to demand changes reduced
- Removal of unnecessary use of warehouse space used by unneeded part of inventory.
- Reduction in excess merchandize stock.
- Taxes and insurance premiums paid on excess merchandize inventory avoided.

- By providing timely accurate information pertaining to inventory location, movement and valuation, receipt of goods, sale and return of goods and profits you can make sure that your inventory is visible throughout a network.

Above paragraph shows the all benefits and objectives of inventory management.

IMPORTANCE OF INVENTORY MANAGEMENT

Inventory management is a very simple concept that don't have too much and too little stock. Since there can be substantial costs that are involved in straying above and below the optimal range, careful inventory management that can make a huge difference in the profitability of a business. Although the concept is simple, the process of getting the right balance can be quite a complex and time consuming process without the right technology.

This topic includes all the reasons by which we known the importance of inventory management.

Finished Goods Inventory

Amount of manufactured product on hand that awaits the sale to customers. Finished goods inventory represents a current asset in the balance sheet. The income statement shows both beginning finished goods and ending finished goods only if cost of goods sold is calculated. When goods that were in process are completed, the entry is to debit finished goods and credit work-in-process. When merchandise is sold, the entry is to debit cost of goods sold and credit finished goods. The difference between the sales and cost of goods sold is the gross profit.

We also discussed this topic of finished goods inventory previously in this chapter. Finished goods inventory is the stage where the raw materials are work in process, after the processing of raw materials, finished goods occurred.

Inventory Analysis

Inventory analysis is the process of understanding the stock/ product mix are combined with the knowledge of the demand for stock/product. It is a method for determining the optimum level of inventory for a firm, it commonly employs one of the two formulas:

(1) Inventory turnover = Cost of goods sold ÷ average inventory.

(2) Number of day's sale in inventory = inventory at the end of an accounting period ÷ average daily cost of goods sold.

Inventory Turnover

Inventory turnover is calculated with the following formula:

Cost of Goods Sold from Stock Sales during the Past 12 Months÷

Average Inventory Investment during the Past 12 Months

There are several things to keep in mind when calculating turnover rates:

1. Only consider cost of goods sold from stock sales which are filled from warehouse inventory. Non-stock items and direct shipments are not included. Sure, these sales are important, but don't involve your warehouse stock (i.e. your investment in inventory).
2. The cost of goods sold figure in the formula includes transfers of stocked products to other branches and quantities of these products that are used for internal purposes such as repairs and assemblies.
3. Inventory turnover is based on the cost of items (what you paid for them) not sales dollars (what you sold them for).

The Inventory Turnover is an equation that equals the cost of goods sold divided by the average inventory. Increased turnover can be just as dangerous as reduced turnover if the business does not have the working capital to support the turnover increase. As turnover increases more working capital and cash is required and if not, overtrading occurs.

Inventory turnover depends on the average value of stocked inventory. To evaluated the average inventory investment:

1. Calculate the total value of every product in inventory (quantity on-hand times cost) every month, on the same day of the month. Be sure to be consistent in using the same cost basis (average cost, last cost, replacement cost, etc.) in calculating both the cost of goods sold and average inventory investment.
2. If your inventory levels tends to fluctuate throughout the month, calculate your total inventory value on the first and fifteenth of every month.

3. Determine the average inventory value by averaging of all of the inventory valuations which are recorded during the past 12 months.

Average inventory equals to the beginning inventory plus ending inventory divided by 2.

TECHNIQUES OF INVENTORY MANAGEMENT

There are two techniques naming economic purchase order quantities and ABC analysis.

1) Economic Purchase Order Quantities: In order to control inventory a decision model has been developed to determine the optimum quantity of materials to be purchased on each purchase order. The model determines the optimum working stock level to be maintained. Each time a purchase order is placed, the company incurs certain costs. In order to minimize the costs of placing purchase orders, the company could increase the order quantity to meet the company's entire needs for the year at one time, incurring only the cost of one purchase order. However, such a practice will lead to having a large average inventory of working stock, resulting in increased carrying costs. The costs of ordering and costs of carrying inventory may be summarized as follows:

Cost of Ordering

- Preparing purchase or production orders, receiving and preparing and processing related documents.

- Incremental costs of purchasing or transportation for frequent orders (Purchase in small lots is often costlier and transportation costs also increase)

- Out of pocket costs of postage, telephones, telegrams, cost of stationery, traveling etc.

- Extra costs of numerous small production runs, overtime, setups, training etc. In addition- fixed costs in form of salaries, wages of employees connected with this work in purchasing, receiving, inspection and Material handling Departments.

Costs of Carrying

- Interest on Investment.

- Losses from obsolescence and deterioration, spoilage.

- Storage-space costs, including Rent, Rates, Taxes, Electricity, etc.

- Insurance, in addition- fixed costs in form of salaries, wages etc of employees connected with this work in stores and Material handling Departments.

It should be noted that in the consideration of the optimum inventory decision, the costs of buying the inventory would usually be irrelevant, because it is assumed that the quantity required for the year would be the same for various alternative. The important relevant costs to be considered are the costs of ordering and the costs of carrying.

2) ABC Analysis:- ABC analysis is a business term used to define an inventory categorized techniques which are frequently used in materials management.

ABC analysis provides a mechanism for identifying items which will have a significant impact on overall inventory cost whilst also providing a mechanism for identifying various categories of stock that will needs different management and controls. When carrying out an ABC analysis, inventory items are valued (items caused multiplied by quantity issued/consumed in period) with the conclusion then ranked. The result are then grouped typically into three bands. These bands are called ABC codes. ABC analysis stands for activity based costing.

Not all stock is equally valuable and therefore doesn't require the same management focus. The results of the ABC analysis provide information that helps evaluate how each inventory part should be monitored and controlled. These controls are typically:Not all stock is equally valuable and therefore doesn't require the same management focus. The results of the ABC analysis provide information that helps evaluate how each inventory part should be monitored and controlled. These controls are typically:

A class items which are critically important and require close monitoring and tight control – while this may account for large value these will typically comprise a small percentage of the overall inventory count. This class accounts 80% of total value and 20% of total items.A class items which are critically important and require close monitoring and tight control – while this may account for large value these will typically comprise a small percentage of the overall inventory count.

B class are of lower criticality requiring standard controls and periodic reviews of usage. This class account 15% of total value and

3% of total items.B class are of lower criticality requiring standard controls and periodic reviews of usage.

C class require the least controls, are sometimes issues as "free stock" or forward holding. This class accounts 5% of remaining or 50% of total items.C class require the least controls, are sometimes issues as freestock or forward holding.

In summary, ABC Analysis is the basis for material management processes and helps to define how stock is managed. It can form the basis of various activity including leading plans on alternative stocking arrangements (consignment stock), reorder calculations and can help determine at what intervals inventory checks are carried out (for example A class items may be required to be checked more frequently than c class stores.In summary, ABC Analysis is the basis for material management processes and helps define how stock is managed. It can form the basis of various activity including leading plans on alternative stocking arrangements (consignment stock), reorder calculations and can help determine at what intervals inventory checks are carried out (for example A class items may be required to be checked more frequently than c class stores.

It is a basic supply chain techniques frequently carried out by inventory controllers/materials managers, and is the starting point in inventory control.

A system of categcrization, with similarities to Pareto analysis, the method usually categorizes inventory into three bands with each band having a different management control associated. Although different criteria may be applied to each category the typical method of "scoring" an inventory item is that of annual consumption value of said item (qty consumed X cost of item) with the result then ranked and then scored (A, B or C).

HOW TO IMPROVE INVENTORY TURNOVER

First, take an end-to-end view in addressing inventory. You need to optimize your supply chain, make your production processes lean, and optimize your relationship to your customers. When you solve the inventory turnover issue correctly from a Lean perspective, everyone benefits in real terms. Your supplier is enabled to produce and deliver materials in a timely, low cost fashion that allows you to minimize your inventory and cost of materials while elevating your supplier's competitiveness as a business. When you establish partnering relationships with your customers, you can enable them to make their demand for products more predictable thereby allowing you to minimize finished product inventory without failing to meet their needs for volume and timeliness.

Second, perfect your value stream operation by following the precepts of Lean. Define value from your customer's perspective, map your value stream, flow the process, establish pull by the customer, and perfect all operations by eliminating waste from the value stream. These steps shrink lead-time, minimize inventory at every point, and drive wastage out. Margins improve, not shrink, as unit cost is reduced. If you follow these guidelines, your improvements in inventory turnover will truly reflect efficient management and the emergence of a Lean enterprise.

TECHNIQUES OF INVENTORY CONTROL

These are the techniques which are developed to maintain the inventory as small as possible in consistent with production schedule and marketing forecast.

There are basically three aspects through which these techniques were framed.

1. Number of variety of items (variety reduction)
2. control of quantities of various items.
3. Cost of each item.

Case Study

Note : knowing more about "Inventory Management" reader can study documentation process of Microsoft company by visiting their site : www.members.microsoft.com

http://www.management-hub.com/inventorymanagement35im.html

http://www.sixsigmasystems.com/case_studies.htm

http://www.inventorymanagementreview.org/2005/09/dell_computers_.html

http://www.icmrindia.org/casestudies/Management.asp?area=Inventory%20Management

http://www.i2.com/solutions/tim/customer_results.cfm

http://www.essays.se/about/Inventory+management+case+study/

10

Product Process Strategy

This chapter includes the key concepts which are shown below:-

- Product
- Product Groups
- National and International Product Classifications
- Production Function
- Stages of Production
- Economies of Scale
- Product Management
- Aspects of Product Management
- Product Life Cycle
- Product Life Cycle Management
- Diffusion of Product Life Cycle Management
- Technology Acceptance Model
- Product development
- Product Data Management
- Product Catalogue Management
- Production Management
- Process Capture Technology
- Manufacturing Operations Management
- Production Scheduling
- Advanced Planning and Scheduling
- Service Product Management

PRODUCT

Product is a term which refers to the thing produced by labor or effort or the result of an act or a process.

In marketing, a product is anything that can be offered to a market that might satisfy a want or need. In retailing, products are called merchandise. In manufacturing, products are purchased as raw materials and sold as finished goods. Commodities are generally raw materials such as metals and agricultural products, but a commodity can also be anything which are widely available in the open market. In project management, products are the formal definition of the project deliverables that make up or contribute to delivering the objectives of the project.

In general usage, product may refer to a single item or unit, a group of equivalent products, a grouping of goods or services, or an industrial classification for the goods or services.

Product is also refer to a single unit as well as group of equivalent product. Product are of raw materials as well as finished goods.

Equivalent or Interchangeable Product

The specific meaning of generic product names varies over time and location. It can be defined as anything that can offer to a market for attention, acquisition. Some products such as bread, milk, and salt have been bartered or sold for centuries, but the meaning of "bread" or "milk" as a product varies. The technologies were not available for pasteurization and homogenization of milk until the 20th century, and these food processing technologies are not used worldwide. Bread varies by type of grain, specific recipe, and size of loaf. In 1924, Morton Salt introduced the iodized table salt, a product previously unavailable. Since 1961, pork bellies have traded on the Chicago Mercantile Exchange, but due to selective breeding and changes in hog feed, today's pork belly is not exactly equivalent to a 1960s pork belly. Some products may be considered equivalent or interchangeable for the purposes of trade, record-keeping, and reporting, despite gradual changes in the product or variations among geographical locations.

Products numbers in many business clearly identify the product by linking to a full description. Each product have their own barcodes number by which we can easily find out the price of that product by using computerized programming.

The distinction between a new product and a minor modification to an existing product is not always clear. Some products have a product life cycle in which the supply and demand for the product increases then decreases over time. The demand for some food products such as bread will tend to increase with population, but the supply and demand for a specific brand of bread may decline over time. In the United States, a patent for a product is recognition that the product is new in a legal sense. "Utility patents may be granted to anyone who invents or discovers any new and useful process, machine, article of manufacture, or composition of matter, or any new and useful improvement thereof; design patents may be granted to anyone who invents a new, original, and ornamental design for an article of manufacture; and, plant patents may be granted to anyone who invents or discovers and asexually reproduces any distinct and new variety of plant." In business an equivalent, interchangeable or fungible product is defined by a company and its customers. A inventory of company is a set of physical products, or goods, that are usually recorded as counts of equivalent unique products, such as 50 8-oz cans of salsa. The equivalent unique products may be assigned a product code or item code, such that "50 8-oz cans of salsa" is recorded as "50 17766443" on the company's records. If the company carries two brands of 8-oz salsa, it may assign the separate item codes to the brands, or it may use a single item code for both brands.

Product identification codes such as Universal Product Code, Global Trade Item Number and International Standard Book Number allow multiple businesses to use a single product identification code to indicate one unit of a mass-produced product.

Lots or Batches

Lot numbers, batch numbers or control numbers are used in manufacturing to sub-divide the equivalent product by its manufacturing batch or run. The publishing page of a book lists the printing run that produced that unique book. Industries such as pharmaceuticals, food processing, and petroleum use certain form of control number to sub-divide the equivalent product for product testing or expiration dating. Two separate lots may vary slightly, but they are not assigned the separate product identification codes because the variation does not give them significantly various features or uses as products.

Barcode labels on vaccines in the UK contain a product code but do not currently contain the batch number or expiry date. Inventory records of controlled substances in the United States must include a "batch number or other appropriate identifying number".

PRODUCT GROUPS

Product is categorized into three groups naming categorizes, sizes and color and product line. Categories are used to defined the function as well as brand. Sizes and color are defined especially for clothes and product line is a group of products that are closely related.

Categories

In its online product catalogue, retailer Sears, Roebuck and Company divides its products into departments, then presents the products to shoppers according to (1) function or (2) brand. Each product has a Sears item number and model number of a manufacturer. The departments and product groupings that Sears uses are intended to help customers to browse products by function or brand within a traditional department or store structure.

Sizes and Colors

A catalog number is used especially for clothing that may group sizes and colors. When ordering the product, the customer specifies size, color and other variables. example: you walk into a store and see a group of shoes and in that group are sections of different colors of that type of shoe and sizes for that shoe to satisfy your need.

Product line

A product line is "a group of products that are closely related, either because they function in a similar way that, are sold to the same customer groups, are marketed through the same types of outlets, or fall within given price ranges."

Many businesses offer a variety of product lines which may be unique to a single organization or may be common across the business's industry. In 2002 the US Census compiled revenue figures for the finance and insurance industry by various product lines such as "accident, health and medical insurance premiums" and "income from secured consumer loans". Within the insurance industry, product lines are indicated by the type of risk coverage, such as auto insurance, commercial insurance and life insurance.

There are the propertied of a product by which a customer, retailers and manufacturers achieve the information about the product.

NATIONAL AND INTERNATIONAL PRODUCT CLASSIFICATIONS

Several classification systems for products have been developed for economic statistical purposes. The North American Industry Classification System (NAICS) classifies the companies by their primary product. The European Union uses a "Classification of Products by Activity" among other product classifications. The United Nations also classifies the products for international economic activity reporting.

The Aspinwall Classification System classifies and rates the products which are mainly based on five variables:

1. Replacement rate (How frequently is the product repurchased?)
2. Gross margin (How much profit is obtained from each product?)
3. Buyer goal adjustment (How flexible are the buyers' purchasing habits with regard to this product?)
4. Duration of product satisfaction (How long will the product produce benefits for the user?)
5. Duration of buyer search behaviour (How long will consumers shop for the product?)

The National Institute of Governmental Purchasing (NIGP) developed a commodity and services classification system for use by state and local governments, the NIGP Code. The NIGP Code is used by 33 states within the United States as well as thousands of cities, counties and political subdivisions. The NIGP Code is a hierarchical schema consisting of a 3 digit class, 5 digit class-item, 7 digit class-item-group and an 11 digit class-item-group-detail. Applications of the NIGP Code include vendor registration, inventory item identification, contract item management, spend analysis and strategic sourcing.

These above are the classification of product at national and international level.

PRODUCTION FUNCTION

Here, function refers to the processing and working either it is product or their production.

A Production function is a function that specifies the output of a firm, an industry, or an entire economy for all combinations of inputs. A meta-production function compares the practice of the existing entities converting inputs X into output y to evaluate the most efficient practice production function of the existing entities, whether the most efficient feasible practice production or the most efficient actual practice production. In either case, the maximum output of a technologically-determined production process is a mathematical function of input factors of production. Put another method which are given the set of all technically feasible combinations of output and inputs, only the combinations which are encompassing a maximum output for a specified set of inputs would constitute the production function. Alternatively, a production function can be defined as the specification of the minimum input requirements which are needed to produce the designated quantities of output, given available technology. It is generally presumed that unique production functions can be constructed for every production technology.

By assuming that the maximum output technologically possible from a given set of inputs is achieved, economists using a production function in analysis are abstracting away from the engineering and managerial problems inherently that are associated with a specific production process. The engineering and managerial problems of technical efficiency are assumed to be solved, therefore, the analysis can focus on the problems of allocative efficiency. The firm is assumed to be making allocative choices that are concerning how much of each input factor to use, given the price of the factor and the technological determinants are represented by the production function. A decision frame, in which one or more inputs are held constant, may be used; for example, capital may be assumed to be fixed or constant in the short run, and only labour variable, while in the long run, both capital and labour factors are variable, but the production function itself remains fixed, while in the very long run, the firm may face even a choice of technologies, represented by various, possible production functions.

The primary purpose of the production function is to address allocative efficiency in the use of factor inputs in production and the resulting distribution of income to those factors. Under some assumptions, the production function can be used to derive a marginal product for each factor, which implies an ideal division of the income generated from output into an income due to each input factor of production.

Production Function as an Equation

There are various methods of specifying the production function.

In a general mathematical form, a production function can be expressed as:

$Q = f(X1,X2,X3,...,Xn)$

where:

Q = quantity of output

X1,X2,X3,...,Xn = factor inputs (such as capital, labour, land or raw materials). This general form does not encompass joint production, that is a production process, which has multiple co-products or outputs. Here, if refers to the function

One method of specifying a production function is simply as a table of discrete outputs and input combinations, and not as a formula or equation at all. Using an equation generally implies the continual variation of output with minute variation in inputs, which is simply not realistic. Fixed ratios of factors, as in the case of laborers and their tools, might imply that only discrete input combinations, and therefore, discrete maximum outputs, are of practical interest.

One formulation is as a linear function:

$Q = a + bX1 + cX2 + dX3,...$

where a,b,c, and d are parameters that are determined empirically and X1, X2, Xn are the factor inputs.

Another is as a Cobb-Douglas production function called multiplicative:

Other forms include the constant elasticity of substitution production function (CES) which is the generalized form of the Cobb-Douglas function, and the quadratic production function which is a particular type of additive function. The perfect form of the equation to use and the values of the parameters (a,b,c, and d) change from company to company and industry to industry. In a short run production function, at least one of the X's (inputs) is fixed. In the long run, all factor inputs are variable at the discretion of management.

STAGES OF PRODUCTION

To simplify the interpretation of a production function, it is common to divide its range into 3 stages. In Stage 1 the variable input is being used with increasing efficiency, reaching a maximum point (since the average physical product is at its maximum at that point). The average physical product of fixed inputs will also be rising in this stage. Because the efficiency of both fixed and variable inputs is improving throughout the stage 1, a firm will always try to operate beyond this stage. In stage 1, fixed inputs are underutilized.

In Stage 2, output increases at a decreasing rate, and the average and marginal physical product is declining. However, the average product of fixed inputs is still rising. In this stage, the employment of additional variable inputs increase the efficiency of fixed inputs but decrease the efficiency of variable inputs. The optimum input/output combination will be in stage 2. Maximum production efficiency must fall somewhere in this stage. Note that this does not define the profit maximizing point. It takes no account of prices or demand. If demand for a product is low, the profit maximizing output could be in stage 1 even though the point of optimum efficiency is in stage 2.

In Stage 3, too much variable input is being used relative to the available fixed inputs: variable inputs are over utilized. Both the efficiency of variable inputs and the efficiency of fixed inputs decline through out this stage. At the boundary between stage 2 and stage 3, fixed input is being utilized the most efficiently and short-run output is maximum.

Shifting a Production Function

As noted above, it is possible for the profit maximizing output level to occur in any of the three stages. If profit maximization occurs in either stage 1 or stage 3, the firm will be operating at a technically inefficient point on its production function. In the short run it can try to alter demand by varying the price of the output or adjusting the level of promotional expenditure. In the long run, the firm has more options that are available to it, most notably, adjusting its production processes so they better match the characteristics of demand. This commonly involves changing the scale of operations by adjusting the level of fixed inputs. If fixed inputs are lumpy, adjustments to the scale of operations may be more significant than what is required to merely balance production capacity with demand. For example, you may only need to increase the production by a million units per year to keep up with demand, but the production equipment upgrades that are available may involve increasing production by 2 million units per year.

If a firm is operating (inefficiently) at a profit maximizing level in stage one, it might, in the long run, choose to reduce its scale of operations (by selling capital equipment). By reducing the amount of fixed capital inputs, the production function will shift down and to the left. The beginning of stage 2 shifts from B1 to B2. The (unchanged) profit maximizing output level will now be in stage 2 and the firm will be operating more efficiently.

If a firm is operating (inefficiently) at a profit maximizing level in stage three, it might, in the long run, choose to increase its scale of operations (by investing in new capital equipment). By increasing the amount of fixed capital inputs, the production function will shift up and to the right.

Classes of Production Function

There are two types classes of production functions that are ofently mentioned. Production function refers to Q = f (X1,X2) is said to be homogeneous of degree n, if given any positive constant k, f(kX1,kX2) = knf(X1,X2). When n > 1, the function exhibits increasing returns, and decreasing returns when n < 1. When it is homogeneous of degree 1, it exhibits the constant returns. Homothetic functions are functions whose marginal technical rate of substitution (slope of the isoquant) is homogeneous of degree zero. Because of this, along rays coming from the origin, the slope of the isoquants will be the same.

These two classes are homogeneous and homothetic production functions.

Diminishing Returns of Product

Diminishing returns can be categorized into three categories:

1. *Diminishing Total returns*, which implies the reduction in total product with every additional unit of input.

2. *Diminishing Average returns*, which refers to the portion of the APP curve after its intersection with MPP curve.
3. *Diminishing Marginal returns,* refers to the point where the MPP curve starts to slope down and travels all the way down to the x-axis and beyond. Putting it in a chronological order, at first the marginal returns start to diminish, then the average returns, followed finally by the total returns

ECONOMIES OF SCALE

This topic is already described in chapter 12 constraint management. But there is also some description in this chapter.

The confusion between the practical concept of economies of scale and the theoretical notion of returns to scale occurs from the fact that large fixed costs, such as occur from investment in a factory or from research and development, are an important source of real world economies of scale. In conventional microeconomic theory, there can be no increasing returns to scale when there are fixed costs, since this refers to at least one input that cannot be increased.

A natural monopoly is frequently defined as a firm which enjoys the economies of scale for all reasonable firm sizes; because it is always more efficient for one firm to expand than for new firms to be established, the natural monopoly has no competition. Because it has no competition, it is likely the monopoly has significant market power. Hence, some industries that have been claimed to be characterized by natural monopoly have been regulated or publicly-owned.

Methods of Economies of Scale

There are two typical methods to achieve economies of scale:

1. High fixed cost and constant marginal cost
2. Low or no fixed cost and declining marginal cost

Economies of scale is defined as to the decreased per unit cost as output increases. More clearly defined the initial investment of capital is diffused (spread) over an increasing number of units of output, and so that, the marginal cost of producing a good or service is less than the average total cost per unit (note that this is only in an industry that is experiencing economies of scale).

AFC is an example economies of scale. It stands for average fixed costs.

Economies of scale tends to occur in industries with high capital costs in which those costs can be distributed across a large number of units of production (both in absolute terms and, especially, relative to the size of the market). A common example is a factory. An investment in machinery is made, and one worker, or unit of production, begins to work on the machine and produces few number of goods. If another worker is added to the machine he or she is able to produce an additional amount of goods without adding significantly to the factory's cost of operation of the factory. The amount of goods which are produced grows significantly faster than the plant's cost of operation. Hence, the cost of producing an additional good is less than the good before it, and an economy of scale emerges.

PRODUCT MANAGEMENT

Product Management is an organizational lifecycle function within a company which are dealing with the planning or marketing of a product or products at all stages of the product lifecycle.

Product management (inbound focused) and product marketing (outbound focused) are variate yet complementary efforts with the objective of maximizing sales revenues, market share, and profit margins. The role of product management spans many activities from strategic to tactical and changes are based on the organizational structure of the company. Product management can be a function which are separate on its own or a member of marketing or engineering.

While involved with the entire product lifecycle, main focus of product management is on launching new product development. According to the Product Development and Management Association (PDMA), superior and differentiated new products - ones that deliver unique benefits and superior value to the customer - is the number one driver of success and product profitability.

Product managements generally refers to the inbound focused whereas product marketing refers too the outbound focused.

ASPECTS OF PRODUCT MANAGEMENT

Depending on the company size and history, product management has a range of functions and roles. Sometimes there is a product manager, and sometimes the role of product manager is held by others. Frequently, there is Profit and Loss (P&L) responsibility as a key metric for evaluating the product manager performance. In some companies, the product management function is the hub of many other activities around the product. In others, it is one of many things that need to happen to bring a product to market.

There are various aspects of product management, if defines. Product planning as well as produced marketing.

Product Planning

Following are the aspects of product planning

- Defining new products
- Gathering market requirements
- Building product roadmaps, particularly Technology roadmaps
- Product Life Cycle considerations
- Product differentiation
- more detail on Product planning

Product Marketing

- Product positioning and outbound messaging
- Promoting the product externally with press, customers, and partners
- Bringing new products to market
- Monitoring the competition
- more detail on Product marketing

These above all the aspects of product marketing.

PRODUCT LIFE CYCLE

Product life cycle is abbreviated as PLC. This includes various stages, i.e., from beginning stage to ending stage, where product tends to be maintained.

A product's life cycle (PLC) can be divided into various stages which are characterized by the revenue that are generated by the product. If a curve is drawn showing product revenue over time, it may take one of several shapes, an example of which is shown below:

Product Life Cycle Curve

The life cycle concept may apply to a brand or to a category of product. Its duration may be as short as a few months for a fad item or a century or more for product categories such as the gasoline-powered automobile.

Product development is the incubation stage of the product life cycle. There are no sales and the firm prepares to introduce the product. As the product progresses through its life cycle, changes in the marketing mix generally are required in terms to adjust to the evolving challenges and opportunities.

There are four stage of PLC which includes introduction stage, growth stage of PLC, maturity stage, decline stage of PLC.

Introduction Stage

It is the first stage of PLC in which produce is introduced and sales well be low because of in appropriate information about product towards the point of view of the customers.

When the product is introduced, sales will be low until customers become aware of the product and its benefits. Some firms may announce their product before it is introduced, but such announcements also alert competitors and remove the element of surprise. Advertising costs typically are high during this stage in terms to rapidly increase the customer awareness of the product and to target the early adopters. During the introductory stage the firm is likely to incur the additional costs which are associated with the initial distribution of the product. These higher costs coupled with a low sales volume that are generally make the introduction stage a period of negative profits.

During the introduction stage, the primary goal is to establish a market and build primary demand for the product class. The following are some of the marketing mix implications of the introduction stage:

- Product - one or few products, relatively undifferentiated
- Price - Generally high, assuming a skim pricing strategy for a high profit margin as the early adopters buy the product and the firm seeks to recoup development costs quickly. In some cases a penetration pricing strategy is used and introductory prices are set low to gain market share rapidly.

- Distribution - Distribution is selective and scattered as the firm commences implementation of the distribution plan.
- Promotion - Promotion is aimed at building brand awareness. Samples or trial incentives may be directed toward early adopters. The introductory promotion also is intended to convince potential resellers to carry the product.

Growth Stage of PLC

The growth stage is a period of rapid revenue growth. Sales increase as more customers that become aware of the product and its benefits and additional market segments are targeted. Once the product has been proven a success and customers begin to asking for it, sales will increase further as more retailers become interested in carrying it. The marketing team may expand the distribution at this point. When competitors enter the market, frequently during the later part of the growth stage, there may be price competition and/or increased promotional costs in terms to convince the consumers that the firm's product is better than that of the competition.

During the growth stage, the major objective is to gain consumer preference and increase sales. The marketing mix may be modified as follows:

- Product - New product features and packaging options; improvement of product quality.
- Price - Maintained at a high level if demand is high, or reduced to capture additional customers.
- Distribution - Distribution becomes more intensive. Trade discounts are minimal if resellers show a strong interest in the product.
- Promotion - Increased advertising to build brand preference.

Maturity Stage of PLC

The maturity stage is the most profitable. While sales continue to increase into this stage, they do so at a slower pace. Because brand awareness is strong, advertising expenditures will be reduced. Competition may conclude in decreased market share and/or prices. The competing products may be very similar at this point, increasing the difficulty of differentiating the product. The firm places the effort into encouraging competitors' customers to switch, increasing usage per customer, and converting non-users into customers. Sales promotions may be offered to encourage the retailers to give the product more shelf space over competing products.

During the maturity stage, the primary goal is to maintain market share and extend the product life cycle. Marketing mix decisions may include:

- Product - Modifications are made and features are added in order to differentiate the product from competing products that may have been introduced.
- Price - Possible price reductions in response to competition while avoiding a price war.
- Distribution - New distribution channels and incentives to resellers in order to avoid losing shelf space.
- Promotion - Emphasis on differentiation and building of brand loyalty. Incentives to get competitors' customers to switch.

Decline Stage of Product Life Cycle

Eventually sales begin to decline as the market that becomes saturated, the product becomes technologically obsolete, or customer tastes the change. If the product has developed brand loyalty, the profitability may be maintained longer. Unit costs may increase with the declining the production volumes and eventually no more profit can be made.

During the phase, the firm generally has three options:

- Maintain the product in hopes that competitors will exit.
- Harvest it, reducing marketing support and coasting along until no more profit can be made.
- Discontinue the product when no more profit can be made or there is a successor product.

The marketing mix may be modified as follows:

- Product - The number of products in the product line may be reduced. Rejuvenate surviving products to make them look new again.
- Price - Prices may be lowered to liquidate inventory of discontinued products. Prices may be maintained for continued products serving a niche market.
- Distribution - Distribution becomes more selective. Channels that no longer are profitable are phased out.

- Promotion - Expenditures are lower and aimed at reinforcing the brand image for continued products.

PRODUCT LIFE CYCLE MANAGEMENT

Product Life Cycle Management is the succession of strategies which are used by management as a product goes through its product life cycle. The conditions in which a product is sold changes over time and must be managed as it moves through its succession of stages. There are two stages naming.

Request for Deviation

In the process of building a product following defined procedure, an RFD is a request for authorization, granted prior to the manufacture of an item, to depart from a specific performance or design requirement of a specification, drawing or other document, for a specific number of units or a specific period of time.

This stage is abbreviated as RFD which refers to the request for authorization which are granted to the manufacturing of product.

Market Identification

A "micro-market" can be used to describe a Walkman, more portable, as well as individually and privately recordable; and then Compact Discs brought increased capacity and CD-R which are offered individual private recording and so the process goes. The below section on the "technology lifecycle" is a most appropriate concept in this context. Most of the context is not in English so you may need a translator.

In short, termination is not always the end of the cycle; it can be the end of a micro-entrant within the grander scope of a macro-environment. The auto industry, fast-food industry, petro-chemical industry, are just a few that demonstrate a macro-environment that overall has not terminated even while micro-entrants over time have come and gone.

DIFFUSION OF PRODUCT LIFE CYCLE MANAGEMENT

Diffusion means the distribution. It is the distribution of new idea into the market. Diffusion is the process by which a new idea or new product is accepted by the market. The rate of diffusion is the speed that the new idea spreads from one consumer to the next. Adoption is similar to diffusion except that it deals with the psychological processes an individual goes through, rather than an aggregate market process. In economics it is more often named "technological change".

Theories of Diffusion

There are various theories that purport to explain the mechanics of diffusion:

1. The two-step hypothesis includes information and acceptance flows, via the media, first to opinion leaders, then to the general population
2. the trickle-down effect - products tend to be expensive at first, and so that only accessible to the wealthy social strata - in time they become less expensive and are diffussed to lower and lower strata
3. The Everett Rogers Diffusion of innovations theory - for any given product category, there are five categories of product adopters:
   - Innovators - venturesome, educated, multiple info sources;
   - Early adopters - social leaders, popular, educated;
   - Early majority - deliberate, many informal social contacts;
   - Late majority - skeptical, traditional, lower socio-economic status;
   - Laggards - neighbours and friends are main info sources, fear of debt.
4. Crossing the Chasm model developed by Geoffrey Moore - This is generally a modification of Everett Rogers' theory applied to technology markets and with a chasm added. According to Moore, the marketer should focus on one group of customers at a time, using each group as a base for marketing to the next group. The most difficult step is making the transition between visionaries (early adopters) and pragmatists (early majority). This is the chasm that he refers to. If successful, a firm can create a bandwagon effect in which the momentum builds and the product becomes a de facto standard.

5. Technology driven models - These are particularly relevant to software diffusion. The rate of acceptance of technology is determined by factors such as ease of use and usefulness.

Rate of Diffusion

According to Everett M. Rogers, the rate of diffusion is influenced by:

- Extent of behavioural changes required.
- Ease of product use - complexity of the product.
- Immediacy of benefits.
- Observability.
- Price.
- Riskiness of purchase.
- Return on investment in the case of industrial products.
- The perceived advantage or benefit of the product.
- Trialability.

Models of Diffusion

There are several types of models of diffusion:

1. Penetration models - use the test market data to develop the acceptance equations of expected sales volume as a function of time. Three examples of penetration models are:
   - Bass trial only model
   - Bass declining trial model
   - Fourt and Woodlock model
2. Trial/Repeat models refers to the number of repeat buyers is a function of the number of trial buyers.
3. Deterministic models defined as assess number of buyers at various states of acceptance - later states are determined from calculations to previous states.
4. Stochastic models used to recognize that many elements of the diffusion process are unknown but explicitly incorporate probabilistic terms.

TECHNOLOGY ACCEPTANCE MODEL

This model is abbreviated as TAM. It is system theory model which is used to know that how users come to accept and use a specific technology.

The Technology Acceptance Model (TAM) is an information systems theory that models how users come to accept and use a technology. The model suggests that when users are presented with a new technology, a number of factors influence their decision about how and when they will use it, notably:

- Perceived usefulness (PU) - This was defined by Fred Davis as "the degree to which a person believes that using a specific system that would enhance his or her job performance".
- Perceived ease-of-use (PEOU) - Davis defined this as "the degree to which a person believes that using a particular system would be free from effort" (Davis, 1989).

PRODUCT DEVELOPMENT

In business and engineering, new product development (NPD) is the term which are used to describe the complete process of bringing a new product or service to market. There are two parallel paths that involved in the NPD process: one involves the idea generation, product design, and detail engineering; the other involves market research and marketing analysis. Companies typically see new product development as the first stage in generating and commercializing new products within the overall strategic process of product life cycle management used to maintain or grow their market share.

There are two ways which are used to describe the complete process of bringing a new product into the market. First way includes the idea generating product design and detail engineering, second methods includes the market research and marketing analysis.

Process is defined as the way to do accomplish a particular task with various methods.

Process

1. Idea Generation is frequently called the "fuzzy front end" of the NPD process

- Ideas for new products can be obtained from basic research using a SWOT analysis . Market and consumer trends, company's R&D department, competitors, focus groups, employees, salespeople, corporate spies, trade shows, or Ethnographic discovery methods may also be used to get an insight into new product lines or product features.
- Idea Generation or Brainstorming of new product, service, or store concepts - idea generation techniques can begin when you have done your OPPORTUNITY ANALYSIS to support your ideas in the Idea Screening Phase.

2. Idea Screening
   - The object is to eliminate unsound concepts prior to devoting resources to them.
   - The screeners must ask at least three questions:
     - Will the customer in the target market benefit from the product?
     - What is the size and growth forecasts of the market segment/target market?
     - What is the current or expected competitive pressure for the product idea?
     - What are the industry sales and market trends the product idea is based on?
     - Is it technically feasible to manufacture the product?
     - Will the product be profitable when manufactured and delivered to the customer at the target price?
3. Concept Development and Testing
   - Develop the marketing and engineering details
     - Who is the target market and who is the decision maker in the purchasing process?
     - What product features must the product incorporate?
     - What benefits will the product provide?
     - How will consumers react to the product?
     - How will the product be produced most cost effectively?
     - Prove feasibility through virtual computer aided rendering, and rapid prototyping

- What will it cost to produce it?

o Testing the Concept by asking a sample of prospective customers what they think of the idea. Usually via Choice Modelling.

4. Business Analysis

o Estimate likely selling price based upon competition and customer feedback

o Estimate sales volume based upon size of market and such tools as the Fourt-Woodlock equation equation

o Estimate profitability and breakeven point

5. Beta Testing and Market Testing

o Produce a physical prototype or mock-up

o Test the product in typical usage situations

o Conduct focus group customer interviews or introduce at trade show

o Make adjustments where necessary

o Produce an initial run of the product and sell it in a test market area to determine customer acceptance

6. Technical Implementation

o New program initiation

o Resource estimation

o Requirement publication

o Engineering operations planning

o Department scheduling

o Supplier collaboration

o Logistics plan

o Resource plan publication

o Program review and monitoring

o Contingencies - what-if planning

7. Commercialization

o Launch the product

- o Produce and place advertisements and other promotions
- o Fill the distribution pipeline with product
- o Critical path analysis is most useful at this stage

these step may iterated means repeated whenever the task completed. Some steps may be eliminated.

To reduce the time that the NPD process, many companies are completing various steps at that time.

Because the NPD process typically needs both engineering and marketing expertise, cross-functional teams are a common method of organizing projects. The team is responsible for all aspects of the project, from initial idea generation to final commercialization, and they generally report to senior management. In those industries where products are technically complex, development research is typically expensive, and product life cycles are relatively short, strategic alliances among various organizations which helps to spread the costs, provide access to a wider skill set, and speeds the overall process.

Also, notice that because engineering and marketing expertise are commonly both critical to the process, choosing a blend of the two is important.

People respond to new products in different ways. The adoption of a new technology can be analyzed using a variety of diffusion theories such as the Diffusion of innovations theory.

PRODUCT DATA MANAGEMENT

This is also abbreviated as PDM, with in the PDM, the main focus is an managing and tracking the creation, change and achieve of all information that are related to the product.

Product Data Management (PDM) is the business function within product lifecycle management that is responsible for the creation, management and publication of product data. Product data management (PDM) is the use of software or other tools to track and control the data which are related to a specific product. The data tracked generally involves the technical specifications of the product, specifications for manufacture and development, and the types of materials that will be required to produce the good. The use of product data management allows a company to track the different costs that are associated with the creation and launch of a product. Product data management is part of product life cycle management, and is primarily used by engineers.

Product data management (PDM) serves as a central knowledge repository for process and product history, and promotes integration and data exchange among all business users who interact with products which includes project managers, engineers, sales people, buyers, and quality assurance teams.

Product data management is focused on capturing and maintaining information on products and/or services through its development and useful life. Typical information managed in the PDM module include

- Part number
- Part description
- Supplier/vendor
- Vendor part number and description
- Unit of measure
- Cost/price
- Schematic or CAD drawing
- Material data sheets

Advantages of PDM:

- Track and manage all changes to product related data
- Accelerate return on investment with easy setup;
- Spend less time organizing and tracking design data;
- Improve productivity through reuse of product design data;
- Enhance collaboration.

Capabilities of PDM

There are various capabilities of PDM which includes the following:-

1. Access control
2. Engineering changes
3. Component/material classification
4. Collaboration

5. Product structure
6. Process management and workflow

(1) Access control—Access control to each element in the product definition data base can be specified. Read only access can be given to personnel not directly involved with the design, development and planning process. Creation and maintenance access can be given to the individuals that are responsible for product and process design. As Product Data Management systems evolve towards Collaborative Product Commerce (CPC) systems which are used across multiple enterprises in a supply chain, access control becomes more critical and requires control to limit access to particular projects, products or parts for a specific supplier or customer.

Access control is the ability to permit or deny the use of a specific resource by a particular entity. Access control process can be used in managing physical resources (such as a movie theater, to which only ticket holders should be admitted), logical resources (a bank account, with a limited number of people authorized to make a withdrawal), or digital resources (for example, a private text document on a computer, which only certain users should be able to read).

(2) Engineering Changes—Engineering changes can be facilitated with this configuration management and administrative control which are embedded within the system. CAE/ CAD tools will enable engineering changes to be more thoroughly developed and analyzed to better define change impact. Once a design has been created, it can be checked-out electronically to a workstation for engineering changes. When the changes have been made, it can be returned to the central database and placed in a queue or an email notification sent for approval by designated parties. In this manner, a Change Control Board (CCB) can even "convene" and provide individual member's input electronically. In addition to supporting engineering analysis, information related to procurement, inventory, manufacturing and cost is available for members of the CCB to evaluate, designate the effectivity of the change and determine the disposition of existing items.

(3) Component / Material Classificatio—Components and materials can be classified and organized and attributes assigned. This supports the standardization by identifying similar components/ materials, eliminating redundancy, and establishing a preferred parts list. Establishing classes and subclasses with attributes allows a designer to search and select a needed material, component or assembly with minimal effort thereby avoiding having to re-specifying an existing or similar component or material

(4) Collaboration—Collaboration can be supported in various manners. First, a PDM system may be the gateway that a team uses to access the information under the discussion avoiding the need to copy and distribute a series of paper documents. Second, the PDM system may provide a synchronous or asynchronous collaboration environment for team members to access, present, review and product feedback on product and process information. Further, this collaboration tool that may incorporate a view and mark-up capability and the provide the ability to store marked-up files or documents by collaborator. Third, what are now described as collaborative product commerce systems (CPC), provide extended PDM functionality and access control outside the enterprise for customers, suppliers and interested third parties (e.g., regulatory agencies). This increase the distribution of information, enhances coordination, and speeds the capture of feedback.

- Storage and retrieval of product information
- Product structure modeling and management
  - Bills of material
  - Product configurations
  - Product variations
  - Product versions
- Project tracking
- Resource planning

(5) Product Structure—Since the relationship of parts of product is a logical one maintained by the information system rather than a fixed physical relationship as represented on a drawing, it is possible to readily maintain more than one relationship. This will allow several views of part relationships in assemblies to correspond to the various departmental needs (e.g., engineering and manufacturing product structures), while maintaining rigor and consistency of the product's definition through this single data base. Thus, this one logical data base can support product and process design requirements as well as maintain part relationships to serve as a manufacturing bill of materials for MRP II/ERP. In other words, PDM provides the ability to hold not just the physical relationships between parts in an assembly but also other kinds of structures; for instance, manufacturing, financial, maintenance or document relationships. So, it is possible for specialist team members to see the product structured from their point of view. Product data can be accessed via this complete Bill of Materials. This access includes assemblies, parts and related documents.An integrated approach to developing, organizing and maintaining part and product definition data facilitates the design process, makes design data more readily usable and enhances integration with process requirements

(6) Process Management and Workflow—PDM systems support that process management by defining process steps that are related to the development, distribution and use of product data. The process is defined in the form of specified process steps and release or promotion levels that the data must achieve. The way in which the process is defined varies with every PDM system. Within a project, responsibilities are defined for the process steps - who needs to approve the data or work on the data before it moves to the next release or promotion level. While, the current process is defined in a company's configuration management or engineering change procedures and in its new product development process, often changes have to be made to take advantage of the communication and coordination capabilities of the PDM system. This new data is moved to the next person's "in basket" within PDM or an email notification is sent.

PRODUCT CATALOGUE MANAGEMENT

Product catalogue management defined as the support of product management in the management of product information in a structured and consistent method in the form of catalogues. This in terms to create a cost-effective means to help customers and channel partners understand what the functionalities and usability of some products or services are. This includes the comparison of product features, advising related products and alternative products and services. The development of online catalogues and open catalogues with multimedia capabilities, have opened completely new horizons. Product catalogue information is typically used in websites, mail order catalogues, webshops, Enterprise resource planning systems, price comparison services, and manufacturer websites.

PRODUCTION MANAGEMENT

Planning, implementation, and control of industrial method production processes are used to ensure smooth and efficient operation. Production management techniques are used in both manufacturing and service industries. Production management responsibilities include the traditional "five M's": men and women, machines, methods, materials, and money. Managers are expected to create an efficient production process with a workforce that can readily adapt to new equipment and schedules. They may use industrial engineering methods, such as time-and-motion studies, to design efficient work methods. They are responsible for managing both physical (raw) materials and information materials (paperwork or electronic documentation). Of their duties involving money, inventory control is the most important. This involves tracking all component parts, work in process, finished goods, packaging materials, and general supplies. The production cycle requires that sales, financial, engineering, and planning departments exchange information - such as sales forecasts, inventory levels, and budgets - until detailed production orders are dispatched by a production-control division. Managers must also monitor the operations to ensure that planned output levels, cost levels, and quality objectives are met.

Effective Production Management

Effective production management involves the understanding of the characteristics of several types of production systems, identification of the dynamics of the various phases of the management process, realizing the potential of different analytical tools, learning the nuances of the implementation of these tools, visualizing the impact of different uncertain situations and developing the ability to react under several scenarios to get the consistently excellent business conclusions. There are evidences to show how a number of organizations achieved world class status by effective management of their production systems. These organizations achieved superior quality, higher productivity, perfect delivery performance, overall customer satisfaction and enterprise excellence all with lower cost.

PROCESS CAPTURE TECHNOLOGY

Optimizing manufacturing processes by using the actual manufacturing process to generate cost estimates. This can allow manufacturing companies to perform trade studies up front in design to lower manufacturing costs when changes are still relatively inexpensive.

MANUFACTURING OPERATIONS MANAGEMENT

It is abbreviated as MOM which acts a methodology for viewing an end to end manufacturing process with a view to optimizing efficiency. There are various types of MOM software.Manufacturing Operations Management (MOM)

There are many types of MOM software, including for production management, performance analysis, quality and compliance, and human machine interface (HMI). *Production management software* provides real-time information about jobs and orders, labor and materials, machine status, and product shipments. *Performance analysis* software displays metrics at the machine, line, plant and enterprise level for situational or historical analysis. *Quality and compliance software* is used to promote compliance with standards and specifications for operational processes and procedures. *HMI software* is a type of manufacturing operations management (MOM) software that enables operators to manage industrial and process control machinery using a computer-based interface.

Manufacturing Process Management

This is abbreviated as MPM which contributes the collection of technology and methods which are used in manufacturing.

Manufacturing Process Management (MPM) is a collection of technology and methods used in the manufacturing and ERP/MRP defines when it is to be made; MPM defines how it will be made.

A cornerstone of MPM is the central repository for the integration of all these tools and activities aids in the exploration of alternative production line scenarios; making assembly lines more efficient with the aim of reduced lead time to product launch, shorter product times and reduced work in progress (WIP) inventories as well as allowing rapid response to product or product changes.

PRODUCTION SCHEDULING

Scheduling is an important tool for manufacturing and engineering, where it can have a major impact on the productivity of a process. In manufacturing, the objective of scheduling is to reduce the production time and costs, by telling a production facility what to make, when, with which staff, and on which equipment. Production scheduling aims to maximize the efficiency of the operation and reduce costs.

Production scheduling tools greatly outperform the older manual scheduling methods. These provide the production scheduler with powerful graphical interfaces which can be used to visually optimize the real-time work loads in different stages of production, and pattern recognition that allows the software to automatically create the scheduling opportunities which might not be apparent without this view into the data. For example, an airline might wish to minimize the number of airport gates required for its aircraft, in order to reduce costs, and scheduling software can allow the planners to see how this can be done, by analyzing time tables, aircraft usage, or the flow of passengers.

Benefits of Production Scheduling : The benefits of production scheduling include:

- Accurate delivery date quotes
- Inventory reduction, leveling
- Increased production efficiency
- Labor load leveling
- Process change-over reduction
- Reduced scheduling effort
- Real time information

Types of Scheduling

In business environment these are two types of scheduling naming forward scheduling and backward scheduling. This type of scheduling are used to allocate the plant and machinery resources, plan production process and for purchase materials.

Forward scheduling is planning the tasks from the date resources become available to determine the shipping date or the due date.

Backward scheduling is planning the tasks from the due date or required-by date to determine the start date and/or any changes in capacity required.

ADVANCED PLANNING AND SCHEDULING

It is abbreviated as APS which are used for manufacturing process.

Advanced Planning & Scheduling are also known as APS and Advanced Manufacturing. It is defined as a manufacturing management process by which raw materials and production capacity are optimally allocated to meet demand. APS is especially well-suited to environments where simpler planning methods cannot adequately address complex trade-offs between competing priorities.

Traditional planning and scheduling systems such as Manufacturing resource planning that utilize a stepwise phenomenon to allocate material and production capacity. This approach is simple but cumbersome, and does not readily adapt to changes in demand, resource capacity or material availability. Materials and capacity are planned separately, and many systems do not consider limited material availability or capacity constraints. Thus, this approach frequently concludes in plans that cannot be executed. However, despite attempts to shift to the new system, attempts have not always been successful, which has called for the combination of management philosophy with manufacturing.

Advanced Planning and Scheduling software enables manufacturing scheduling and advanced scheduling optimization within these environments.

SERVICE PRODUCT MANAGEMENT

Service Product Management deals with managing a service product across it's complete life cycle. This organizational function is equally common between Business-to-business as well as Business-to-consumer businesses. A service product, unlike a hardware or software product, is intangible and manifests itself as pure professional services or as a combination of services with necessary software and/or hardware. The Service product management practice ensures that the management of a profitable service in the market place. Service Product manager identifies profitable service space, packages services in a productized form and deliver's the same to the market. The function is a core service business management fucntion and is a mix of sales and marketing functions. The function interfaces with various organizational groups like Strategy, Planning, Financial controls /Management Accounting, Sales, Marketing Communications etc.

Important functions of a Service Product Manager

1. Business Management System Support
2. Demand Supply Planning
3. Knowledge Management
4. Marketing and Market Communications
5. Service Ramp Down
6. Service Productization
7. Service Ideal Generation/Management
8. Service Sales Support

Business Management System Support : Efficient management of service product cost and revenues according to service contract and incurred costs. The same is generally needs a service product manager to provide product data management for Enterprise resource planning systems.

Demand Supply Planning : Services profitability management by supporting balance between service demand and supply of necessary service resources.

Knowledge Management : Manage the knowledge management process and best practices for the service.

Marketing and Market Communications : Industry event participation, press release, consensus building, delivering service messaging through various available marketing channels.

Service Ramp Down : Manage the decision process of ramping down service product, and executing the service ramp down thus ending the service product management process.

Service Productization : Potentially saleable service features are captured and productized. That means creation of necessary product documentation like executive materials, service product document, technical services document, service scope etc.

Service Ideal Generation/Management : The function deals with capturing market's unmet and/or under-served needs, filtering the ideas based on business viability, business feasibility and potential, scalability, company strategy, and capital rate of return considerations. The end result is a potential set of market feasibility and market features captured in a marketing requirement document.

Service Sales Support : Service product management supports service sales by providing accurate resource estimate and in the right mix to provide an efficient product cost base on which to baseline the customer pricing.

Case Study

Note : knowing more about "Product Process Strategy" reader can study documentation process of Microsoft company by visiting their site : www.members.microsoft.com

http://www.slideshare.net/G20Technologies/insead-sales-strategy-case-study

http://www.cheshirehenbury.com/publications/ebmanrep/ebmrprodinfo.html

http://www.nomad-marketing.com/product_strategy.html

http://www.visionandexecution.com/success.html

http://www.deloitte.com/view/en_US/us/Insights/Browse-by-Content-Type/Case-Studies/case-study/a69d71308efd2210VgnVCM100000ba42f00aRCRD.htm

http://www.wipro.com/microsoft/psa/psa.htm

http://www.macadamian.com/process/

11

Maintenance Management

This chapter includes the key concept which are shown below:-

- Introduction
- Total Productive Maintenance
- Similarities and differences between TQM and TPM
- Types of Maintenance
- TPM Targets
- Steps in Introduction of TPM in a Organization
- Conclusion of TPM

INTRODUCTION

Maintenance management encompasses and supplies the various solutions for the planning and control of activities that are associated with the maintenance activities of a plant or facility. Usually, it incorporates the labor and materials that may include the management of maintenance stores.

Maintenance Management addresses various competencies and areas of expertise. These are vehicle maintenance, shop operations, environmental issues, inventory management section, benchmarking section and finally, outsource maintenance activities. These all competencies are described below as much information:-

The first competency concentrates on vehicle maintenance, including particular maintenance functions, preventive maintenance program implementation and effective administration of warranty programs. This potentially affects all aspects of fleet management including the financial and safe operation of a fleet and the end user's productivity.

First competency includes vehicle maintenance which refers to the maintenance functions and preventive maintenance.

The second competency is shop operations, which review the various practices of shop that are related to efficiency, staffing levels, and the decision to outsource a shop operation. This process appraises all the operations to determine the optimum staffing levels and advantageous outsourcing opportunities.

Second competency includes shop operations which refers to all the practices of shops that includes the efficiency and staffing levels.

The third competency is environmental issues that provides greater comprehension and addresses the environmental regulatory affairs and environmentally-responsible fleet/shop operations. Its requirements guarantee is not only a clean and healthy environment, but also the safety of employee.

The inventory management section identifies the importance of effective materials management. It makes use of professionally managed parts to operate at peak efficiency. It is an important contributing element to the progress of maintenance facility. This the fourth competency of maintenance management.

After the inventory management the benchmarking section offers the valuable principles for an in-house fleet maintenance operation. It is a key function to retain the productivity and effectively maintain all the operations. Benchmarking includes proper data collection, comparison, and analysis to evaluate the performance status and standards. It is the fifth competency of maintenance management, i.e., bench making which allows the properdars collection, comparison and analysis of performance status.

And the last competency is outsourcing maintenance activities which is the outsourcing, reviews and understands all the factors and elements that are influencing the settlements on outsource fleet maintenance activities. Its results depends on a vast range of factors but its ultimate goal is efficiency.

Another element making up the maintenance management is its processes. It includes the Preventive Maintenance and Condition Monitoring; Maintenance Planning and Scheduling; Root Cause Analysis and Materials Management. First of all we have to described about preventive management and collection monitoring.

Preventive maintenance and condition monitoring begins out by creating the implementation plan that identifies the measurable success indicators for the condition monitoring and preventive maintenance program. The objectives is to achieve a condition monitoring and preventive maintenance program that is documented, executed and tracked. And this may be done by the process of setting up, executing and measuring an effective program.

After studying, the preventive maintenance and condition monitoring, now we are discus about the maintenance planning and scheduling.

Maintenance Planning and scheduling is an important element in developing a well functioning maintenance organization. In order for it to work, the organization should do the inspections of equipment through preventive maintenance, technical database such as bill of materials, work order history, and standard job plans. Advanced methods are also must in leading focus of the company on simplifying the planning and scheduling process to make it truly effective.

Now we are studied about the root cause analysis and materials management after studying the maintenance planning and scheduling.

Root cause analysis is the another process of maintenance management, if properly implemented conclusion to the reduction of maintenance planner's work load; decrease in inventory-replenishment purchase orders; deduction of manually-prepared direct purchase requisitions; condensation of maintenance storeroom inventories, while increasing reliability; and generation of new measures for tracking plant reliability.

To complete the maintenance management processes is materials management. This comprises the educational maintenance audit and benchmarking tools. Its goal is, to train and educate the organization in best practices for reliability and maintenance; and to conduct a maintenance audit of reliability and maintenance performance of the company.

Efficiency and effectiveness of maintenance management relies heavily on total comprehension and the ability to address the competencies or areas of expertise involved; and the proper calculation, assembly and conduction of each of its processes.

TOTAL PRODUCTIVE MAINTENANCE

Total productive maintenance is also the concept of maintenance management. It resembles to TQM, i.e., total quality management. It is way of looking at the maintenance.

TPM brings the maintenance into focus as a essential and vitally important part of the business. It is no longer regarded as a non-profit activity. Down time for maintenance is scheduled as a part of the manufacturing day and, in some cases, as an integral part of the manufacturing process. It is no longer simply squeezed in whenever there is a break in material flow. The objective is to hold emergency and unscheduled maintenance to a minimum.

Total Productive Maintenance is a new way of looking at maintenance, or conversely, a reversion to old methods but on a mass scale. In TPM, the machine operator performs much, and sometimes all, of the routine maintenance tasks themselves. This auto maintenance ensures the suitable and effective efforts that are expended since the machine is wholly the domain of one person or team. TPM is a critical adjunct to lean manufacturing. If machine uptime is not predictable and if process capability is not sustained, the process must keep extra stocks to buffer against this uncertainty and flow through the process will be interrupted.. One method to think of TPM is "deterioration prevention" and "maintenance reduction", not fixing the machines. For this reason many people refer to TPM as "Total Productive Manufacturing" or "Total Process Management". TPM is a proactive approach that necessary aims to prevent any kind of slack before occurrence. Its aim is "zero error, zero work-related accident, and zero loss".

SIMILARITIES AND DIFFERENCES BETWEEN TQM AND TPM

TPM resemble to the TQM (Total Quality Management) in various aspects. These aspects are:-

1. Total commitment to the program by upper level management is required
2. Employees must be empowered to initiate corrective action, and
3. A long range outlook must be accepted as TPM may take a year or more to implement and is an on-going process.

TYPES OF MAINTENANCE

There are 4 types of maintenances such as breakdown maintenance, corrective maintenance, preventive maintenance and maintenance prevention.

1. Breakdown maintenance : It means that people waits until equipment fails and repair it. Such a thing could be used when the equipment failure does not significantly affect the operation or production or generate any significant loss other than repair cost.

2. Corrective maintenance : It improves the equipment and its components so that preventive maintenance can be carried out reliably. Equipment with design weakness must be redesigned to improve the reliability or improving maintainability. As the name implies, it is the maintenance of equipments and its components.

3. Preventive maintenance: It is a daily maintenance, i.e., cleaning, inspection, oiling and re-tightening which are design to retain the healthy condition of equipment and prevent failure by the prevention of deterioration, periodic inspection or equipment condition diagnosis, to measure the deterioration. It is further categorized into periodic maintenance and predictive maintenance. Just like human life is extended by preventive medicine, the equipment service life can be prolonged by doing preventive maintenance.

a. Periodic maintenance is also known as Time based maintenance which is abbreviated as TBM: Time based maintenance consists of periodically inspecting, servicing and cleaning equipment and replacing parts to prevent the sudden failure and process problems.

b. Predictive maintenance : This is a method in which the service life of important part is predicted based on inspection or diagnosis, in terms to use the parts to the limit of their service life. Compared to periodic maintenance, predictive maintenance is are condition based maintenance. It manages the trend values, by measuring and analyzing data about deterioration and employs a surveillance system that are designed to monitor the conditions by an on-line system.

4. Maintenance prevention: It indicates the design of a new equipment. Weakness of current machines are sufficiently studied on site information which are leading to failure prevention, easier maintenance and prevents of defects, safety and ease of

manufacturing and are incorporated before commissioning a new equipment.

Implementation of TPM

To begin applying TPM concepts to plant the maintenance activities, the entire work force must first be convinced that upper level management is committed to the program. The first step in this effort is to either hire or appoint a TPM coordinator. The responsibility of the coordinator is to sell the TPM concepts to the work force through an educational program. To do a thorough job of educating and convincing the work force that TPM is just not another "program of the month," that will take time, perhaps a year or more.

Once the coordinator is convinced that the work force is sold on the TPM program and that they understand it and its implications, the first study and action teams are formed. These teams are generally made up of people who directly have an impact on the problem being addressed. Operators, maintenance personnel, shift supervisors, schedulers, and upper management might all be included on a team. Each person becomes a "stakeholder" in the process and is encouraged to do his or her best to contribute to the success of the team effort. Usually, the TPM coordinator heads the teams until others become familiar with the process and natural team leaders emerge.

The action teams are charged with the responsibility of pinpointing problem areas, detailing a course of corrective action, and initiating the corrective process. Recognizing problems and initiating solutions that may not come easily for some team members. They will not have had experiences in other plants where they had opportunities to see how things could be done differently. In well run TPM programs, team members often visit cooperating plants to observe and compare TPM methods, techniques, and to observe work in progress. This comparative process is part of an overall measurement technique called "benchmarking" and is one of the greatest assets of the TPM program.

The teams are encouraged to start on small problems and keep meticulous records of their progress. Successful completion of the team's initial work is always recognized by management. Publicity of the program and its results are one of the secrets of making the program a success. Once the teams are familiar with the TPM process and have experienced success with a small problem, problems of ever increasing importance and complexity are introduced.

Training for TPM coordinators is available from various sources. Most of the major professional organizations are associated with manufacturing as well as private consulting and educational groups that have information which are available on TPM implementation. The Society of Manufacturing Engineers (SME) and Productivity Press are two examples. Both offer tapes, books, and other educational material that tell the story of TPM. Productivity Press conducts frequent seminars in most major cities around the United States. They also sponsor plant tours for benchmarking and training purposes.

TPM TARGETS

TPM Targets	
TPM Objectives	1. Achieve Zero Defects, Zero Breakdown and Zero accidents in all functional areas of the organization.
	2. Involve people in all levels of organization.
	3. Form different teams to reduce defects and Self Maintenance.
Motives of TPM	1. Adoption of life cycle approach for improving the overall performance of production equipment.
	2. Improving productivity by highly motivated workers which is achieved by job enlargement.
	3. The use of voluntary small group activities for identifying the cause of failure, possible plant and equipment modifications.
Direct benefits of TPM	1. Increase productivity and OPE (Overall Plant Efficiency) by 1.5 or 2 times.
	2. Rectify customer complaints.
	3. Reducethe manufacturing cost by 30%.

	4. Satisfy the customers needs by 100 % (Delivering the right quantity at the right time, in the required quality.)
	5. Reduce accidents.
	6. Follow pollution control measures.
Indirect benefits of TPM	1. Higher confidence level among the employees.
	2. Keep the work place clean, neat and attractive.
	3. Favorablechange in the attitude of the operators.
	4. Achieve goals by working as team.
	5. Horizontaldeployment of a new concept in all areas of the organization.
	6. Share knowledge and experience.
	7. The workers get a feeling of owning the machine.
Uniqueness of TPM	The major difference between TPM and other concepts is that the operators are also made to involve in the maintenance process. The concept of "I (Production operators) Operate, You (Maintenance department) fix" is not followed.

STEPS IN INTRODUCTION OF TPM IN A ORGANIZATION

There are four steps of introducing TPM, which includes preparatory stage, introduction stage, implementation and institutionalizing stage.

Step A - Preparatory Stage

STEP 1 - Announcement by Management to all about TPM introduction in the organization :

Proper understanding, commitment and active involvement of the top management in required for this step. Senior management should have awareness programmes, after which announcement is made to all. Publish it in the house magazine and put it in the notice board. Send a letter to all concerned individuals if required.

STEP 2 - Initial education and propaganda for TPM :

Training is to be done based on the need. Some need intensive training and some just an awareness. Take people who matters to places where TPM already successfully implemented.

STEP 3 - Setting up TPM and departmental committees :

TPM includes improvement, autonomous maintenance, quality maintenance etc., as part of it. When committees are set up it should take care of all those needs.

STEP 4 - Establishing the TPM working system and target :

Now each area is benchmarked and fix up a target for achievement.

STEP 5 - A master plan for institutionalizing :

Next step is implementation leading to institutionalizing wherein TPM becomes an organizational culture. Achieving PM award is the proof of reaching a satisfactory level.

Step B - Introduction Stage

This is a ceremony and we should invite all. Suppliers as they should know that we want quality supply from them. Related companies and affiliated companies who can be our customers, concerns etc. Some may learn from us and some can help us and customers will get the communication from us that we care for quality output.

Step C – Implementation Stage

In this stage eight activities are carried which are called eight pillars in the development of TPM activity.

Of these four activities are for establishing the system for production efficiency, one for initial control system of new products and equipment, one for improving the efficiency of administration and are for control of safety, sanitation as working environment.

Step D - Institutionalizing Stage

By all there activities one would has reached the maturity stage. Now is the time for applying for PM award. Also think of challenging level to which you can take this movement.

CONCLUSION OF TPM

Ford, Eastman Kodak, Dana Corp., Allen Bradley, Harley

Davidson; these are just certain of the companies that have implemented the TPM process successfully. All report an increase in productivity using TPM. Kodak reported that a $5 million investment resulted in a $16 million increase in profits which could be traced and directly contributed to implementing a TPM program. One appliance manufacturer reported the time which are needed for die changes on a forming press that are went from various hours down to twenty minutes! This is the same as having two or three additional million dollar machines that are available for use on a daily basis without having to buy or lease them. Texas Instruments reported the increased production figures of up to 80% in some areas. Almost all the above named companies reported 50% or greater reduction in down time, reduced spare parts inventory, and increased on-time deliveries. The need for out-sourcing part or all of a product line was greatly reduced in many cases.

Today, with competition in industry at an all time high, TPM may be the only thing that stands between success and total failure for some companies. It has been proven to be a program that works. It can be adapted to work not only in industrial plants, but in construction, building maintenance, transportation, and in a range of other situations. Employees must be educated and convinced that TPM is not just another "program of the month" and that management is totally committed to the program and the extended time frame necessary for full implementation. If everyone involved in a TPM program does his or her part, an unusually high rate of return that are compared to the resources which are invested may be expected or not.

Case Study

Note : knowing more about "Maintenance Management" reader can study documentation process of Microsoft company by visiting their site : www.members.microsoft.com

http://portal.acm.org/citation.cfm?id=98373

http://www.icmrindia.org/courseware/Operations%20Management/Operations%20Management-DS20.htm

http://www3.interscience.wiley.com/journal/113445580/abstract?CRETRY=1&SRETRY=0

http://whitepapers.businessweek.com/rlist/term/Equipment-Maintenance-Management-Software.html

http://searchvirtualdesktop.bitpipe.com/rlist/term/Computer-Maintenance-Management-(CMMS).html

12

Constraint Management

This chapter includes the key concepts which are described below:-

- Introduction
- Theory of Constraints (TOC)
- Assumptions of Constraint Management
- Criticism of TOC
- Economies of Scale
- Goals and Necessary Condition
- Tools of Constraint Management

INTRODUCTION

In twenty-first century "quality" has come to encompass much more than first product or process conformance. And with the widespread acceptance of higher product and process quality as a way of life among commercial companies, not for profit organizations and government agencies. For the customer, this means that it can be more difficult to differentiate between the product quality offered by competitors.

In many cases, the difference between winning and losing a customer's business (or continued loyalty) resides in the quality of the interaction between customer and supplier. In other words, service can be as important an element in customer satisfaction as product quality. Once managers venture beyond product and process conformance (or quality), they move up from process improvement to system-level improvement.

Constraint management seeks to help managers at all levels of an organization maintain proper focus on the factors that are most critical to overall success, i.e., system constraints. Constraint management is an outgrowth of theory of constraint.

THEORY OF CONSTRAINTS (TOC)

Theory of Constraints (TOC) is an overall management philosophy which was introduced by Dr. Eliyahu M. Goldratt in his 1984 book titled *The Goal*, that is geared to help the organizations which continually achieve their goal or objectives. The title comes from the contention that any manageable system is limited in achieving more of its goal by a very small number of constraints, and that there is always at least one constraint. The TOC process seeks to identify the constraint and restructure the rest of the organization around it, through the use of the Five Focusing Steps.

ASSUMPTIONS OF CONSTRAINT MANAGEMENT

The underlying assumption of Theory of Constraints is that organizations that can be measured and controlled by variations on three measures: Throughput, Operating Expense, and Inventory. Throughput is money or goal units which are generated through sales. Operating Expense is the money that goes into the system to ensure its operation on an ongoing basis. Inventory is money the system invests in order to sell its goods and services.

Constraint management is based ion four assumptions about how system function. These assumptions are:-

1. Every system has a goal and a finite set of necessary conditions that must be satisfied to achieve that goal. Effective effort to improve system performance is not possible without a clear understanding and consensus about what the goal and necessary conditions are.

2. The sum of a system's local optima does not equal the global system optimum. In other words, the most effective system does not come from maximizing the efficiency of each system component individually, without regard to its interaction with other components.

3. Very few variables—maybe only one—limit the performance of a system at any one time. This is equivalent to the "weakest link" concept discussed earlier.

4. All systems are subject to logical cause-and-effect. There are natural and logical consequences to any action, decision, or event. For those events that have already occurred, these consequences can be visually mapped to aid in situation or problem analysis. For those decisions that have yet to occur, or which are contemplated, the result of these actions, decisions or events can be logically projected into the future and visually mapped as well.

All of the description and prescription are contained in constraint management is predicted on these assumption.

Five Focusing Steps

Theory of Constraints is based on the premise that the rate of goal achievement is limited by at least one constraining process. Only by increasing flow through the constraint can overall throughput be increased. Assuming the goal of the organization has been articulated the steps which are following below.

Theory of Constraints is based on the premise that the rate of goal achievement is limited by at least one constraining process. Only by increasing flow through the constraint can overall throughput be increased. [1]

Assuming the goal of the organization has been articulated (e.g., "Make money now and in the future") the steps are:

1. IDENTIFY the constraint (the resource/policy that prevents the organization from obtaining more of the goal). It is used to identify the system's constraint. Once the system constraint is identified, if it can be broken without much investment.

2. Decide how to EXPLOIT the constraint (make sure the constraint's time is not wasted doing things that it should not do). It describes that how to exploid the system constraint. Exploit means to get the most out of constrain implement without additional investment.

3. SUBORDINATE all other processes to above decision (align the whole system/organization to support the decision made above). Once decision on how to exploit the constraint has been made, subordinate everything else to that decision.

4. ELEVATE the constraint (if required/possible, permanently increase capacity of the constraint; "buy more"). After completing step 3, the original constraint is still the system constraint at this point, the best you can be assured of is that you're ringing as much productivity out of it as possible.

5. If, as a result of these steps, the constraint has moved, return to Step 1. Don't let inertia become the constraint.

The five focusing steps aim to ensure ongoing improvement efforts are centered around the organization's constraints. In the TOC literature, this is referred to as the Process of Ongoing Improvement (POOGI). These focusing steps are the key steps which are used to developing the specific applications including constraints, buffer.

A constraint is anything that prevents the system from achieving more of its goal and objecyive. There are various method that constraints can show up, but a core principle within TOC is that there are not tens or hundreds of constraints. There is at least one and at most a few in any given system. Constraints can be internal or external to the system. An internal constraint is in evidence when the market demands more from the system than it can deliver. If this is the case, then the focus of the organization should be on discovering that constraint and following the five focusing steps to open it up (and potentially remove it). An external constraint exists when the system can produce more than the market will bear. If this is the case, then the organization should focus on mechanisms to create more demand for its products or services.

Types of (internal) constraints

- Equipment: The way equipment is currently used limits the ability of the system to produce more salable goods / services.
- People: Lack of skilled people limits the system.
- Policy: A written or unwritten policy prevents the system from making more.

The concept of the constraint in Theory of Constraints differs from the constraint that shows up in mathematical optimization. In TOC, the constraint is used as a focusing process for management of the system. In optimization, the constraint is written into the mathematical expressions to limit the scope of the solution (X can be no greater than 5).

Remember that Organizations have many problems with equipment, people, policies, etc. But the constraint is the thing that is preventing the organization from getting more Throughput (typically, sales).

Buffers are used throughout the TOC. They appear as part of EXPLOIT and SUBORDINATE steps of five focusing step. Buffers are placed before the key constraint thus ensuring that the constraint is never starved.

Buffers can be a bank of physical objects before a work center, waiting to be processed by that work center. Buffers can also be represented by time, as in the time before work reaches the constraint. There should always be enough (but not excessive) work in the time queue before the constraint.

Buffers are *not* the small queue of work that sits before every work center in a Kanban system. The assumption in Theory of Constraints is that with one constraint in the system, all other parts of the system have sufficient capacity to keep up with the work at the constraint. In a balanced line, as dictated by Kanban, when one work center goes down, then the entire system must wait until that work center is restored. In a TOC system, the only situation where work is in danger is if the constraint is unable to process (either due to malfunction, sickness or a "hole" in the buffer).

Thinking Processes of TOC

The Thinking Processes are a set of tools which are used to help managers walk through the steps of initiating and implementing a project. When used in a logical flow, the Thinking Processes help walk through a buy-in process:

1. Gain agreement on the problem
2. Gain agreement on the direction for a solution
3. Gain agreement that the solution solves the problem
4. Agree to overcome any potential negative ramifications
5. Agree to overcome any obstacles to implementation

TOC practitioners sometimes refer to these in the negative as working through *layers of resistance* to a change.

CRITICISM OF TOC

Criticism of TOC includes various points. Criticism that have been leveled against TOC include:-

Heading :- It is not the part of main stream business education.

While TOC has been compared favorably to linear programming techniques or methods D. Trietsch from University of Auckland argues that DBR methodology is inferior to competing methodologies.

ECONOMIES OF SCALE

It is the discipline of economies of scale which refers to the reduction in unit cost as the size of facility or scale, increases.

In microeconomics, **economies of scale** are the cost advantages that a business obtains due to expansion. They are factors that cause a producer's average cost per unit to fall as scale is increased. Economies of scale is a long run concept and refers to reductions in unit cost as the size of a facility, or scale, increases. Diseconomies of scale are the alternative of it. Economies of scale may be utilized by any size firm expanding its scale of operation. The common ones are purchasing (bulk buying of materials through long-term contracts), managerial (increasing the specialization of managers), financial (obtaining lower-interest charges when borrowing from banks and having access to a greater range of financial instruments), and marketing (spreading the cost of advertising over a greater range of output in media markets). Each of these factors reduces the long run average costs (LRAC) of production by shifting the short-run average total cost (SRATC) curve down and to the right.

Economies of scale increasing a facility's size decrease the average unit cost. There are four principle reasons including:-

1. Spreading fixed cost
2. Reducing construction cost
3. Cutting costs of purchased materials
4. Finding process advantages

Economies of scale is a practical concept that is inevitable for explaining the real world phenomena or mechanisms such as patterns of international trade, the number of firms in a market, and how firms get "too big to fail". Economies of scale is related to and can easily be confused with the theoretical economic notion of returns to scale. Where economies of scale refer to costs of firm, returns to scale describe the relationship between inputs and outputs in a long-run (all inputs variable) production function. A production function has the *constant* returns to scale if increasing all inputs by some proportion concludes in output increasing by that same proportion. Returns are *decreasing* if, say, doubling inputs concludes in less than double the output, and *increasing* if more than double the output. If a mathematical function is used to represent the production function, returns to scale are represented by the degree of homogeneity of the function. Production functions with constant returns to scale are first degree homogeneous; increasing returns to scale are represented by degrees of homogeneity greater than one, and decreasing returns to scale by degrees of homogeneity less than one.

The confusion between the practical concept of economies of scale and the theoretical notion of returns to scale occurs from the fact that large fixed costs, such as occur from investment in a factory or from research and development, are an important source of real world economies of scale. In conventional microeconomic theory there can be no increasing returns to scale when there are fixed costs, since this implies at least one input that cannot be increased.

There are two methods to achieve the economies of scale:-

1. High fixed cost and constant marginal cost
2. Low or no fixed cost and declining marginal cost

Economies of scale refers to the decreased per unit cost as output increases. More clearly, the initial investment of capital is diffused (spread) over an increasing number of units of output, and therefore, the marginal cost of producing a good or service is less than the average total cost per unit remember that this is only in an industry that is experiencing the economies of scale). Average fixed cost is the example of economies of scale.

Economies of scale tends to occur in industries with high capital costs in which those costs can be distributed across a large number of units of production both in absolute terms and, especially, relative to the size of the market. A common example is a factory. An investment in machinery is made, and one worker, or unit of production, starts to work on the machine and produces a few number of goods. If another worker is added to the machine he or she is able to produce an additional amount of goods without adding significantly to cost of operation of the factory. The amount of goods produced grows significantly faster than cost of operation of the plant. Hence, the cost of producing an additional good is less than the good before it, and an economy of scale emerges. Economies of scale are also derived partially from learning by doing. The exploration companies prow large on some industries.

Diseconomies of Scale

There are some characteristics of diseconomies of scale. It is the alternative of economies of scale.

a. Excessive size can bring complexity, loss of focus, and inefficiencies, which raise the average unit cost.

b. Characterized by loss of agility, less innovation, risk avoidance, and excessive analysis and planning at the expense of action.

c. Nonlinear growth of overhead leads to employee ceilings.

d. Loss of focus

GOALS AND NECESSARY CONDITION

The first assumption holds that every system has a goal and a set of necessary condition that must be satisfied to achieve that goal.

While this assumption is undoubtedly valid in most cases, there are obviously some organizations that have not expended the time or effort to clearly and unequivocally define what their goal is.

And even if they have defined a goal, most have not gone the extra step to define the minimum necessary or essential conditions, or critical success factors, for achieving that goal. Necessary conditions are critical success factors. They are actually necessary to achieve the goal.

For instance, customer satisfaction is unquestionably essential to continued the progress toward a financial goal. Employee satisfaction might be considered necessary for achieving the goal. Including necessary conditions like these as part of the goal hierarchy gives it credibility, identifying it as something that is not just temporary but must be satisfied throughout the lifetime of the organization.

Necessary conditions differs from the goal. While the goal itself generally has no limit it's normally worded in such a way that it's not likely ever to be fully realized, necessary conditions are more finite, i.e., fixed. They might be characterized as a "zero-or-one" situation: It's either there or it isn't (a "yes-or-no" state). For example, a for-profit organization might want to make as much money as it can—no limits. But employee security and satisfaction, as necessary conditions, should be established at a well-defined minimum level.

A for-profit company's goal can't expect to satisfy its employees without limit, but the organization should recognize the need to achieve a certain level of employee security and satisfaction as one minimum requirement for achieving the goal. This is not to say that all necessary conditions are zero-or-one in nature. Some, such as customer satisfaction, can be increased, and doing so can be expected to improve progress toward the goal. But even such variable necessary conditions have practical limits.

TOOLS OF CONSTRAINT MANAGEMENT

1. *The Current Reality Tree (CRT).* Designed to help identify the system constraint, especially when that constraint is a policy of some kind.

2. *The "Evaporating Cloud" (EC).* A kind of conflict resolution diagram. Helps create breakthrough solutions to resolve hidden, underlying conflicts that tend to perpetuate the constraint. Figure 1 illustrates a typical Evaporating Cloud.

3. *The Future Reality Tree (FRT).* Tests and validates potential solutions. Provides logical verification that a proposed solution will actually deliver the desired results.

4. *The Negative Branch (NB).* Actually a subset of the FRT. Helps identify and avoid any new, devastating effects that might result from the solution.

5. *The Prerequisite Tree (PRT).* Helps to surface and eliminate obstacles to implementation of a chosen solution. Also time-sequences the actions required to achieve the objective.

6. *The Transition Tree (TT).* Can facilitate the development of step by step implementation plans. Also helps explain the rationale for the proposed actions to those responsible for implementing them. This can be especially important when those charged with executing a plan are not the same people who developed it. Figure 3 contains a typical Transition Tree. Either the Transition Tree or the Prerequisite Tree can form the basis of a project activity network for implementation of change.

ASSUMPTIONS:

1. *The FAST supplier is more expensive than other supplier*
2. *Buying from the FAST supplier is ALWAYS more costly*
3. *Purchase costs are significant*
4. *All cost savings are important*

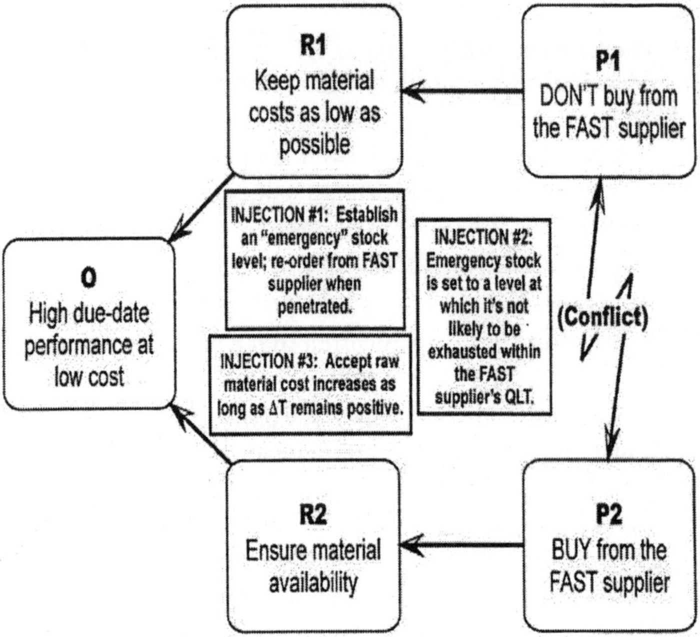

ASSUMPTIONS:

5. *The regular supplier is unreliable*
6. *The regular supplier takes too long to deliver*
7. *We never know about peak demands in time to order from the regular supplier*
8. *Purchase cost is less important than the cost of a missed delivery*

(Adapted from Schragenheim and Dettmer, 2000)

Figure : 1 "Evaporating Cloud" - "Unreliable Supplier"

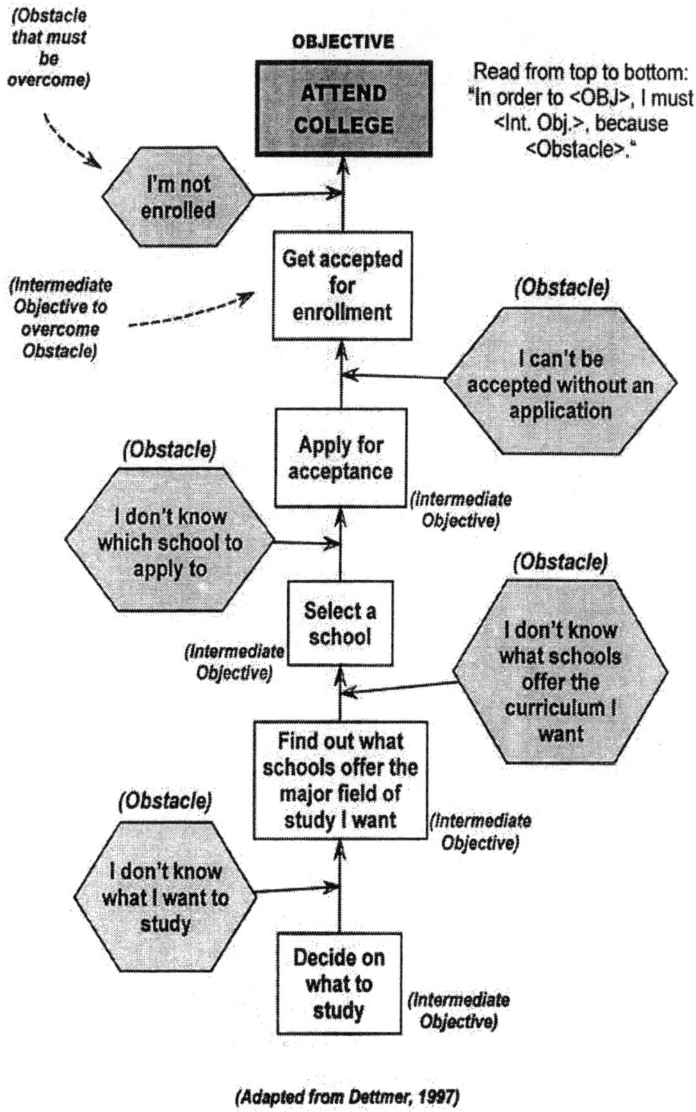

Figure : 2 Prerequisite Tree (Example)

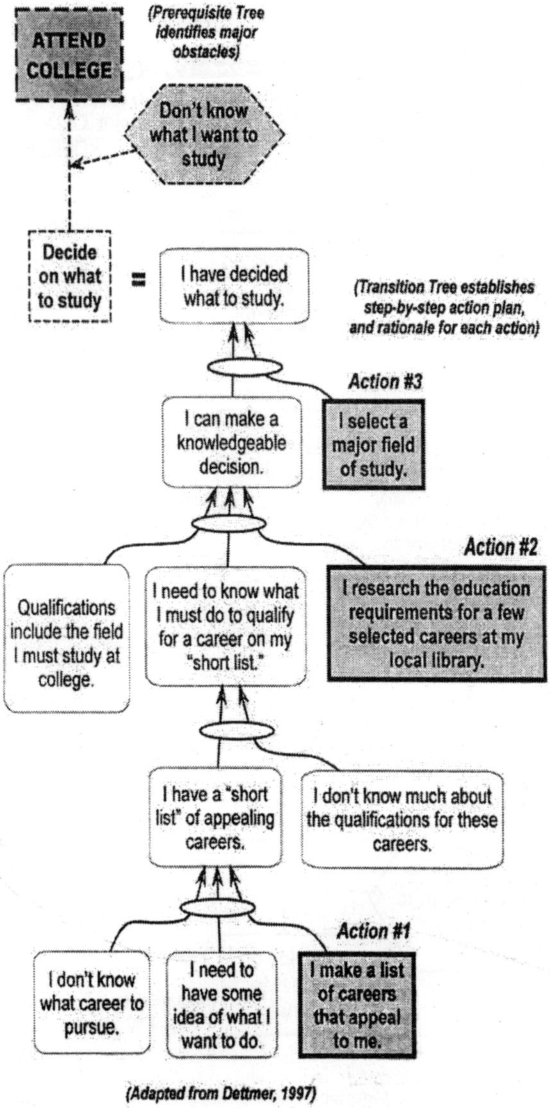

Figure : 3 Transition Tree (Example)

Bibliography

Abernathy, W. J., K. B. Clark and A. M. Kantrow. 1981. The new industrial competition. Harvard Business Review (September-October): 68-81. (These authors discuss how Japanese and European competition has affected U.S. manufacturers in automobiles, machine tools, minicomputers, commercial aircraft, textile machinery, and color TV sets. Using autos as an example they attribute Japanese success to superiority in manufacturing processes and work force management).

Abramovitch, I. 1994. Beyond kaizen. Success (January/February): 85-88.

Ahmadjian, C. L. and P. Robinson. 2001. Safety in numbers: Downsizing and the deinstitutionalization of permanent employment in Japan. Administrative Science Quarterly 46(4): 622-654. (JSTOR link).

Akao, Y. 1991. Hoshin Kanri: Policy Deployment for Successful TQM. Productivity Press.

Amar, A. D. 1984. Japanese production management - Just-in-time and total quality control: Review and critique. Mid-Atlantic Journal of Business (Summer): 55-59.

Arnold, W. J. 1961. Japanese management rates itself - An experiment in appraising "business efficiencies". The Journal of the Academy of Management 4(2): 144-148. (JSTOR link).

Asada, T. J. C. Bailes and K. Suzuki. 2000. Implementing ABM with Hoshin management. Management Accounting Quarterly (Winter): 6-11. Note: Hoshin management is a Japanese concept.

Barton, M. F., S. P. Agrawal and Lynn Rockwell. 1988. Meeting the challenge of Japanese Management concepts. Management Accounting (September): 49-53.

Benedict, R. 1946. The Chrysanthemum and the Sword: Patterns of Japanese Culture. Rutland, VT: Charles E. Tuttle Company Inc.

Bensaou, M. and M. Earl. 1998. The right mind-set for managing information technology. Harvard Business Review (September-October): 119-128. (Compares the western approach with how Japanese companies manage information technology). (Summary).

Bergevin, P. M. 1993. The stockholders' equity section of a Japanese company: The Minolta Camera Company case. Journal of Accounting Education 11(2): 301-311.

Birnbaum, P. H. 1987. Review: The Behavioral Science of Leadership: An Interdisciplinary Japanese Research Program, by J. Misumi. Administrative Science Quarterly 32(3): 455-456. (JSTOR link).

Brett, J. M. and T. Okumura. 1998. Inter- and intracultural negotiation: U.S. and Japanese negotiators. The Academy of Management Journal 41(5): 495-510. (JSTOR link).

Brinker, B. J. 1990. ABCs, thanks, and Japanese baseball. Journal of Cost Management (Summer): 3.

Brown, T. 2008. Design thinking. Harvard Business Review (June): 84-92.

Chang, S. J. 1995. International expansion strategy of Japanese firms: Capability building through sequential entry. The Academy of Management Journal 38(2): 383-407. (JSTOR link).

Charitou, A. 2000. The impact of losses and cash flows on dividends: Evidence for Japan. 36(2): 198-225.

Chew, D. H. 1997. Studies in International Corporate Finance and Governance Systems: A Comparison of the U.S., Japan, and Europe. Oxford University Press.

Chow, C. W., Y. Kato and K. A. Merchant. 1996. The use of organizational controls and their effects on data manipulation and management myopia: A Japan vs. U.S. comparison. Accounting, Organizations and Society 21(2-3): 175-192. (Summary).

Christopher, R. C. 1987. Second to None. Rutland, VT: Charles E. Tuttle Company Inc.

Chrysler, M. 1988. Japan's 'shame' society. Tokyo Journal (August).

Finch, B. 1986. Japanese management techniques in small manufacturing companies: A strategy for implementation. Production and Inventory Management (3rd Quarter): 30-38.

Johnson, H. T. 2006. Sustainability and "Lean Operations". Cost Management (March/April): 40-45. (Summary).

Monden, Y. 1981. Kanban system. Industrial Engineering (May): 29-46.

Monden, Y. 1981. Production smoothing, Part II. Industrial Engineering (September): 22-30.

Monden, Y. 1981. Production smoothing. Industrial Engineering (August): 42-51.

Monden, Y. 1981. What makes the Toyota production system really tick. Industrial Engineering (January): 36-48.

Monden, Y. 1983. Toyota Production System. Atlanta, GA: Industrial Engineering Press.

Monden, Y. 1998. Toyota Production System: An Integrated Approach to Just-In-Time. Atlanta, GA: Industrial Engineering Press.

Murrin, T. 1982. Rejecting the Traditional Ways of Doing Business. American Production and Inventory Control Society.

Nicholas, J.M. "JIT: Value added and waste elimination" Chapter 3, Competitive Manufacturing Management, Irwin McGraw-Hill, 1998.

Nicholas, J.M. "MRP based production planning & scheduling " Appendix, Competitive Manufacturing Management, Irwin McGraw-Hill, 1998.

Nicholas, J.M. "Pull production systems" Chapter 8, Competitive Manufacturing Management, Irwin McGraw-Hill,

Nicholas, J.M. "Race without a finish line" Chapter 1, Competitive Manufacturing Management, Irwin McGraw-Hill, 1998.

Noori, H. and Radford, R. "Aggregate Planning", Chapter 14, Production & Operations Management: Total Quality and Responsiveness, McGraw Hill Book Company, 1995.

Noori, H. and Radford, R. "Demand Management", Chapter 4, Production and Operations Management: Total Quality and Responsiveness, McGraw Hill Book Company, 1995.

Noori, H. and Radford, R. "Shop Floor Management", Chapter 17, Production and Operations Management: Total Quality and Responsiveness, McGraw Hill Book Company, 1995.

Ohno, T. 1988. Toyota Production System: Beyond Large Scale Production. Cambridge, MA: Productivity Press.

Public Affairs Division and Operations Management Consulting Division. 1998. The Toyota Production System: Leaner Manufacturing for a Greener Planet. Toyota Motor Corporation.

Shingo, S. and A. P. Dillion. 1989. A Study of the Toyota Production System from the Industrial Engineering Viewpoint. Productivity Press.

e-bibliography

http://tutor2u.net/business/production/pom_introduction.htm

http://en.wikipedia.org/wiki/Operations_management

http://www.bized.co.uk/learn/business/production/index.htm

http://managementhelp.org/ops_mgnt/ops_mgnt.htm

http://www.poms.org/

http://www.oup.co.in/search_detail.php?id=144262

http://www.iimb.ernet.in/areawise/list/productions

http://www3.interscience.wiley.com/journal/121568272/home?CRETRY=1&SRETRY=0

http://en.wikipedia.org/wiki/Operations_management

http://www.siom.in/

http://managementhelp.org/ops_mgnt/ops_mgnt.htm

http://mbaalliance.com/operations-management.html

http://bx.businessweek.com/sales-operation-management/

http://www.apics.org/resources/careercenter.htm

http://www.business.com/directory/management/operations_management/employment/

http://www.tropmet.res.in/~caipeex/pm2.html

http://www.senatehall.com/journals.php?journal=6

http://en.wikibooks.org/wiki/Operations_Strategy/What_is_operations_strategy%3F/Operations_strategy

http://www.businessinsights.biz/Sample%20Reports/PDF/SAMP001.pdf

http://www.prtm.com/strategiccategory.aspx?id=77&langtype=1033

http://www.docstoc.com/docs/8079294/Chapter-2-Operation-Strategy

http://www.flipkart.com/operations-strategy-slack-nigel-mike/0273695193-jsw3fmihhc

http://www.seawun.org/Home/AboutSEAWUN/OperationStrategy/tabid/56/Default.aspx

http://www.netmba.com/operations/process/analysis/

http://www.asq.org/learn-about-quality/process-analysis-tools/overview/overview.html

http://en.wikipedia.org/wiki/Business_analysis

http://www.statsoft.com/TEXTBOOK/stprocan.html

http://changingminds.org/disciplines/hr/job_analysis/process_analysis.htm

http://oeas.ucf.edu/process_analysis/what_is_pa.htm

http://www.metastorm.com/products/business_process_analysis.asp

http://www.oracle.com/technology/software/products/bpa/index.html

http://www.mega.com/index.asp/l/en/c/ea/p/bpa

http://en.wikipedia.org/wiki/Project_management

http://www.pmi.org/Pages/default.aspx

http://managementhelp.org/plan_dec/project/project.htm

http://www.projectscenter.com/

http://www.pmearth.com/

http://www.getafreelancer.com/projects/by-job/Project-Management.html

http://www.bpubs.com/Management_Science/Project_Management/

http://www.mindtools.com/pages/main/newMN_PPM.htm

http://en.wikipedia.org/wiki/Quality_management

http://www.iitb.ac.in/~cep/brochures/2005/asb-qm-bro.html

http://managementhelp.org/quality/quality.htm

http://www.iso.org/iso/iso_catalogue/management_standards/iso_9000_iso_14000/qmp.htm

http://www.tqmc.org/index.php

http://www.oup.co.in/search_detail.php?id=143418

http://www.iqmsindia.com/

http://www3.interscience.wiley.com/journal/60500185/home

http://en.wikipedia.org/wiki/Supply_chain_management

http://lcm.csa.iisc.ernet.in/scm/supply_chain_intro.html

http://www.supplychainseminars.com/

http://www.supplychainmanagement.in/

http://logistics.about.com/

http://www.infosysblogs.com/supply-chain/

http://www.sap.com/solutions/business-suite/scm/index.epx

http://en.wikipedia.org/wiki/Inventory

http://www.invatol.com/

http://www.inventorymanagement.com/

http://www.inventorymanagementreview.org/

http://www.effectiveinventory.com/

http://www.netsuite.com/portal/products/netsuite/inventory-management.shtml

http://www.oracle.com/applications/logistics/inventory-management.html

http://www.simba.org/

http://www.inventoryops.com/

http://www.pragmaticmarketing.com/publications/magazine/3/4/0508ec.pdf

http://www.npd-solutions.com/pdstrategy.html

http://www.nickwebb.com/Keys4.html

http://www.ies.luth.se/log/courses/iet065/Krajweski%20Chapter%204.ppt

http://hypermanymedia.wku.edu/Paglialunga_MGT314_Chapter_7.ppt

http://www.emeraldinsight.com/Insight/viewContentItem.do?contentType=Article&contentId=854819

http://www.igorinternational.com/process/company-product-names.php

Index

A

Aesthetics 5

B

Business continuity 54
Business Plan 41

C

Capability Study 173
Chain Dynamics 208
Chain Methodology 154
Commercialization 255
Competitive Weapon 62
Conclusion of Decision Tree 59
Constraint Management 285
Corporate Strategy 71
Cost and Quality 72
customization 3

D

Decision Making 80
Decision Theory 107
Decision Tree 55
Dimension of Quality 74
Diminishing Returns 243
Diseconomies of Scale 293
Distressed Inventory 226

E

Economies of Scale 282
Entrepreneur 9
Evaluating 58
Evaluating Quantitatively 90
Execution 161

F

Facilitated Risk 48
Feasibility Studies 67
Field Analysis 85
Final Design 67
Finished Goods 217

G

Gantt Charts 25
Global Strategy 72
Grid Analysis 104

H

Historical Development 159
Human capital 12

I

Idea Generation 67
Idea Screening 254
Implementation 52
Intellectual capital 12
Inventory Credit 227
Inventory Turnover 230

L

Labor services 9

M

Machinery 9
Market Testing 67
Measured Criteria 84
Monitoring 154

N

Necessary Condition 284
Next queue 25
Normative and Descriptive 112

O

Operation Strategy 61
Operational Levels 193
Operational Planning 19
Operational Risk 20
Operations Scheduling 21
opportunity costs 73

P

Paired Comparison Analysis 96
Paradoxes of Uncertainty 119
Priority Rules 24
Prototype Design 67

Q

Quality 5, 74
Quality Assurance 181
Quantity 5

R

Reliability 5
Risk Analysis 21
Risk assessment 20
Risk Management 20
Risk reduction 49
Row materials 9

S

separately 19
Sequencing 23
Setting Priorities 104
Structural Elements 209

T

Tactical Levels 192
Technology Selection 68
Traditional Approach 146
Transportation Decisions 196